Rebellion, revolution and a new world order

Edited by Toby Manhire
with an introduction by Ian Black

Published by Guardian Books 2012

2 4 6 8 10 9 7 5 3 1

Copyright © Guardian News and Media 2012

First published in Great Britain in 2012 by
Guardian Books
Kings Place, 90 York Way
London N1 9GU

www.guardianbooks.co.uk

A CIP catalogue record for this book is available from the British Library

ISBN 978-0852-65254-1

Text design by seagulls.net
Cover design by Two Associates

CONTENTS

INTRODUCTION

Ian Black

Spontaneous, unforeseen and contagious, the uprisings of the Arab Spring took everyone – participants included – by surprise. Like revolutions in other times and places, they seemed impossible beforehand and inevitable afterwards. In mid-December 2010 the desperate act of a young Tunisian barely featured on the global news agenda. But it set off a chain reaction of extraordinary events that would unseat dictators, reshape the political landscape of North Africa and the Middle East and affect the lives of millions of people. The Guardian has been running, often breathlessly, to follow the story and to explain it ever since.

It is a story of many chapters in a book that has not yet been completed. Individual countries had their own distinctive experiences, which have been seen collectively as a defining phenomenon of the early 21st century. Yet as the summer and autumn of 2011 gave way to a bloody and inconclusive winter the future of what some preferred to call the "Arab awakening" remained deeply uncertain. No single outcome across the region could be predicted, let alone guaranteed.

Egypt, the largest and most important country of them all, faced a hard road long after its 18 days of revolution in January and February, their human and political drama powerfully covered by Cairo correspondent Jack Shenker – a young man in instinctive sympathy with the youthful activists of Tahrir Square. On the back of huge interest, the Guardian launched its pioneering Middle East live blog – rolling online news, comment, tweets, video and sound, edited in London – which quickly attracted audiences across the world.

Egyptian emotions and expectations ran high, peaking when Mubarak's once loyal generals persuaded him to relinquish power – haughty and peevish at the masses who had the temerity to demand his departure after 30 years' loyal service. It was the unforgettable "Berlin Wall" moment of the Arab world.

In August, the next time Mubarak appeared live on TV – as millions again watched in slack-jawed amazement – the deposed Pharoah was being carried on a stretcher into a caged dock to face criminal charges. Yet ominously, months later, the Supreme Council of the Armed Forces was still assuming that transition to democracy could accommodate the military's continued dominance – that the ancien régime, in other words, could survive. Free elections did finally get under way after another spasm of violence in and around Tahrir – by then a standing inspiration for other manifestations of people power from Wall Street to Tel Aviv. But that was only the beginning of a complex and drawn-out process. Cairenes often call their chaotic city by its Arabic nickname – *umm ad-dunya* (mother of the world). What happens there will continue to be closely watched as a bellwether for wider trends.

The outlook was far better in Tunisia. Its "Jasmine" revolution was triggered by the self-immolation of 26-year-old Mohammed Bouazizi, whose terminal misery seemed emblematic of a generation of young people with no hope of a decent job or independence under a regime which branded itself, at home and abroad, as a bulwark of stability against extremism.

Paris correspondent Angelique Chrisafis flew in in mid-January to document the "confusion, fear and horror" before the fall and flight of Zine al-Abidine Ben Ali, president since 1987. (Ben Ali and his family's reputation for corruption and nepotism had been devastatingly exposed weeks earlier in a WikiLeaks cable written by the US ambassador and published by the Guardian – generating fierce debate over whether this was a "WikiLeaks revolution".) Chrisafis was back in Tunis in October to report on the first free election since Ben Ali's departure for a gilded retirement in Saudi Arabia.

By any sober assessment, however, Tunisia looked to be the exception not the norm of the Arab Spring. Its smooth transition from dictatorship to democracy was built on a sizeable middle class, a homogeneous population, relatively advanced women's rights, a civil society and non-political generals who did the right thing at the crucial moment – ditching a president whose sell-by date suddenly expired. Links to the former colonial power France played a role, too – though the tin-eared offer from Paris of riot police "knowhow" to help Ben Ali underlined Europe's collective failure to understand the sheer novelty of what was going on in its backyard.

Next door, Libya's February 17 revolution was a different kind of exception – not only for the Maghreb but the whole Arab world. Until then conventional wisdom – so often proved wrong in this turbulent year – was that the country was too repressive, too tribal and too divided to see a successful uprising. Libya's oil wealth allowed it easily to pay to solve problems. Yet the spirit of its hard-up Tunisian and Egyptian neighbours was catching. And Muammar Gaddafi's eccentricities and isolation meant that the suppression of protests on a "day of rage" in Benghazi galvanized Arab as well as western opinion against him. Defecting troops looting government arsenals, captured mercenaries – and at least 230 dead – all featured in a vivid Guardian dispatch from Martin Chulov, the first western journalist to report from free Benghazi. Chris McGreal, a Middle East veteran, spent dangerous weeks roaring up and down the coastal road to Tripoli – covering vicious but largely inconsequential skirmishes around oil terminals on the shifting front line between the ragtag rebels and Libyan government forces.

In the end, rare UN security council unity and Nato's intervention – supported by Qatar and the United Arab Emirates and blessed by the Arab League – helped a temporarily united opposition defeat Gaddafi. In Britain and other western countries, some criticised yet another war in another Muslim country as being about oil and self-interest, not protecting vulnerable civilians. Remembering the US-led invasion of Iraq, they saw not the exercise of the UN's "responsibility to protect", but regime change by stealth. Gaddafi's propaganda machine dubbed it the "colonialist-Crusader aggression".

But many ordinary Libyans cheered Nato's (impressively precise) airstrikes as the "brother leader of the revolution" ranted at opponents he called "greasy rats". Gaddafi's death in his hometown of Sirte – where Observer correspondent Peter Beaumont witnessed the final days of fighting in October – represented closure for exultant Libyans. It was a brutal end to a brutal 42-year rule. Enormous challenges loomed for the National Transitional Council, not least in bringing the undisciplined rebel brigades under control. But the mood was ecstatic: "Whatever happens next, things can't be worse then they were under Gaddafi," I was told repeatedly in Tripoli in the following weeks.

Further afield, impoverished, wild Yemen looked like another special case. Its experience of the Arab Spring reflected its political and geographic complexities, and combined mass street protests with the intertwined conflicts of elites, regions and tribes. "For months the sandbagged streets of downtown Sana'a have witnessed running battles," Tom Finn reported. It was November when Ali Abdullah Saleh, president for 33 years, finally agreed to go – securing an amnesty deal that would spare him Mubarak's humiliation in court. Saleh's exit was a big change but not a revolutionary rupture as his own family and the old ruling party and opposition were still jockeying for power with independent newcomers. It was Saleh, after all, who famously compared ruling Yemen to "dancing on the heads of snakes". The agreement was brokered by Saudi Arabia and backed by a United States worried about a residual al-Qaida threat.

Geopolitical considerations also shaped the outcome in Bahrain, the island state that straddles the region's sectarian divide, its Sunni Muslim minority ruling over a restive Shia majority. Bahraini politics are determined as much by the presence of the US Fifth Fleet and an assertive Iran across the Gulf as by any domestic struggle. Outrage flared in February as initially peaceful protests were violently crushed. Medical staff in Manama's main hospital were accused of siding with rioters, though the charges were later dropped. Months afterwards the competing narratives of the two sides, as polarised as those that divide Israelis and Palestinians or Catholics and Protestants in Northern Ireland, could still not be reconciled, I discovered. In November an independent report commissioned by King Hamad found that torture and other human rights abuses had been committed by security forces during the "Pearl revolution". That Gulf revolt may have been crushed or contained. But its root causes have not yet been tackled.

Containment was the watchword elsewhere in the region. King Abdullah of Saudi Arabia earmarked $130bn for economic and social benefits to deflect anger at lack of housing and jobs, promising more positions in the religious bureaucracy and the security services. Riyadh also blamed Iran for stirring Shia unrest in the oil-rich eastern province, close to Bahrain, where hundreds were arrested and only released after pledging not to protest again. Many faced travel bans. "Anyone hoping for major upheaval soon is likely to be disappointed," Jason Burke concluded after a reporting trip in June. "The word that recurs in Saudi Arabia is 'gradual'." Political parties remained illegal; women were still banned from driving.

The poorer western-backed Arab kingdoms acted more boldly. Jordan's King Abdullah II, vulnerable like Mubarak because of the unpopular peace treaty with Israel, pledged to allow parliament to appoint a future prime minister – a dilution of direct royal control. In Morocco King Mohammed VI allowed modest constitutional amendments. Feted in Washington, London and Paris with their aura of legitimacy and settled mechanisms for succession, these monarchs proved more adept than the Arab republics in adapting to demands for change.

It was a different story in Syria, where at least 5,000 people, according to UN figures, had been killed by December. Peaceful protests erupted in March at Deraa in the south and spread. President Assad dismissed what he called "armed terrorist gangs" as a conspiracy by his western, Israeli and Arab enemies, though as time went on the rebels did launch military actions. Assad offered reforms but they were too little and too late. Yet in contrast to Libya, Syria saw no defections of senior loyalists. Nor was there any prospect of outside military intervention. Outwardly, the regime appeared resilient, with sectarianism a real danger and the opposition divided. Damascus and Aleppo, the country's second city, remained relatively calm. But for how long? The Arab League and Turkey both turned against Assad, even if he could still count on being defended from punitive UN action by Russia and China. And economic sanctions were starting to hurt.

Syria's uprising posed grave problems for the media, kept out except on rare occasions when the government agreed to self-serving interviews or strictly controlled access for carefully selected outlets. Nonetheless, pseudonymous Guardian correspondents Katherine Marsh and Nour Ali reported discreetly from Damascus for months at some risk to their own security. Ghaith Abdul-Ahad found villagers in the north manufacturing roadside bombs to use against tanks, smuggling in guns – and warning of civil war to come unless Assad goes.

The story so far, then, has been mixed. The variety of the Arab Spring was neatly encapsulated one day in November in a split-screen image broadcast on al-Jazeera TV – the Qatar-based satellite channel that was simultaneously dedicated reporter and unabashed cheerleader for the uprisings: one side showed the solemn opening of Tunisia's new constituent assembly, dominated by once-banned parties; the other recorded choking clouds of tear-gas in Cairo as Egypt's generals resisted demands for civilian rule.

And there were other striking and poignant juxtapositions: jerky video clips filmed on mobile phones and posted on YouTube showed Syrians weeping over the mutilated corpses of loved ones or demanding freedom as the crackle of gunfire rings out; mass rallies of flag-waving Assad loyalists in central Damascus. Bahrain's government mounted a slick PR campaign to advertise reforms while Shia protesters continued to clash nightly with the riot police. The dominant narrative of the uprisings was written defiantly in the streets, but the regimes' fightback – a counter-revolution some called it – continued.

If circumstances differed from country to country, some common themes stood out. Security "solutions" do not work for long – or not unless followed by meaningful concessions. Activists across the Arab world spoke of breaking through the barrier of fear so that even the harshest repression no longer deters. And one revolution inspired another in a domino effect of sympathy and solidarity: Tunisia, Egypt; Egypt, Bahrain; Libya, Syria, and so on. "Dear

Arab dictator, take a long hard look at Mubarak," one Bahraini tweeted as he watched the deposed Egyptian leader being wheeled into court. "He was just as powerful as u were. Your time is up if u don't change." A common language worked its unifying magic, too: crowds everywhere chanted the same simple Arabic demand: *Ash-sha'ab yurid isqat al-nizam* (The people want the overthrow of the regime).

For most, parliamentary democracy was the goal. Angry and humiliated subjects aspire to become citizens enjoying human rights, an end to corruption and the establishment of the rule of law. "Our weapons are our dreams," went one of the most intoxicating Tahrir slogans. Rashid Khalidi, the Palestinian-American historian, explained in March why what was unfolding felt so empowering: "Arab youth at the end of the day have been shown to have hopes and ideals no different from the young people who helped bring about democratic transitions in Eastern Europe, Latin America and south, southeast and east Asia," he wrote. "These voices have been a revelation only to those deluded by the propaganda of the Arab regimes themselves, or by the western media's obsessive focus on Islamic fundamentalism and terrorism whenever it deals with the Middle East. This is thus a supremely important moment not only in the Arab world, but also for how Arabs are perceived by others. A people that has been systematically maligned in the west for decades is for the first time being shown in a positive light."

Still, the role of Islamists is a hot topic. Egypt's long-suppressed and well-organised Muslim Brotherhood was predictably the biggest winner in the first round of elections. Having survived in an authoritarian environment it faced having to adapt to a pluralistic one. Worried liberals and secularists hope that freedom from dictatorship will encourage moderation and pragmatism. But the alarming strength of conservative Salafists – dour fundamentalists many believe are being discreetly financed by the Saudis – will have its effect too.

In Tunisia the An-Nahda party underwent a remarkable rehabilitation. Its leader, Rachid Ghannouchi, returned home from exile in Britain while his colleague Hamadi Jebali, a political prisoner under Ben Ali, became prime minister after October's election. In Morocco, which has had only sporadic protests, elections saw victory for the like-minded Justice and Development party. Islamists also look like playing a big role in post-Gaddafi Libya. Abdul Hakim Belhaj, head of Tripoli's military council, abandoned a jihadi world view to make the case for representative government. All insist they are committed to democracy, tolerance and coalition politics. Turkey's AK party is cited by many as a significant influence.

Algeria, which shares many of its neighbours' problems but saw only sporadic unrest, looked on nervously: it suffered the tragedy of tens of thousands killed in a bloody civil war that erupted after the Islamic Salvation Front, poised to take power, was banned by the military in 1991. May's killing of Osama bin Laden in his Pakistani hideout was not only a hammer blow to an already faltering al-Qaida and its hateful ideology – but also a well-timed reminder that political Islam can take many forms.

Looking ahead, it is clear that simplistic slogans like "Islam is the solution" are not enough to deal with the problems of the least developed Arab economies and societies – high birth rates, poverty and illiteracy. Protesters everywhere have demanded bread as well as dignity. The Arab revolutions risk losing support if expectations for higher living standards, fairer wealth distribution and more jobs are not met. As commentator Rami Khouri put it: "The really important phase of Arab political transformation is not the Islamists' victories, but the fact that Islamists share executive power and are subjected for the first time to the unforgiving test of incumbency." Social justice can not be just an afterthought when tyrants fall.

No account of the Middle East can be complete without mentioning the Israel-Palestine conflict, for so long the most closely scrutinised story in the region – and its most intractable conflict. Overshadowed by the Arab uprisings, it went nowhere slowly, though the mood hardened against Barack Obama, who had promised but failed to pursue a just peace settlement and an end to occupation. The PLO registered diplomatic progress with its bold bid for UN membership but saw no change on the ground in the West Bank, where Israeli colonisation continued apace. Its Islamist rival Hamas, still running the besieged Gaza Strip, won plaudits for securing the release of 1,100 prisoners in exchange for its single captive Israeli soldier, boosting hopes for inter-Palestinian reconciliation. That in turn was a byproduct of an Arab political climate invigorated by unprecedented demonstrations of the possibility of smashing the status quo.

Israel fretted about the uncertainties of post-Mubarak Egypt – would the 1979 peace treaty survive? – and the implications of Assad's overthrow – even if that would discomfit and weaken his ally Iran. Tehran's nuclear ambitions, a direct challenge to Israel's nuclear hegemony, continued to fuel international alarm – and divisions over how to deal with it. Iran treated – and misrepresented – the Arab uprisings (except Syria's) as an "Islamic awakening" against the US and Israel while continuing to repress its own people.

Catchy names and labels tend to stick, so 2011 looks likely to be remembered as the year of the Arab Spring, of stirrings and hope after decades of stagnation – though euphoria has given way to more nuanced and differentiated expectations of what happens next. "The revolution can be tweeted," someone quipped, "but the transition cannot." Forecasting is risky, but the political weather in the Middle East and North Africa will stay turbulent well into 2012 – and probably far beyond. Yet if much remains to be decided, it is clear that the genie of Arab people power is out of the bottle. It does not look likely to be stoppered up again any time soon.

Ian Black is the Guardian's Middle East editor

EDITOR'S NOTE

Toby Manhire

Still a nascent journalistic form, the live blog is a story told online as it happens –updating regularly with the latest developments and coverage on the given subject or event. Rarely can there have been a more ambitious live blog than the Guardian's account of the biggest and most dramatic story of 2011: the uprisings in the Middle East and north Africa.

Combine the daily blogs through the year and you have a giant article of more than two million words, penned by more than 20 reporter-bloggers – a contextualised, rolling aggregation of spoken and written dispatches from Guardian correspondents, wire reports (and here the breadth, authority and bravery of agency reporters is as clear as ever), other media organisations, blogs, tweets, videos, and anything else they can lay their hands on.

In the first part of this book that mammoth effort is boiled down to around one thirtieth of its original length. Inevitably it cannot retain the depth of the original, but I hope it still manages to convey something of the unique energy and immediacy of the daily posts as they unfolded.

The words are almost all drawn from the live blog, though on a handful of occasions I have amended or added material from Guardian reports to capture important moments that passed when the blog was not in operation.

It is impossible to byline the live blog in the usual manner, so here is the roll of honour: Richard Adams, Jo Adetunji, David Batty, Sean Clarke, Lizzy Davies, Rowenna Davis, Alan Evans, Adam Gabbatt, Jonathan Haynes, Tim Hill, Sam Jones, Saeed Kamali Dehghan, Mona Mahmood, Warren Murray, Alex Olorenshaw, Paul Owen, Ben Quinn, James Randerson, Haroon Siddique, Matthew Taylor, Mark Tran, Peter Walker, Matthew Weaver and Matt Wells. I'm bound to have left at least one live-blogger out. If that's you: apologies.

Through the second half of the year especially, as the blog became a staple part of the Guardian coverage under the banner "Middle East Live", the lion's share of the task was completed by Haroon Siddique and Matthew Weaver.

The second part of the book is a more orthodox anthology of journalism on the Arab unrest in 2011 – selected from the hundreds of pieces that have appeared in the Guardian, the Observer, and online.

Thanks to the many people at the Guardian who advised on the contents, especially Ian Black, Natalie Hanman, Paul Owen, Haroon Siddique and Brian Whitaker.

Personal thanks to Lisa Darnell and Katie Roden at Guardian Books for backing this unconventional collection, and to Emily Anderton for support and advice.

The story continues at www.guardian.co.uk/world/middle-east-live.

PART ONE

Middle East Live

The Guardian Live Blog 2011

THURSDAY 30 DECEMBER, 2010

10.00am: "The biggest story from the Middle East this week – no, the biggest, most important and most inspiring story from the Middle East *this year* – is one that most readers may only vaguely have heard of, if at all," writes the Guardian's Brian Whitaker at Comment Is Free. "It's the Tunisian uprising."

In his weekly roundup of events in the Middle East, Brian writes:

> For almost two weeks now, people up and down the country have been protesting, some of them rioting, others demonstrating peacefully – and all in a police state where the penalties for defying the regime are severe.
>
> You won't find much about it in the western media (or the Arab media, for that matter) though you can piece together much of the story from snippets on Twitter and videos on YouTube …
>
> What we have in Tunisia today is the birth of a genuine, national, indigenous, popular movement, not against colonialists or foreign occupiers but against their own repressive regime, and one which is not tainted (as in Iran) by international power games. This is something new, which is why it's so important.

Two days ago, Brian Whitaker wrote about the roots of the emerging rebellion:

> The riots and demonstrations that have swept through Tunisia during the past 10 days … began with a small incident. Twenty-six-year-old Mohammed Bouazizi, living in the provincial town of Sidi Bouzid, had a university degree but no work. To earn some money he took to selling fruit and vegetables in the street without a licence. When the authorities stopped him and confiscated his produce, he was so angry that he set himself on fire.

Rioting followed and security forces sealed off the town. On Wednesday, another jobless young man in Sidi Bouzid climbed an electricity pole, shouted "no for misery, no for unemployment", then touched the wires and electrocuted himself.

On Friday, rioters in Menzel Bouzaiene set fire to police cars, a railway locomotive, the local headquarters of the ruling party and a police station. After being attacked with Molotov cocktails, the police shot back, killing a teenage protester. By Saturday, the protests had reached the capital, Tunis – and a second demonstration took place there yesterday …

Ben Ali may try to cling on, but his regime now has a *fin de siècle* air about it. He came to power in 1987 by declaring President Bourguiba unfit for office. It's probably just a matter of time before someone else delivers that same message to Ben Ali.

FRIDAY 31 DECEMBER

10.00am: Sudanese commentator Nesrine Malik has written at Comment Is Free of "Tunisia's inspiring rebellion":

There are few moments in the political atmosphere of the Middle East that fill me with genuine pride. While eyes have long been fixed on opposition movements in Iran and Egypt, suddenly Tunisia has provided one of the most inspiring episodes of indigenous revolt against a repressive regime …

Even if nothing comes of the Tunisian revolt, it is proof that the resignation is not an inevitability, that it is not hardwired into our DNA, that the "Arab malaise" is not terminal.

TUESDAY 11 JANUARY, 2011

Simon Tisdall, in his Guardian World Briefing, says this:

Despite Ben Ali's assertions, there is no evidence so far of outside meddling or Islamist pot-stirring. What is abundantly plain is that many Tunisians are fed up to the back teeth with chronic unemployment, especially affecting young people; endemic poverty in rural areas that receive no benefits from tourism; rising food prices; insufficient public investment; official corruption; and a pseudo-democratic, authoritarian political system that gave Ben Ali, 74, a fifth consecutive term in 2009 with an absurd 89.6% of the vote.

WEDNESDAY 12 JANUARY

10.00am: Reuters news agency reports that violence has rocked the Tunisian capital for the first time, with protesters attacking government buildings.

12.04pm: Brian Whitaker has been tracking events via Twitter. He writes:

> With reporting on the ground severely curtailed by the authorities, with the western media slow to catch on to the significance of the events, and the Arab media – with a few rare exceptions such as al-Jazeera – nervously wondering what they can safely say, Twitter has become the first port of call for information …
>
> The discourse about Tunisia on Twitter is unlike any you would find in the mainstream Arab media where journalists, for the most part, are heavily constrained and constantly looking over their shoulders. It's free and uninhibited, much more like a private conversation among friends in some smoke-filled shisha cafe – except that it's happening on the internet and the whole world can listen in.

FRIDAY 14 JANUARY

2.48pm: Things seem to have taken a serious turn for the worse. The Guardian's Angelique Chrisafis, who is in Tunisia, is tweeting:

\# Gunshots are now ringing around us and in the other sidestreets around interior ministry.

An earlier tweet from her:

\# Running battles amid extreme violence from police. Protesters being chased onto rooftops. This is turning very, very bad.

This is very bad news for Ben Ali who must have been hoping that his concessions announced yesterday would calm things down. Instead the protesters seem to have been emboldened.

3.41pm: Ben Ali has said that elections will be held in six months – a big concession since last night when he said he would leave leave office at the end of his term in 2014. But will demonstrators be satisfied with that? Today they are demanding his immediate departure.

5.59pm: In a television address, the prime minister, Mohamed Ghannouchi, has said he has taken over from Ben Ali on an interim basis. This is what he said, according to Reuters:

> I vow that I will respect the constitution and implement the political, economic and social reforms that have been announced … in consultation with all political sides including political parties and civil society.

6.31pm: Some more information on the new president. He is a long-term ally of the former president, having joined the cabinet when Ben Ali assumed power in 1987. Ben Ali appointed him prime minister in 1999. Ghannouchi has had a high profile role during the unrest of the past few days, announcing the sacking of the interior minister earlier this week. Ghannouchi also gave interviews to the international media defending Tunisia's handling of the protests.

7.48pm: Angelique Chrisafis reports that French police are awaiting the arrival of Ben Ali's plane in Paris. The French president, Nicolas Sarkozy, said France – the former occupying power – recognises the "constitutional transition" in Tunisia.

SUNDAY 16 JANUARY

10am In a piece for the Observer, Peter Beaumont points to the potential for a ripple effect:

> What has happened in Tunisia, a country which Ben Ali and his cronies controlled since he seized power in 1987, has a message for other regimes whose democratic credentials are less than shining. While it is not clear what Tunisia's path will be after Friday's insurrection, the complaints of the protesters are familiar across the region and have also, in some cases, prompted demonstrations. Algeria, home to an often restless young population, has seen protests about unemployment and food prices which

began on 5 January and prompted a harsh crackdown. In Jordan, which saw demonstrations last week in five cities, the calls were very similar. There, too, the country's leader was assailed with demands to resign.

Nowhere has the link between the removal of Ben Ali and other countries been clearer than in Cairo, where on Friday night protests were held by opposition members outside the Tunisian embassy. Their message was explicit: President Mubarak should follow Ben Ali's example and leave his country, too.

1.07pm: The Libyan leader, Muammar Gaddafi, has condemned the uprising in neighbouring Tunisia amid reports today of unrest on the streets of Libya. In a speech last night Gaddafi, an ally of the ousted president, Ben Ali, said he was "pained" by the fall of the Tunisian government. He claimed protesters had been led astray by WikiLeaks disclosures detailing the corruption in Ben Ali's family and his repressive regime.

8.37pm: Angelique Chrisafis has filed for tomorrow's paper from Tunis. She writes:

> For the first time in the Arab world, a people [have] forced out a leader by spontaneously and peacefully taking to the street. But although Ben Ali has fled, the diehards of his brutal police force have not. During the day random yellow taxi-loads of militia loyal to the ousted leader had careered through the capital and some suburbs, firing randomly into the air. Armed gangs broke into homes and ransacked them, or fired shots in the street.
>
> Meanwhile, the full horror of repression over four weeks of demonstrations is beginning to emerge. Human rights groups estimate at least 150–200 deaths since 17 December. In random roundups in poor, rural areas youths were shot in the head and dumped far from home so bodies could not be identified. Police also raped women in their houses in poor neighbourhoods in and around Kasserine in the rural interior.

MONDAY 17 JANUARY

8.55am: There's more evidence that the Tunisian unrest is spreading with another self-burning protest, this time in Egypt. The unrest started in Tunisia started on December 17 when an unemployed student, Mohammed Bouazizi, set fire to himself to protest at economic conditions. He later died.

Today an Egyptian man set fire to himself near the parliament building in Cairo in an apparent copycat protest. It comes after a man died yesterday in Algeria, after setting fire to himself after failing to find a job and a house.

10.17am: Supporters of the ousted president Ben Ali are expected to take to the streets of Tunis later today in what could become a flashpoint for more violence, according to Sky News. Its foreign affairs editor Tim Marshall says:

> This is the key day now because if the president's supporters, if they exist, come out on to the streets, it will be very interesting to see what the police, the army and the people do. Supporters are claiming 15,000 will be on the streets so it's a critical day if we get those numbers. Instinct tells me they won't get those numbers but it's a volatile situation, so let's see.

11.05am: Al-Jazeera's correspondent in Tunis says around 1,000 protesters turned out. Water cannons were used against them when they tried to move from trade union headquarters towards the interior ministry, Ayman Mohyeldin told the broadcaster. He said the protest is generally being tolerated, but the security forces will not let demonstrators get near government buildings. He also confirmed that protesters are demanding that the new government should not contain any representatives from the old regime.

11.43am: More teargas has been fired, according to an email from Angelique: "Teargas here is extreme, on Friday afternoon, people's eyes and lungs were burning, some totally lost their voice until the next morning."

3.34pm: Reuters is reporting the following:

> The ministers of defence, interior, finance and foreign affairs will keep their posts in Tunisia's new government but opposition leaders including Najib Chebbi will have posts, the prime minister has said.

4.33pm: Many protesters are objecting to the retention of figures from the old Ben Ali regime in the new government. But, as the New York Times points out, "after more than 50 years of one-party rule, there are few people outside the ruling party with the experience and expertise to steer the government until elections are held." In addition, outlawed Communist and Islamist parties were also excluded from the talks, the paper reports.

TUESDAY 18 JANUARY

11.41am: It didn't take long for the interim unity government to begin to totter.

There are conflicting reports about ministerial resignations. Al-Jazeera is reporting that three ministers, from the trade union movement, have resigned in protest at the presence of members from Constitution Democratic Rally, the party of the ousted president. Al-Arabiya is reporting that as many five ministers have left the government.

The apparent resignations come amid continuing protests on the streets of Tunis. Once again teargas has been used to break up the demonstration, as Angelique Chrisafis reports from Tunis:

> About 200 leftwing opposition party supporters and unionists gathered in Avenue Bourguiba this morning, carrying banners denouncing the presence of the ruling RCD party in the new government. "The new government is a sham. It's an insult to the revolution that claimed lives and blood," said one, a student named Ahmed al-Haji.

12.41pm: Protests in Tunis appear to be coming and going in waves. CNN's Ben Wedeman tweets:

> \# Anti-government protests have now been going on for 3-hours center Tunis. Every time tear scatters them, they return.

Similarly the BBC's Lyse Ducet tweets:

> \# Protests started again centre Tunis … for hours starting/stopping and growing bigger/louder.

12.44pm: Nicolas Sarkozy's government has responded to accusations that it was trying to prop up the Ben Ali's regime in Tunisia, writes Kim Willsher in Paris.

> French foreign minister Michele Alliot-Marie has defended her contro-versial offer to help Tunisia's deposed president restore order a few days before he was ousted … She fended off opposition calls for her resigna-tion and told parliamentarians that France, along with other countries,

had "not seen events coming" ... She added she was "scandalised" by how her comments had been distorted.

1.44pm: Another man has set fire to himself in protest in Cairo, according to Reuters. This is third self-immolation protest in Cairo in the last two days, and the second today.

5.28pm: Reuters has confirmed that state TV is reporting that Tunisia's newly appointed interim president, Fouad Mebazaa, and the prime minister, Mohamed Ghannouchi, have both resigned from the RCD party of the former Ben Ali regime. The news agency characterises this as "a move to meet demands of opposition politicians and union leaders who threatened to bring down the interim government". They remain in their positions as president and prime minister.

6.18pm: The Guardian's Jack Shenker has interviewed Egyptian dissident Mohamed ElBaradei, who warns of a "Tunisia-style explosion" in his country as self-immolation protests continue and anti-government activists announce plans for a nationwide "day of anger" next week.

> But the former UN nuclear weapons chief stopped short of calling on his supporters to take to the streets, prompting scathing criticism from opposition campaigners who believe ElBaradei is squandering a rare opportunity to bring an end to President Mubarak's three decades of autocratic rule ... He said: "I still hope that change will come in an orderly way and not through the Tunisian model. But if you keep closing the door to peaceful change then don't be surprised if the scenes we saw in Tunisia spread across the region."

WEDNESDAY JANUARY 19

10.02am: Delegates at an Arab League meeting have been warned to heed the economic and social problems that led to the uprising in Tunisia. Reuters reports:

> What is happening in Tunisia in terms of the revolution is not an issue far from the issues of this summit which is economic and social development," the League's Egyptian secretary general, Amr Moussa, told the summit in Sharm el-Sheikh.

"It is on everyone's mind that the Arab self is broken by poverty, unemployment and a general slide in indicators," he said, referring to events in Tunisia as an example of "big social shocks that many Arab societies are exposed to".

1.13pm: Two more people have tried to set fire to themselves in Algeria, according to a tweet from the broadcaster al-Arabiya. It says there have been seven self-immolation protests this week.

3.08pm: The security forces have been much more tolerant towards the protests today, in a marked change of attitude, according to Angelique Chrisafis, who tweets:

\#   Real change: for 4 hours peaceful protesters on Bourguiba ave have been chanting "RCD out". No teargas. Police letting them demonstrate.

4.15pm: The Egyptian dissident Mohamed ElBaradei seems to changing his line on street protests, which he now appears to support.

He just tweeted this in Arabic and this in English:

\#   Fully support call 4 peaceful demonstrations vs repression & corruption. When our demands for change fall on deaf ears what options remain?

THURSDAY 20 JANUARY

3.30pm: Reuters has news of a "blanket amnesty" being offered by the interim Tunisian government "to all political groups including the banned Islamist opposition":

The pledge came in the ruling coalition's first cabinet meeting. Protesters have complained that despite a promised amnesty, only a few hundred of those imprisoned for political reasons during the 23-year rule of Ben Ali had been released …

The announcement followed another day of protests, with police firing shots into the air to try to disperse hundreds of demonstrators demanding that ministers associated with the rule of Ben Ali leave the government.

4.55pm: The Guardian datablog has analysed some important statistics relating to Tunisia's neighbours. Among the findings is this:

> Libya is the only country with a higher unemployment rate than Tunisia, and a similar population size. However the GDP per capita is lower than Tunisia in every country compared, except Libya where GDP per capita is running at a relatively healthy $14,000.

SATURDAY 22 JANUARY

11.00am: From Reuters:

> Thousands of Tunisian police, national guard, firemen and street cleaners thronged central Tunis today, distancing themselves from deposed President Ben Ali in the largest demonstration for days. The protest marks a turning point in the Tunisian uprising, throughout which Ben Ali loyalists in the police force fired on crowds, beat protesters with batons and shot teargas even at relatively small and peaceful gatherings.
>
> Tunisia's interior minister has said 78 people have been killed since the start of the demonstrations, but the UN high commissioner for human rights put the number at 117, including 70 killed by live fire.

MONDAY 24 JANUARY

4.42pm: Tomorrow is shaping up as a big day in Egypt. Jack Shenker has filed from Cairo:

> Egypt's authoritarian government is bracing itself for one of the biggest opposition demonstrations in recent years, as thousands of protesters prepare to take to the streets demanding political reform. An unlikely alliance of youth activists, political Islamists, industrial workers and hardcore football fans have pledged to join a nationwide "day of revolution" on a national holiday to celebrate the achievements of the police force.
>
> With public sentiment against state security forces at an unprecedented level following a series of high-profile police brutality cases and the torture of anti-government activists, protest organisers are hoping that a large number of Egyptians will be emboldened to attend rallies, marches and flash mobs across the country in a sustained effort to force concessions from an increasingly unpopular ruling elite.

TUESDAY 25 JANUARY

11.55am: Protesters in Cairo have broken through police ranks and are heading towards the Nile, says Jack Shenker, who has just been in touch. Some have been beaten by police but the demonstrators remain defiant, chanting at the police, most of whom are from very poor neighbourhoods, to join them. Many have sat down in the face of the amassed police ranks. Shenker says that what started as a protest with three specific aims is now seen by many as an opportunity to bring down the Mubarak regime.

12.57pm: There is intense activity on Twitter, particularly with respect to Egypt, using the #jan25 hashtag.

\# **ashrafkhalil** #Jan25 crowds overwhelming police cordons outside courthouse downtown!

\# **sandmonkey** Security tried to storm protesters. Failed. Regrouping. #jan25

\# **salmander** If you are in a cab or speaking with people in the st tell them to break the barriers of fear #jan25

And from Jack Shenker, reporting for the Guardian:

\# Protesters marching past min of foreign affairs chanting 'Tunis' and revelling in their control of the street #jan25

3.37pm: Martin Chulov, the Guardian's Iraq correspondent, reports that there were high hopes last week in cyberspace that Egypt's demonstrations would be replicated in Syria today. But according to our people in Damascus, he says, there is "not a peep of protest" there.

4.07pm: Jack Shenker has just sent this dramatic update from Egypt:

Downtown Cairo is a war zone tonight – as reports come in of massive occupations by protesters in towns across Egypt, the centre of the capital is awash with running street battles. Along with hundreds of others I've just been teargassed outside the parliament building, where some youths were smashing up the pavement to obtain rocks to throw at police.

We've withdrawn back to the main square now where thousands more demonstrators are waiting and a huge billboard advertising the ruling NDP party has just been torn down. Security forces are continuing to use sound bombs and teargas to disperse the crowd, but so far to no avail.

5.40pm: US secretary of state Hillary Clinton has spoken about Egypt:

We support the fundamental right of expression and assembly for all people and we urge that all parties exercise restraint and refrain from violence. Our assessment is that the Egyptian government is stable and is looking for ways to respond to the legitimate needs and interests of the Egyptian people.

7.01pm: There are reports that Twitter has been blocked in Egypt in a bid to quell the demonstrations. The protests have been organised in part through Twitter and Facebook, but TechCrunch says the Twitter website and mobile site have been blocked in the country.

Facebook is still working in Egypt, however, with the group We Are all Khaled Said posting updates every 15 minutes or so. Khaled Said was an Egyptian activist who died in 2010, allegedly at the hands of police.

7.20pm: The video journalist Mohamed Abdelfattah has posted some distressing tweets from the scene of the protests, where he says he has been arrested. Here are some of his posts – all filed within minutes of each other and presented here in chronological order.

\# Teargas

\# I'm suffocating

\# We r trapped inside a building

\# Armored vehicles outside

\# Help we r suffocating

\#   I will be arrested

\#   Help !!!

\#   Arrested

\#   Ikve been beaten alot

10.19pm: Here's Jack Shenker's latest from Cairo:

> As midnight approaches thousands of protesters are still occupying Tahrir Square, vowing to remain in place until the government falls …
>
> Pamphlets widely distributed amongst protesters declared that "the spark of intifada" had been launched in Egypt. "We have started an uprising with the will of the people, the people who have suffered for 30 years under oppression, injustice and poverty," read the Arabic-language texts. "Egyptians have proven today that they are capable of taking freedom by force and destroying despotism."

1.05am: Police have used teargas and rubber bullets to clear Tahrir Square. Protesters fled to side streets and bridges across the river Nile, some pledging to continue protesting on Wednesday.

WEDNESDAY 26 JANUARY

9.58am: Egypt's interior ministry has warned of zero tolerance for protests today. From AP:

> The interior ministry said in a statement that police would not tolerate any gatherings, marches or protests Wednesday, suggesting that security forces would immediately resort to force to at the first sign of protesters gathering. Thousands of policemen in riot gear and backed by armored vehicles could be seen on bridges across the Nile, at major intersections and squares.

12.03pm: Interpol has a warrant for the arrest of the former Tunisian president Ben Ali, reports Reuters. He is wanted for "possessing of (expropriated) property and transferring foreign currency abroad".

2.43pm: An update from Jack Shenker:

> Things are kicking off again in downtown Cairo as protesters attempting to rally are met with fierce police resistance. Security forces are repeating yesterday's tactics, using sound bombs and teargas to disperse crowds; protesters that can get access to Twitter are calling desperately for help. There are reports of hundreds of beatings and arrests, with many fearful that violence will intensify as darkness begins to fall.

3.03pm: If you're wondering why Jack Shenker, reporting from Cairo for the Guardian, has been relatively quiet today, he was arrested and beaten by the police in the early hours of the morning. He was taken in the back of a police van. He writes:

> We were being dragged towards a security building on the edge of the square, just two streets away from my apartment, and as I approached the doorway of the building other security officers took flying kicks and punches at me. I spotted a high-ranking uniformed officer and shouted at him that I was a British journalist. He responded by walking over and punching me twice, saying in Arabic, "Fuck you and fuck Britain."

4.31pm: The Associated Press is reporting that 860 protesters have been "rounded up" by police since yesterday.

7.41pm: Peter Beaumont arrived today in Cairo. Demonstrators are playing "cat and mouse" with police, he reports:

> Tonight groups of demonstrators and police are still playing a violent game of cat and mouse through the city centre's streets – with protesters quickly regrouping after being broken up.
>
> The sound of police sirens and detonating teargas canisters could be heard across the city, in the biggest protests against the regime of 82-year-old president Mubarak in three decades.

12.09am: The We are all Khaled Said opposition protest group is updating its Facebook page constantly. Here's its latest post on Suez.

Urgent News: Suez is completely cut off. Police have been evacuated … Some sad speculations say that a massive crackdown will take place in Suez on protesters which could end up with a REAL Massacre. Suez now is Egypt's Sidi Bouzid.

THURSDAY 27 JANUARY

8.29am: Political reform campaigner Mohamed ElBaradei, who lives in Vienna, is expected to return to the country today. ElBaradei, who was awarded the 2005 Nobel Peace Prize along with the UN's International Atomic Energy Agency, which he headed at the time, told the Daily Beast:

> I am going back to Cairo, and back on to the streets because, really, there is no choice. You go out there with this massive number of people, and you hope things will not turn ugly, but so far, the regime does not seem to have gotten that message … This week the Egyptian people broke the barrier of fear, and once that is broken, there is no stopping them.

10.10am: First Tunisia, then Egypt and now Yemen. Here's Reuters:

> Thousands of Yemenis today took to the streets of the capital, Sana'a, to demand a change of government, inspired by the unrest that ousted the Tunisian leader and spread to Egypt this week. "The people want a change in president," protesters chanted at Sana'a University in one of a series of demonstrations across the city – the largest in a wave of anti-government protests. President Ali Abdullah Saleh, a key ally of the US in a battle against the resurgent Yemeni arm of al-Qaida, has ruled the impoverished Arabian Peninsula state for more than 30 years.

1.27pm: Despite widespread reports of use of teargas and police brutality, Egypt's cabinet spokesman has said today officers were showing maximum restraint in dealing with anti-government protesters but intervening "strongly" in Suez in response to vandalism.

2.13pm: The outlawed Muslim Brotherhood, the biggest opposition group in Egypt, has thrown its weight behind tomorrow's planned demonstration. People are spreading the world via Twitter, trying to get a million people onto the streets after Friday prayers.

2.49pm: Egypt's interior minister Habib al-Adli, whose resignation is being demanded by the protesters, has dismissed the demonstrations, reports Reuters. He told Kuwait's al-Rai newspaper:

> Egypt's system is not marginal or frail. We are a big state, with an administration with popular support. The millions will decide the future of this nation, not demonstrations even if numbered in the thousands. Our country is stable and not shaken by such actions.

FRIDAY 28 JANUARY

7.45am: Overnight several senior members of the Muslim Brotherhood were arrested after the organisation pledged to take part in the demonstrations for the first time. To date the demonstrations have been largely secular, as they were in Tunisia. The involvement of the Muslim Brotherhood could change that, according to the New York Times:

> The support of the Brotherhood could well change the calculus on the streets, tipping the numbers in favour of the protesters and away from the police, lending new strength to the demonstrations and further imperiling president Mubarak's reign of nearly three decades.

9.39am: CNN's Ben Wedeman says he "momentarily" has access to the internet. He just tweeted:

\#   Just saw blue fiat entering main tv building in Maspiro when guards opened trunk, full of baseball bats. Car allowed in #egypt

\#   Cairo in COMPLETE lockdown. Security everywhere, including special forces. Government once again warning protests BANNED.

11.12am: Within seconds of Friday prayers finishing teargas, water cannons, and "sound bombs" were used against protesters, Jack Shenker reports from Cairo. Protesters continued to chant "down, down, Hosni Mubarak", despite the crackdown. "It was obvious the regime was not going to tolerate any protests today," Jack said. ElBaradei's whereabouts are unknown.

3.30pm: Egyptian state media are reporting a curfew starting at 6pm tonight (about 30 minutes away) and running until 7am tomorrow in Cairo, Alexandria and Suez. The way it's looking on the streets at the moment suggests there is little chance of people obeying the order.

4.22pm: Army tanks are rolling into the centre of Cairo and Suez, al-Jazeera reports. Mubarak has supposedly ordered them in to restore order but people have been cheering the army hoping it will side with them against the police.

4.45pm: A downtown police station in Cairo, police cars and gas tanks outside the police station are on fire, which could account for the number of loud explosions being heard, al-Jazeera reports.

9.09pm: Three tweets from CNN's Ben Wedeman in the last 10 minutes:

\# Teenager showed me teargas canister "made in USA". Saw the same thing in Tunisia. Time to reconsider US exports?

\# One man said he graduated from college 4 years ago, hasn't worked a day since. Has been in streets since Tuesday protesting.

\# Saw boys with massive seal of the republic looted from State TV. If this isn't the end, it certainly looks and smells like it.

9.19pm: Reuters are reporting that "Egyptian medical sources" estimate there have been 1,030 people wounded today in today's protests.

10.17pm: Mubarak now appears on television, with little warning. It's a single camera shot of him standing at a podium, reading from a statement, lit from below in a gloomy room. No indication if this is live or taped. He begins:

I have been closely following the protests and what they were asking for and calling on. My instructions to the government have stressed providing it with an opportunity to express the opinions and demands of the citizens … I deeply regret the loss of innocent lives among protesters and police forces.

10.27pm: Mubarak says the government will resign tomorrow and a new government will be appointed. The key statement:

> I have asked the government to present its resignation today [Friday] and I will name a new government starting from tomorrow … to effectively deal with the priorities of this current phase.

Mubarak has announced that he will force the government to resign and appoint a new one. But he gave no sign whatsoever that he would be going with them. Quite the opposite.

11.32pm: Barack Obama has just given a short briefing at the White House. Here's a selection of what the president said:

> I just spoke to President Mubarak, after his speech, and told him he has a responsilibilty to give meaning to his words …
>
> When I was in Cairo, after I became president, I said that all governments must maintain power through consent, not coercion, and that is how they will achieve the future. The US will continue to stand up to the rights of the Egyptian people, and work with the government to ensure a future that is more hopeful.

SATURDAY 29 JANUARY

10.25am: Peter Beaumont has just rung in from Cairo with the latest from Tahrir Square. He said that although a number of army tanks are parked around the square the military has so far not intervened in the clashes between protesters and the police.

11.21am: At least 74 people have been killed in the protests to date and 2,000 have been wounded, Reuters has calculated from medical sources, hospitals and witnesses. The agency cautions that this is not an official figure but notes that 68 deaths were reported in Cairo, Suez and Alexandria during yesterday's unrest, with at least six deaths prior to that.

12.01pm: Jack Shenker, who's covering the protests in Cairo, has just called. He says there was a "surreal air of normalcy" on the streets of the capital first thing this morning. But within hours this gave way to the charged atmosphere seen over the past few days as thousands once again gathered to protest:

> By mid-morning the atmosphere had changed, with tens of thousands returning to the streets and clambering on top of the tanks which are now stationed all over downtown Cairo. As during last night's protests, people were chanting: "The army and the people are as one." But there is growing confusion over what exactly the millitary's stance is.

12.29pm: King Abdullah of Saudi Arabia has, unsurprisingly, backed Mubarak, according to the official Saudi Press Agency. He said:

> No Arab or Muslim can tolerate any meddling in the security and stability of Arab and Muslim Egypt by those who infiltrated the people in the name of freedom of expression, exploiting it to inject their destructive hatred … The Kingdom of Saudi Arabia and its people and government declares it stands with all its resources with the government of Egypt and its people.

12.35pm: Al-Jazeera reports that China has blocked the term "Egypt" from its equivalent of Twitter, the Sina microblogging site, because it is "sensitive to any potential source of social unrest".

3.34pm: Mubarak has appointed his intelligence chief and confidante, Omar Suleiman, as vice president, the official Egyptian news agency reports. There has not been a vice president since Mubarak took office in 1981. Mubarak held the post before he was appointed president.

3.43pm: Fawaz Gerges, professor of Middle Eastern politics and international relations at the London School of Economics, has said this is "the Arab world's Berlin moment". He told Reuters:

> The authoritarian wall has fallen – and that's regardless of whether Mubarak survives or not. It goes beyond Mubarak. The barrier of fear has been removed. It is really the beginning of the end of the status quo in the region. The introduction of the military speaks volumes about the failure of the police to suppress the protesters. The military has stepped in and will likely seal any vacuum of authority in the next few weeks. Mubarak is deeply wounded. He is bleeding terribly. We are witnessing the beginning of a new era.

4.23pm: Ahmed Shafiq, the former air force commander and civil aviation minister in the outgoing cabinet, has been appointed as prime minister, state television has reported.

SUNDAY 30 JANUARY

9.38am: The government plans to shut down al-Jazeera's operations in Egypt, according to Reuters, citing the state news agency Mana. "The information minister ordered … suspension of operations of al-Jazeera, cancelling of its licences and withdrawing accreditation to all its staff as of today," a statement said.

9.46am: Al-Jazeera has denounced the closure of its Cairo bureau. In a statement it said:

> Al-Jazeera sees this as an act designed to stifle and repress the freedom of reporting by the network and its journalists … The closing of our bureau by the Egyptian government is aimed at censoring and silencing the voices of the Egyptian people.

9.58am: Brian Whitaker, writing on his blog, addresses talk of a military crackdown:

> Rumours have been circulating that the army will take a much tougher line with protesters today – what some are calling the Tiananmen Square option. However, I am sceptical about that. For one, thing, the US has warned strongly against it, and though Mubarak may not listen to Washington I think his commanders are more likely to.

1.18pm: Peter Beaumont is in Tahrir Square:

> People clearly sense that something different is going on. People feel very uncomfortable about all these tanks trying to enter the square.

1.56pm: Fighters jets are flying very low over central Cairo, Peter Beaumont reports. A tweet from al-Jazeera confirms this:

\# 2 egyptian airforce fighter planes currently flying above crowds at #Tahrir Square, defiant chants and roars from protesters.

4.34pm: ElBaradei has arrived in Tahrir Square, reports Jack Shenker from Cairo:

> It's still unclear at the moment what his reception will be. He's popular among some people, but there are those who felt he has joined the protests too late and is only arriving now once the danger is apparently over. Either way this is a special moment … Many people in the crowd feel these are the final hours of the Mubarak regime.

4.58pm: Reuters has some quotes from ElBaradei's address:

> Change is coming in the next few days. You have taken back your rights and what we have begun cannot go back … We have one main demand – the end of the regime and the beginning of a new stage, a new Egypt. I bow to the people of Egypt in respect. I ask of you patience.

5.13pm: Egyptian TV viewers can't see the footage of ElBaradei because al-Jazeera continues to be blocked. State TV has been showing footage of security guards outside a government building, the network said.

7.50pm: Human Rights Watch's Egypt researcher, Heba Fatma Morayef, says the mood in Tahrir Square is orderly and cooperative:

> Several thousand people remain in Tahrir Square, many say they're planning to spend the night and stay till Mubarak resigns. There was a huge cheer when we heard Mohamed ElBaradei was coming but unfortunately most of us couldn't hear what he said – no loudspeakers, apparently. The square has emptied out since the afternoon but it's still a great atmosphere, a sense of solidarity, and very well-behaved – people are sitting around bonfires, or walking around picking up rubbish.

MONDAY 31 JANUARY

9.48am: Syria's president, Bashar al-Assad, says the protests in Tunisia and Egypt are ushering in a "new era" in the Arab world, but he claims his country is immune.

In a rare interview Assad tells the Wall Street Journal that Syria is stable despite having more "difficult circumstances" than the rest of the Arab world. He says:

If you want to make a comparison between what is happening in Egypt and Syria, you have to look from a different point: why is Syria stable, although we have more difficult conditions? Egypt has been supported financially by the United States, while we are under embargo by most countries of the world. We have growth although we do not have many of the basic needs for the people. Despite all that, the people do not go into an uprising. So it is not only about the needs and not only about the reform. It is about the ideology, the beliefs and the cause that you have.

11.18am: A coalition of opposition groups are backing calls for a million people to take to Cairo's streets tomorrow, while politicians talk of deals with the army. AP reports:

The coalition of groups including the outlawed Muslim Brotherhood said it wants the march from Tahrir, or Liberation Square, to force Mubarak to step down by Friday. The groups also called for a general strike today, although much of Cairo remained shut down, with government officers and private businesses closed.

11.38am: On Twitter, friends express concerns for Egyptian blogger and Google Middle East staffer Wael Ghonim, who has been missing since Thursday. Ghonim, who studied in Cairo and is now Head of Marketing at Google's UAE office, had tweeted his intent to be at the January 25 protests.

12.04pm: Tahrir Square is now packed with protesters, reports the Guardian's Harriet Sherwood.

Lots of people, including women and children, are carrying signs, urging Mubarak to go. The military are tolerating the demonstration with good humour.

Some estimates suggest there might be 100,000 people gathered there.

3.55pm: While protests continue today and there are hopes that one million will take to the streets tomorrow, there are already plans for Friday. Protesters have said the army must choose to take the people's side by Thursday or else demonstrators will march on the presidential palace in Heliopolis after Friday prayers. The statement from youth-led groups says:

We the people and the youth of Egypt demand that our brothers in the national armed forces clearly define their stance by either lining up with the real legitimacy provided by millions of Egyptians on strike on the streets, or standing in the camp of the regime that has killed our people, terrorised them and stole from them.

5.37pm: Twitter co-founder Biz Stone has posted a blog entry defending Twitter and freedom of expression, in the wake of events in Egypt last week (though he doesn't explicitly mention Egypt):

Our goal is to instantly connect people everywhere to what is most meaningful to them. For this to happen, freedom of expression is essential. Some Tweets may facilitate positive change in a repressed country, some make us laugh, some make us think, some downright anger a vast majority of users. We don't always agree with the things people choose to tweet, but we keep the information flowing irrespective of any view we may have about the content.

6.10pm: Sky News in the UK is quoting Egypt's state news agency, something that may be hugely significant, tweeting:

\#   Egypt's army says it will not use force against tens of thousands of people demonstrating around country – state news agency.

On TV, Sky is sourcing this to the AFP news agency, which in turn is sourcing it to state television.

6.49pm: Reuters confirms reports regarding the Egyptian army's stance, and the army's statement that it would not use force against protesters demanding that Mubarak step down:

[The statement] said "freedom of expression" was guaranteed to all citizens using peaceful means.

It was the first such explicit confirmation by the army that it would not fire at demonstrators who have taken to the streets of Egypt since last week to try to force Mubarak to quit.

"The presence of the army in the streets is for your sake and to ensure your safety and wellbeing. The armed forces will not resort to use of force against our great people," the army statement said.

6.54pm: The Associated Press's correspondent Hamza Hendawi files from Tahrir Square:

> The mood in Tahrir Square, surrounded by army tanks and barbed wire, was celebratory and determined as more protesters filtered in to join what has turned into a continual encampment despite a curfew, moved up an hour to 3pm on its fourth day in effect. Some protesters played music, others distributed dates and other food to their colleagues or watched the latest news on TVs set up on sidewalks.

8.14pm: New Egyptian vice president Omar Suleiman appears on state television, and announces: "I have been asked by the president to contact all the political parties regarding constitutional reform."

Suleiman then says the government will "fight corruption and unemployment" and go ahead with elections "in contested districts in Egypt in the coming weeks" – although it's unclear what that means.

10.08pm: Al-Jazeera English is reporting that there is a pro-Mubarak demonstration taking place in Cairo right now, and suggestions that it could be headed towards Tahrir Square, where thousands of anti-Mubarak protesters remain tonight.

10.23pm: The pro-Mubarak demonstrators are outside the information ministry, with a nearby resident telling al-Jazeera English that they only amounted to 300 or so people gathered near the building. Another witness reported hearing pro-government chanting but said that the army had blocked off the routes to Tahrir Square, making it difficult for anyone to get through. Nonetheless, this is the first sign of pro-government forces even attempting to organise opposition on the streets of Cairo.

TUESDAY 1 FEBRUARY

8.34am: "A lot of protesters are hoping and believing that this could be the final hours of the Mubarak regime," Jack Shenker reports from Cairo.

> Tens of thousands of people have defied a strict night curfew after night. Right now in Tahrir, there is a huge presence, far bigger than it has been at this time before. There are tens of thousands certainly. Thousands from different directions are streaming towards the square.

9.46am: The Observer's foreign affairs editor, Peter Beaumont, is in Tahrir Square. He sent these Twitter updates in the last few minutes:

\# Huge crowd in square. Hearing mobile phone net might come down again shortly

\# Soldiers frisking everyone going into tahrir sq but v dif feeling to friday, laid back not tense and no police

\# Egyptian army sent out txt message last night saying with egypt against thugs and thieves

\# Steady stream of people heading to Tahrir square. Scores of tanks on road to airport

10.57am: Egypt's key ally, Turkey, has urged Mubarak to meet the popular demands for change. AP has this:

Prime minister Recep Tayyip Erdogan said Mubarak should act immediately and prevent "exploiters, groups with dirty aims, [and] those sections that have dark designs over Egypt to take the initiative." He did not elaborate.

11.46am: "It certainly feels like close to a million people are crammed into the square," Jack Shenker reports. But he says there is confusion about what they do next:

It is quite clear they have broken past that fear barrier. But now debates are breaking out everywhere about what to do next. There was a plan to march on the presidential palace – about 10 miles. There are a lot of people who are against that because it's too far. And there is also a fear that if they leave the square, riot police will reoccupy it.

There is no one leader; it has been a leaderless movement from the start and it still a leaderless movement here in the square. A huge amount of energy but not much of an outlet at the moment as to where it should be taken next.

1.12pm: A new government has been formed in Jordan. From our Middle East editor Ian Black:

Jordan's prime minister has been replaced by King Abdullah as the political shockwaves from Egypt continue to reverberate across the Arab world. Marouf al-Bakhit was asked to form a new government following the sudden resignation of Samir al-Rifai after weeks of protests by Jordanians calling on the government to step down.

Demonstrators had demanded Rifai's departure in weekend demonstrations, the latest in a series which have been given added impetus by the dramatic events in Egypt and Tunisia.

1.23pm: It's not just Cairo, there are reports of huge demonstrations in several other Egyptian cities including: Suez, Alexandria, Ismailiya, Mansoura, Damietta, and Mahalls.

3.10pm: "This is absolutely massive, it's extraordinary; it's just heaving with people as far as the eye can see," Harriet Sherwood reports from Alexandria. "People are confident that it is only a matter of time before Mubarak goes."

3.13pm: Syrians are planning their own "day[s] of rage" in Damascus this week, reports AP:

> The main Syrian protest page on Facebook is urging people to protest in Damascus on 4 and 5 February for "a day of rage". It says the goal is to "end the state of emergency in Syria and end corruption".

5.13pm: A giant TV screen has reportedly just been put up in Tahrir Square. No prizes for what it is showing – al-Jazeera. The revolution will be televised.

8.09pm: Jack Shenker, in Tahrir Square, has asked locals if Mubarak's expected announcement that he will now step down at the next election, in September, will suffice. "The overwhelming consensus is that is absolutely not enough." On the phone from Cairo, he says:

> They are really fired up, they're really emboldened by the fact that, assuming Mubarak announces this, they've secured a major concession from him and it's only spurred them on to continue the protests and stick it out till the bitter end.

9.02pm: Mubarak is speaking. He said the protests were started by "honest youths and men" but were taken over by those "who wanted to take advantage".

The protests were "manipulated and controlled by political forces", he says.

9.07pm: Mubarak says he will instruct the police apparatus "to protect and serve the citizens in absolute dignity". He says:

I pray to God to guide me to the successful right path to end my career in a way that is applicable to God and the people. I have exhausted my life serving Egypt but I am totally prepared to end my career.

The translation is halting but he is saying he will not run for another term as president.

9.09pm: Mubarak finishes speaking and immediately people in Tahrir Square begin chanting their opposition to him. They are shouting, "Leave, leave" and "Get out".

9.47pm: Jack Shenker has called in again from Tahrir Square:

People were bursting with hostility, many people held up their shoes in the air, which is, as you probably know, is one of the gravest insults you can show people in Arab culture, and as he announced that he would not be running in the September elections many of those shoes were hurled at the screen.

11.51pm: Barack Obama has just spoken. It was a brief statement, just a few minutes, but the highlight was this:

What is clear – and what I indicated tonight to President Mubarak – is my belief that an orderly transition must be meaningful, it must be peaceful, and it must begin now.

That is perhaps the clearest statement to date from the administration, although it's hardly going to satisfy the administration's critics, who define change as starting with Mubarak leaving office.

WEDNESDAY 2 FEBRUARY

7.45am: Mubarak's decision to tough it out for now has been greeted by rage from protesters and international calls for more immediate change. Egypt's key ally Turkey today urged Mubarak to heed protesters' calls. Last night Barack Obama said "change must begin now". Not everyone is calling for Mubarak to stand down now. Speaking to CNN Tony Blair described him as "immensely courageous and a force for good".

8.03am: Yemeni president Ali Abdullah Saleh has done a Mubarak, by saying he won't seek to extend his presidency. Eyeing protests that brought down Tunisia's leader and threaten to topple Egypt's president, Saleh also vowed not to pass on the reins of government to his son, Reuters reports:

> "No extension, no inheritance, no resetting the clock," Saleh said, speaking ahead of a planned rally in Sana'a today that has been dubbed a "Day of rage".

8.53am: "Thousands" of people have been involved in a number of pro-Mubarak rallies, according to AP.

> The small rallies appeared to be the start of an attempt by Mubarak's three-million-member National Democratic party to retake momentum from protesters demanding Egypt's nearly 30-year ruler step down immediately.

10.16am: The Egyptian military is calling for an end to more than a week of demonstrations, AP reports. Internet service is also returning to Egypt after days of an unprecedented cut-off by the government.

10.55am: Al-Jazeera appears to be available again in Egypt. The channel is no longer showing constant coverage of the unrest.

12.10pm: Tahrir Square is changing hands, according to Peter Beaumont:

> Thousands and thousands of pro-Murabak demonstrators are now pouring into the square. It seems to have been heavily choreographed.

12.42pm: Peter Beaumont again:

I've seen one guy with a pole with a knife attached to it. It's quite clear some of these people came prepared for a violent confrontation.

12.59pm: The writer Ahdaf Soueif emails to express concern.

This is urgent news: the Mubarak thugs are now suddenly out in force. I say "thugs" because their behaviour immediately is radically different from everything we have seen in the last week.

They are in microbuses and trucks and are keeping up a deafening wall of sound with their claxons. They are armed with sticks and various bits of weaponry and are waving them and shouting and honking their horns. They carry large well-made banners – replicas of the banners that are used in the rigged elections, proclaiming for Mubarak.

2.29pm: Pro-Mubarak supporters are recognisably police, says Peter Beaumont by phone from Cairo.

There is no question in my mind that they're police, they are central security forces. These are the same guys that were out in force all last week and they have filtered back in again. They are very, very recognisable.

4.26pm: Some recent tweets on the continuing violence, from Cairo:

\# **Ssirgany** Until last night, Tahrir was the safest place in Egypt, with pro-change protesters staying there for 8 days. Now Mubarak people go in & WAR

\# **sandmonkey** The egyptian state TV are on a different universe, showing pictures of pro-Mubarak protesters all over egypt.

\# **bencnn** All indications are that what is happening in Tahrir Square is government-sanctioned.

4.43pm: We've just spoken to Karim Ennarah, a pro-democracy protester in Tahrir Square. He says the protesters opposed to Mubarak are still in control of the square but it is an "ugly and messy scene".

Both groups are pelting each other with rocks, it's extremely violent here. People are unsure about the army position ... I don't see this coming to an end, it's been going on for hours now. There are hundreds of people injured, literally hundreds of people.

10.05pm: CNN's Anderson Cooper, looking down on Tahrir Square, reports that the anti-Mubarak groups have retaken the large area around the Egyptian Museum, and have put up barricades, while several cars have been set on fire.

"I'm sorry I've got to duck down, some shoots have been fired," says Cooper, who seems not to have slept for three days.

10.23pm: The toll of those injured today in Cairo has reached more than 1,500 people, a doctor at an emergency clinic at the scene has told Reuters.

11.10pm: Malcom Gladwell, the New Yorker sociological popularist, is trying to dismiss the influence of social media in events in Tunisia and Egypt:

Right now there are protests in Egypt that look like they might bring down the government. There are a thousand important things that can be said about their origins and implications: as I wrote last summer in the New Yorker, "high risk" social activism requires deep roots and strong ties. But surely the least interesting fact about them is that some of the protesters may (or may not) have at one point or another employed some of the tools of the new media to communicate with one another. Please. People protested and brought down governments before Facebook was invented. They did it before the internet came along.

11.48pm: The Guardian's Jack Shenker reports from central Cairo:

It's almost 2am in Egypt, and amid all the drama on our screens and rumours zipping around on the web, we shouldn't lose sight of one basic and incredible fact – for the ninth night running, ordinary Egyptians are on the streets in their thousands, still bound together with remarkable social solidarity, still battling their three-decade-old dictatorial regime, still holding their ground even as it is rained on by rocks and Molotov cocktails.

Downtown Cairo is aflame tonight, its streets playing host to block-by-block, roof-by-roof, corner-by-corner urban warfare – but it's the bravery behind those fighting the battle that should really be leaving people open-mouthed.

THURSDAY 3 FEBRUARY

7.42am: Egyptian blogger SandMonkey urges fellow protesters not to give up:

> If you are in Egypt, I am calling on all of you to head down to Tahrir today and Friday. It is imperative to show them that the battle for the soul of Egypt isn't over and done with. I am calling you to bring your friends, to bring medical supplies, to go and see what Mubarak's gurantees look like in real life. Egypt needs you. Be Heroes.

8.01am: Thousands of anti-government demonstrators have gathered in the Yemeni capital Sana'a to take part in a "day of rage". They claim that President Saleh's offer to step down in 2013 was not enough.

9.17am: "It's all kicked off again," says Jack Shenker:

> People are starting to throw stones, lots of stones. This definitely started from the pro-Mubarak side. They have rushed into the no man's land. The army are not intervening, in fact they are moving back. The pro-Mubarak side are pelting the anti-Mubarak protesters with rocks. The anti-Mubarak supporters are throwing them back.

11.10am: The British telecommunications company Vodafone is being accused of sending out text messages urging pro-Mubarak supporters to "confront" protesters.

According to a Flickr gallery, this is what some of them said.

\# The Armed Forces asks Egypt's honest and loyal men to confront the traitors and criminals and protect our people and honor and our precious Egypt.

\# Youth of Egypt, beware rumors and listen to the sound of reason –
Egypt is above all so preserve it.

\# To every mother-father-sister-brother, to every honest citizen preserve
this country as the nation is forever.

12.05pm: In a statement, Vodafone says they were powerless to prevent these
"unacceptable" texts being sent out.

> Under the emergency powers provisions of the Telecoms Act, the Egypt-
> ian authorities can instruct the mobile networks of Mobinil, Etisalat and
> Vodafone to send messages to the people of Egypt …
>
> Vodafone Group has protested to the authorities that the current situa-
> tion regarding these messages is unacceptable.

2.15pm: Pro-Mubarak forces are being pushed further and further back,
Peter Beaumont reports from Cairo. He says forces loyal to the president
haven't come out in the numbers that they did yesterday. Some of the groups
are only a few hundred strong:

> The army has been trying to put themselves in between them. Tanks are
> not the greatest crowd-control weapons. Tanks are driving in and swing-
> ing their turrets around, trying to intimidate people by waggling round
> the main gun. Occasionally we'll see groups of soldiers run down trying
> to break up a knot of people, or we will hear warning shots.

4.38pm: Ian Black, the Guardian's Middle East editor, writes:

> The feeling in the Egyptian capital today is that Suleiman and other lead-
> ers are now digging in behind the embattled president. "They are rattled
> and under pressure but there is no sign of them giving up in the face of
> the criticism from foreign capitals," one western official said. "There is
> a sense of disconnect."

4.49pm: Vice president Omar Suleiman is on state TV. He has held out the
prospect of the presidential election taking place in August (rather than
September) but holding it any earlier would leave a "constitutional vacuum".

He says the wishes of the January 25 movement are "acceptable" and blamed outside forces for trying to foster instability.

4.58pm: Suleiman blamed the recent violence on "some other opportunists carrying their own agenda. It might be related to outside forces or other domestic affairs". He said it was "a conspiracy".

This approach was predicted in this morning's Guardian by the novelist Ahdaf Soueif, who wrote:

> Their next trick will be to say that the young people in Tahrir are "foreign" elements, that they have connections to "terrorism", that they've visited Afghanistan, that they want to destabilise Egypt. But by now the whole world knows that this regime lies as naturally as it breathes.

FRIDAY 4 FEBRUARY

7.32am: Anti-government protesters are today hoping they can force Mubarak from office, on a day they have dubbed "departure Friday" or the "day of departure". Fridays after midday prayers are traditionally an explosive point in Middle Eastern countries, with masses taking to the streets after attendance at mosques.

8.45am: Jack Shenker sends this from Cairo:

> I'm standing with about 2,000 protesters in a queue to get into Tahrir Square. Spirits are high and people are queuing patiently – not usually a common sight in Egypt – all the way across the Kasr al-Nile bridge. The army are searching people as they enter for weapons, but are letting people in. This is just one entrance to Tahrir Square; there will be similar queues all the way round.

9.18am: Our correspondent in Damascus, who we are not naming, sends this update on the situation in Syria:

> Syrians woke to a calm and rainy day in Damascus this morning, with so far, no signs of unrest.
>
> Over 15 Facebook groups have emerged this week rallying people to take to the streets for a "day of rage" today and tomorrow, calling for solidarity with Egypt and an end to emergency law in the country.

Our correspondent goes on to say that, with security tightened around the country and Facebook and other networking sites blocked, turnout is expected to be low.

10.13am: Ayatollah Ali Khamenei told worshippers at Friday prayers in Tehran that he saluted what he termed an "Islamic liberation movement" in the Arab world, Reuters reports. Khamenei advised the people of Egypt and Tunisia to unite around their religion and against the west. Iran's supreme leader said:

> The awakening of the Islamic Egyptian people is an Islamic liberation movement and I, in the name of the Iranian government, salute the Egyptian people and the Tunisian people.

10.15am: Omar Suleiman, the Egyptian vice president, has said force will not be used against the pro-democracy protesters today.

11.40am: Silvio Berlusconi, the embattled and scandal-plagued Italian prime minister, has praised Mubarak and said the Egyptian president should remain in place during the country's transition to democracy.

> I hope there can be continuity in government. I hope that in Egypt there can be a transition toward a more democratic system without a break from President Mubarak, who in the west, above all in the United States, is considered the wisest of men and a precise reference point.

11.48am: Egyptian state TV is now covering the demonstrations in Tahrir square. But it is billing the scenes as "demonstrations to support stability", according to Draddee on Twitter. State TV is living in an "alternate reality", he says.

1.34pm: Al-Jazeera is reporting that their Cairo office has been stormed by "gangs of thugs". In a statement, the news channel says its office and the equipment inside has been set on fire:

> It appears to be the latest attempt by the Egyptian regime or its support-ers to hinder al-Jazeera's coverage of events in the country ... Al-Jazeera has also faced unprecedented levels of interference in its broadcast signal as well as persistent and repeated attempts to bring down its websites.

2.08pm: Our correspondent in Damascus reports that protests in the Syrian capital have not materialised.

3.37pm: Amr Moussa, secretary general of the Arab League, who was in Tahrir Square today, is considering running for president, Egyptian newspaper al-Masry al-Youm reports.

Amr Moussa says he expects Mubarak to remain in his post until his term ends in seven months, though "there are extraordinary things happening and there is chaos, maybe he will make a different decision."

7.22pm: Omar Suleiman will meet a group of prominent independent figures tomorrow, promoting a solution to the country's crisis in which he would assume the president's powers for an interim period, one of the group said, reports Reuters. They appear to think Suleiman taking over is "the only way forward". It seems unlikely that many of the protesters would agree with that.

9.05pm: Sad news in the form of more details on the death of Ahmed Mohammed Mahmoud, an Egyptian journalist shot and killed while covering the protests. AP reports:

> State-run newspaper Al-Ahram says an Egyptian reporter shot during clashes earlier this week has died of his wounds, the first reported journalist death in 11 days of turmoil surrounding Egypt's wave of anti-government protests.
>
> Al-Ahram says Ahmed Mohammed Mahmoud, 36, was taking pictures of clashes on the streets from the balcony of his home, not far from central Tahrir Square when he was "shot by a sniper" four days ago.

SATURDAY 5 FEBRUARY

10.33am: The immediate removal of Mubarak from office will not be sufficient to stop the mass protests in Egypt, Jack Shenker writes in the Guardian. In a piece filed late last night, Shenker notes that the coalition of protesters have drawn up a common list of radical demands.

These include:

- The resignation of the entire ruling party, including the new vice president Omar Suleiman, whom the Obama administration believes is best placed to oversee a transition of power.

- A broad-based transitional government appointed by a 14-strong committee, made up of senior judges, youth leaders and members of the military.
- The election of a founding council of 40 public intellectuals and constitutional experts, who will draw up a new constitution under the supervision of the transitional government, then put it to the people in a referendum, to be followed by fresh elections at a local and national level.
- The trial of key regime leaders, including Mubarak.

11.44am: Protest leaders say they have met Egypt's prime minister to discuss ways to ease Mubarak out of office so negotiations can begin on the nation's future, AP reports:

> A self-declared group of Egypt's elite called the "group of wise men" has circulated ideas to try to break that deadlock. Among them is a proposal that Mubarak "deputise" his vice president Omar Suleiman with his powers and, for the time being at least, step down in everything but name.
>
> The "wise men," who are separate from the protesters on the ground, have met twice in recent days with Suleiman and the prime minister, said Amr el-Shobaki, a member of the group.

SUNDAY 6 FEBRUARY

2.22pm: Ayman Nour, leader of the el-Ghad (Tomorrow) party, has rejected the deal opposition leaders made with Suleiman. According to a Twitter update from the journalist Sultan Soooud Al Qassemi, Nour said: "No one has the right to make decisions on behalf of the youth who have led the uprising."

4.57pm: Amnesty International has warned that a Google employee in Cairo, reportedly arrested at the start of the protests, faces a "serious risk of torture". Wael Ghonim was arrested by Egyptian security forces on 27 January during protests in Cairo, eyewitnesses said.

Hassiba Hadj Sahraoui, deputy director of Middle and North Africa at Amnesty International says:

> The Egyptian authorities must immediately disclose where Wael Ghonim is and release him or charge him with a recognisable criminal

offence. His case is just one of many that highlight the continued crackdown by the Egyptian authorities on those exercising their right to protest peacefully.

6.09pm: Issandr El Amrani posts an update from Tahrir Square on the Arabist website:

> The mood in Tahrir is, as ever, uplifting and ebullient. It's a veritable tent city in the grassy parts, and the atmosphere is reminiscent of a moulid – the celebrations of saints that are part of the more Dionysian side of the way Islam is practiced in Egypt. Or, in western terms, it's Glastonbury out there.

MONDAY 7 FEBRUARY

11.35am: As part of a Q&A, Reuters asks, how united is the opposition?

> Two broad trends seem to be emerging between youths – who can reasonably claim to have been the driving force for the protests – and the more formal opposition groups ranging from liberals and leftists to Islamists, which are more pragmatic and more ready to engage in political horse-trading.

9.33pm: Wael Ghonim – the Google executive arrested on 27 January and released today – has made an extraordinary appearance on Egyptian TV. Here's Jack Shenker:

> Egyptian activist Wael Ghonim – released today from detention – has just given a television interview about his experiences and served up a tour de force of calm but explosive political passion.
>
> The internet is already abuzz with talk of Ghonim's performance, which ended with him being overcome with emotion as he was shown images of some of those who died in the uprising. Many are saying the regime will regret the day they ever allowed him out, others are calling for the Google employee to run for president, and everybody agrees that his TV appearance is certain to boost crowds in Tahrir tomorrow.

Ghonim was an administrator of the highly influential "We are all Khaled Said" Facebook group, and spent up to 12 days in captivity.

10.01pm: AP has more on Wael Ghonim's electrifying interview with Mona Shazli on Egypt's Dream TV:

> He insisted he had not been tortured and said his interrogators treated him with respect. "This is the revolution of the youth of the internet and now the revolution of all Egyptians," he said.

TUESDAY 8 FEBRUARY

8.21am: Wael Ghonim's release could help relaunch the revolution, argues Issandr El Amrani on his Arabist blog.

> This cathartic moment may be the spark that was needed to revive Egypt's revolutionary fervour. … I thought that the next step for the people in Tahrir would have been to retake the initiative by suggesting its own road map for transition, or focusing on the many deaths and reports of the use of snipers that are coming out. After two weeks, the world's media is getting tired of this story and there needed to be a relaunch. Who better than a marketing executive from Google to do that?

9.08am: Back in Tunisia, Angelique Chrisafis reports on the problems for their unfinished revolution from the border town of Kasserine:

> As the world spotlight turns to Cairo, Tunisia's rural interior fears its revolution could disintegrate.
> Kasserine finds itself at the heart of the attempts by Ben Ali's former ruling RCD party to stir fresh violence to disrupt the revolution. In the past three days, at least five people have died in Tunisia in the worst violence since Ben Ali fled on 14 January. The interim government has blamed the wave of violence on a plot by old figures in the RCD party to stir panic and damage the revolution.

10.35am: "There are thousands pouring into the square. In the background you can hear the chants of 'welcome'," Chris McGreal reports from Tahrir Square.

There is a man here dressed as a referee waving a red card with Mubarak's name on it. There's a lot of determination that he has to go, despite the political negotiations.

The army has a much lower profile today than in the past. It has been possible for foreign reporters to get into the square, simply because the army has withdrawn from checking the people entering the square. It is much more relaxed.

4.41pm: Omar Suleiman has offered more concessions to the protesters. They include a supposed plan and timetable for the peaceful transfer of power, a pledge not to pursue protesters and a new committee created to discuss and recommend constitutional changes that would relax eligibility rules governing who can run for president and limit the number of presidential terms.

WEDNESDAY 9 FEBRUARY

8.00am: Wael Ghonim, the released activist and newly anointed voice of the revolution, has urged protesters to keep up the pressure for Mubarak to stand down. He tweets:

\#   This is not the time to "negotiate", this is the time to "accept" and
    "enforce" the demands of the Egyptian Youth movement #Jan25

His comments come after Suleiman, who has been leading those negotiations with the opposition, warned that protests were "very dangerous" and ominously said the only alternative to dialogue was "a coup".

4.21pm: The April 6 Youth movement has sent a defiant reply in response to vice president Omar Suleiman's warning that the protests were "very dangerous" and the only alternative to dialogue was "a coup". In an email sent to followers of its Facebook page it says:

We reaffirm our rejection of … this comic speech, made by Omar Soleiman and some cartoon parties who do not represent us … We refuse any negotiations until Mubarak and his regime leaves. Our rights and demands which have not been implemented, and the blood of our martyrs, are not negotiable.

9.10pm: Talks between the Egyptian regime and opposition figures are on the brink of collapse, according to a new report from Cairo just filed by Jack Shenker and Chris McGreal:

> A prominent member of a key opposition group, the Council of Wise Men, said negotiations had "essentially come to an end". A western diplomat said Washington was alarmed by the lack of political progress and Suleiman's warning of a coup.
>
> Diaa Rashwan, of the Council of Wise Men, said he offered Suleiman a compromise in which Mubarak would have remained president but with his powers transferred to a transitional government. Rashwan said this proposal was rejected at the weekend and there had been no further movement.

THURSDAY 10 FEBRUARY

12.44pm: Reuters is reporting that one of the Egyptian opposition parties has pulled out of the talks on reform with the government, saying Mubarak's administration has not responded to "the minimum level of popular demands".

Explaining why it was pulling out of the talks, the Tagammu party criticised the government's handling of the dialogue, saying official announcements on what had been agreed were inaccurate. "Unacceptable statements" by officials had put participants "in confrontation with the popular revolution", it said.

3.45pm: According to various reports, General Hassan al-Roueini, the military commander for the Cairo area, has told thousands of protesters in central Tahrir Square: "All your demands will be met today."

3.59pm: Chris McGreal confirms there has been a sudden change in the atmosphere since the news from the military in the last half an hour. The feeling now in Cairo is "Boom: this changes everything", he says.

4.09pm: Blogger SandMonkey is confident:

\# I am going to tahrir. It started there and will end there tonite. #jan25

4.25pm: The prime minister, Ahmed Shafiq, says Mubarak is still in power and no decisions have been taken that would change that. Shafiq said:

> Everything is normal. Everything is still in the hands of the president. The supreme leader [Mubarak] is informed of everything going on inside the Higher Military Council.

4.36pm: Egyptian state TV says Mubarak will speak to the nation from his palace in Cairo this evening.

5.21pm: Jack Shenker calls in from Tahrir Square. He says that in contrast to previous days when people have ebbed away from the square in the evening, tonight people are "streaming in". There is triumph and celebration, but also uncertainty as rumours swirl around the square.

7.45pm: Only 15 minutes until Mubarak is due to speak on television – but don't be surprised if there's a delay.

8.02pm: This from Chris McGreal in Cairo on the will-he-stay-or-will-he-go question:

> It might be a question of nuance. If Mubarak transfers powers but retains the title then technically he hasn't stepped down.

8.20pm: State television is now reporting that Mubarak's speech will begin shortly. We'll see.

On Twitter the hashtag #reasonsmubarakislate is trending. Here are some of the many suggestions:

\# You think it's easy packing gold bullion bars into vintage Louis Vuitton luggage?

\# Plucking embarrassing nasal hair

\# Checking the sofa cushions to make sure he isn't leaving any change behind

\# He is in de Nile

8.46pm: Mubarak has begun speaking. He says he will "respond to your demands and your voices".

8.49pm: Mubarak reaffirms that he's not standing for election as president and that power will be transfered to "whoever the electorate chooses in the new fair and square elections".

8.58pm: "I have spent most of my life in defence of our homeland," says Mubarak. "I have never succumbed to any international pressure … I have my dignity intact."

So he's not stepping down, it seems.

9.02pm: No one in Tahrir Square is listening to the rest of the Mubarak speech. The chant is: "Get out, get out."

"We will be dignified until the very end, may God preserve Egypt, may peace be upon you," is Mubarak's final remark.

9.05pm: There was little that was new in Mubarak's speech, and he granted some powers to Omar Suleiman, but little else and far less than many expected. None of this meshes with the statements issued by the military leadership today that hints at a palace civil war going on behind the scenes.

9.10pm: Tahrir Square is filled with a huge, angry crowd – although state television isn't showing any of it. Same in Alexandria.

9.15pm: Here is the key quote from Mubarak's speech:

> Satisfied with what I have offered the nation in more than 60 years, I have announced I will stay with this post and that I will continue to shoulder my responsibilities.

At that point protesters erupted in jeers and shoe-waving.

9.20pm: The Guardian's Brian Whitaker gives his analysis:

> It was a seriously bad speech. Mubarak seems to have totally misjudged the situation. His start, saying he was speaking as a father to his children, was shockingly patronising. The crowd in Tahrir became

increasingly angry as they realised he was offering nothing more than minor concessions.

He also came out with the bizarre assertion that "the current situation" is not about his personality. Everyone else can see that it is about him.

9.29pm: This from Jack Shenker in Tahrir Square:

When it became clear that Mubarak intended to stay on until September, the square shook with fury. "We are not going until he goes," they chanted.

10.00pm: The Guardian's Ewen MacAskill reports on a humiliation for the White House:

The Obama administration was embarrassingly wrong-footed when the Egyptian president confounded expectations by refusing to leave office. Mubarak's speech came only hours after Barack Obama and the director of the CIA, Leon Panetta, appeared to give credence to the rumours that the Egyptian president was heading for the exit …

Mubarak's response provides a graphic illustration of America's slow decline from its status as the world's sole superpower, unable to decisively influence events in Egypt in spite of that country being one of the biggest recipients of US military aid.

10.16pm: There seems to be huge confusion over what Mubarak really did say this evening, and exactly what power he handed over to the vice president.

CNN is saying that it has now got a "precise translation" with Mubarak saying he was "delegating power" to Suleiman – not "the power" or "all power," but a frustratingly vague use of language.

AP also says it has a better translation of Mubarak's exact words, which it says read:

I saw fit to delegate the authorities of the president to the vice president, as dictated in the constitution.

According to AP, the Egyptian constitution allows the president to transfer his powers if he is unable to carry out his duties "due to any temporary obstacle," but it does not mean his resignation.

11.36pm: Opposition leader Mohamed ElBaradei gives his reaction via Twitter:

\#   Egypt will explode. Army must save the country now

12.53am: A long-awaited statement from Barack Obama finally lands – and it is mildly critical of Mubarak's sluggish and stubborn response, saying that "it is not yet clear that this transition is immediate, meaningful or sufficient".

FRIDAY 11 FEBRUARY

9.07am: The April 6 youth movement has issued a furious response to Mubarak's speech last night. In a communique sent to its Facebook followers it says "a general strike is needed to bring him down" and that Mubarak's speech was "an astonishing piece of hypocritical filth".

9.24am: As everyone awaits the army's next move the people in Tahrir Square in Cairo are chanting that the people and the army are "together". There are also reports of army officers joining the protests.

9.45am: The Guardian's Chris McGreal, in Cairo, says people will not just be listening to what the supreme military council has to say in its announcement, expected shortly, but will also be scrutinising the army's behaviour on the streets:

> A lot of people will be interested to hear what they have to say, about how they react to Mubarak's announcement but they will also be looking at how the military behaves, particularly around Tahrir Square. Will they just stand back as they have done on previous days? Are they going to try to prevent it, control it? It will be very telling about where the military leadership is.

9.51am: The military statement has just been read out. The supreme military council essentially seems to be saying it will help see through the transition to democracy but there is no indication that it is opposed to Mubarak and/or Suleiman being involved in that transition.

10.09am: Chris McGreal, calling from Cairo, says the army has "thrown its weight behind the status quo for now". However, he adds, the army may be warning Mubarak that he must carry out the reforms that he has promised.

10.39am: Apparently the following joke is doing the rounds among Egyptians:

> Communique No 2 from the Armed Forces: "A message from the Armed Forces to the Noble Egyptian People: our next Communique to you will be No 3."

11.50am: Chris McGreal has been on the phone with an update from Tahrir Square. He says signs are that the protests are spreading across Cairo:

> At the moment this square is packed, almost full, and that's before the large number on a Friday after prayers and the square tends to fill up through the afternoon. The protesters' organisers are hoping to take advantage of that and move into other areas and keep hold of them.

2.20pm: A local government official has confirmed that Mubarak is in the Red Sea resort of Sharm el-Sheikh, AP reports.

4.02pm: Omar Suleiman is making a statement now. "President Mubarak has decided to waive the office of the republic."

4.03pm: There are huge cheers in Tahrir Square.

4.12pm: The full text of the vice president's very brief statement:

> In these difficult circumstances that the country is passing through, President Mubarak has decided to leave the position of the presidency. He has commissioned the armed forces council to direct the issues of the state.

4.20pm: From Chris McGreal in Tahrir Square:

> Cairo erupts in celebration as 18 days of defiant protest finally delivers a revolution after 24 hours of euphoria, dashed hopes and victory.

4.23pm: The Egyptian pro-democracy campaigner Mohamed ElBaradei has cheered Mubarak's resignation. "This is the greatest day of my life. The country has been liberated after decades of repression," he has told AP. He says he expects a "beautiful" transition of power.

4.28pm: From amidst a cacophony of cheers, Jack Shenker describes the reaction of the crowd outside the presidential palace.

> There was a complete eruption of humanity, I have never seen anything like it. The world's biggest street party has really kicked off here. There are huge huge crowds of people jumping up and down suddenly as one. Suddenly everyone rushed into the road. I'm being slapped in happiness and bounced around.

4.50pm: Wael Ghonim has tweeted, simply:

\# Welcome back Egypt.

6.29pm: A spokesman for Egypt's military has just appeared on television to read a new statement, "Communique Number Three".

Read aloud in a flat monotone, the statement said that the supreme council of the armed forces was "currently studying the situation to achieve the hopes of our great people" and will issue further statements to clarify its position:

> The council will issue a statement outlining the steps and procedures and directives that will be taken, confirming at the same time that there is no alternative to the legitimacy acceptable to the people.

The statement made no mention of vice president Suleiman.

7.04pm: Egyptian state TV has bowed to the inevitable and is just showing al-Jazeera's feed. A week ago the government banned the channel from operating.

8.06pm: Obama has just begun his delayed statement on Egypt, being delivered from the White House's Grand Foyer, which is reserved for set-piece presidential apperances:

The people of Egypt have spoken. Their voices have been heard. And Egypt will never be the same ... But this is not the end of Egypt's transition, this is a beginning. Egyptians have made it clear that nothing less than genuine democracy will carry the day.

9.32pm: After the overthrow of regimes in Tunisia and Egypt, how are the region's other governments reacting? The Guardian's Julian Borger tweets some fascinating news from Bahrain:

Reports say Bahrain's King Hamad has offered a grant of $2,600 to every family ahead of Bahrain's day of rage due on Monday. Panic spreads.

9.45pm: Algeria is another country with a nervous government, ahead of a day of protest planned for Saturday. The government and security forces are leaving nothing to chance according to an online AFP report:

Large numbers of police were deployed in central Algiers Friday ahead of a pro-democracy march planned by opposition groups in defiance of a government ban. The head of the opposition Rally for Culture and Democracy, Said Sadi, said the authorities had ringed the capital in a bid to prevent people joining Saturday's march from outside.

10.00pm: Tahrir Square is still full of celebrating people, just after midnight in the Egyptian capital.

SATURDAY 12 FEBRUARY

11.04am: There are protests today in Yemen and Algeria, inspired by the Egyptian and Tunisian revolutions.

Thousands of demonstrators in the Yemeni capital, Sana'a, have clashed with government supporters. The protesters chanted: "The people want the fall of the government. A Yemeni revolution after the Egyptian revolution."

Meanwhile in Algeria, thousands of riot police have been deployed in the capital, Algiers, to stop an anti-government demonstration from gathering momentum, Reuters reports.

12.22pm: Pro-democracy activists in Cairo's Tahrir Square have vowed to stay there until the higher military council accepts their agenda for reform, Reuters reports.

12.39pm: More details about the list of demands issued by protest leaders has emerged, Reuters reports.

> "People's Communique No 1" demands the dissolution of the cabinet Mubarak appointed on 29 January and the suspension of the parliament elected in a rigged poll late last year.
>
> The reformists want a transitional five-member presidential council made up of four civilians and one military person. The communique calls for the formation of a transitional government to prepare for an election to take place within nine months, and of a body to draft a new democratic constitution.

1.39pm: Saudi Arabia welcomes the peaceful transition of power in Egypt, its state news agency has reported. "The government of the kingdom of Saudi Arabia welcomes the peaceful transition of power in the Arab republic of Egypt, and expresses hope in the efforts of the Egyptian armed forces to restore peace, stability and tranquility," the news agency said, according to Reuters.

3.53pm: Here are some important lines from the Supreme Council of the Armed Forces' statement about their role in the transition of power:

> The current government, and governors, shall continue as a caretaker administration until a new government is formed.
>
> The Supreme Council of the Armed Forces aspires to guaranteeing a peaceful transition of authority within a free and democratic system that allows for the assumption of authority by a civilian and elected authority to govern the country and the build of a democratic and free state.
>
> The Arab Republic of Egypt is committed to all regional and international obligations and treaties.

3.58pm: The Egyptian protest organisers have announced they are forming a council to defend the revolution and negotiate with the military council now running the country, Reuters reports, quoting academic Khaled Abdel Qader Ouda:

> The purpose of the Council of Trustees is to hold dialogue with the Higher Military Council and to carry the revolution forward through

the transitional phase. The council will have the authority to call for protests or call them off depending on how the situation develops.

4.00pm: Egypt's Muslim Brotherhood has released an intriguing statement about its intention during and after a transition of power:

> The Muslim Brotherhood … are not seeking personal gains, so they announce they will not run for the presidency and will not seek to get a majority in the parliament and that they consider themselves servants of these decent people. We support and value the sound direction that the Higher Military Council is taking on the way to transfer power peacefully to create a civilian government in line with the will of the people.

SUNDAY 13 FEBRUARY

9.51am: There have already been signs of discord this morning. As so often over the past 20 days, the focus is once more on Tahrir Square, where protesters have been resisting army attempts to clear the plaza, Reuters reports:

> Hundreds of Egyptian soldiers shoved pro-democracy protesters aside to force a path for traffic to start flowing through central Cairo's Tahrir Square on Sunday for the first time in more than two weeks.
>
> Protesters chanted "Peacefully, peacefully" as the soldiers and military police in red berets moved in to disperse them. Scuffles broke out and some soldiers lashed out with sticks.

11.07am: An update from Chris McGreal, in Tahrir Square:

> Many more people are coming in to Tahrir square apparently in response to a call from the remaining protesters not to let the army force them out. The military had got the traffic flowing earlier today but the demonstrators are now sitting down in the road and blocking the roundabout after soldiers ripped up their tents and told them to go home.
>
> There is also a counter-demonstration of about 100 people, chanting at the protesters to go home.

2.08pm: Egypt's military rulers have dissolved parliament and suspended the constitution. The announcement came in their latest public statement. They have said they will run the country for six months, or until presidential and parliament elections can be held.

4.53pm: The organisers of protests that toppled President Mubarak have called for a "march of victory" across Egypt on Friday. Reuters quotes leading activist Khaled Abdelkader Ouda:

> We salute the armed forces for their serious steps to meet the demands of the people. We call on Egyptians to do their part and give the army a chance to proceed with the next stage. We call for a Friday march of victory in the millions across Egypt to celebrate the gains of the revolution. We will announce the members of the council of trustees on Friday.

7.53pm: Wael Ghonim, the Google executive who played a key role in the protests across Egypt, has been tweeting about his activities tonight.

\# Egypt changed, 8 young guys sitting with 2 generals from the higher council of the armed forces and freely exchanging our opinions.

MONDAY 14 FEBRUARY

8.57am: At least 14 people have been injured in clashes on Bahrain's "Day of Rage", Reuters reports:

> Police clashed late on Sunday with residents in Karzakan village, where security forces regularly skirmish with Shia youths, and one protester was injured, witnesses said. Police said three officers were hurt. In the village of Nuweidrat, police used teargas and rubber bullets on Monday to disperse a crowd demanding the release of Shia detainees, witnesses said.

9.09am: The 19-year-old state of emergency in Algeria will end within days, foreign minister Mourad Medelci said. There were running battles between police officers and about 2,000 demonstrators in Algiers on Saturday.

10.10am: Guardian Middle East editor Ian Black has provided some interesting analysis of the situation in Bahrain and the prospects of the protests escalating:

Bahrain's Day of Rage today is unlikely to take on the dimensions of the unrest in Cairo, but it will be closely watched to see if the small island state lives up to its reputation for being the odd man out in the Gulf ...

Bahrain's distinction is that the Sunni Al-Khalifa dynasty rules over an often restive Shia majority that has long complained about discrimination for jobs and housing. Precise figures are not available but the population has grown from 750,000 to more than 1 million in a few years while the number of Shias in senior jobs has decreased. Large numbers of non-Bahraini Sunnis have been naturalised. This sectarian division puts Bahrain on a major regional fault line, with Iran glowering across the Gulf at a state which is also home to the US 5th fleet.

10.52am: The Iranian security apparatus is out in force on the streets of Tehran already in anticipation of the planned opposition rally, Reuters reports.

"There are dozens of police and security forces in the Vali-ye Asr Avenue ... they have blocked entrances of metro stations in the area," a witness told Reuters by telephone, referring to a large thoroughfare that cuts through Tehran. Another witness said police cars with windows covered by black curtains were parked near Tehran's notorious Evin prison.

11.36am: Iraq can be added to the list of countries where people are protesting today. From AP:

Hundreds of Iraqis rallied in central Baghdad against corruption and the lack of government services that have plagued this country for years. Many of the demonstrators carried banners that bore the image of a broken red heart, alluding to the fact that the protest took place on Valentine's Day.

12.40pm: There are disturbing reports of gangs of government thugs attacking protesters in Yemen. From Reuters:

Government backers armed with broken bottles, daggers and rocks chased down thousands of pro-reform demonstrators in Yemen's capital on Monday, turning unrest inspired by Egypt's uprising increasingly violent.

1.00pm: Demonstrators are trying to move into the centre of Tehran, Reuters reports:

> Hundreds of demonstrators marched down Azadi (Freedom) Street, a wide boulevard, towards Azadi Square, a traditional rallying point for protests dominated by a huge white marble arch, in central Tehran.

6.14pm: According to the Arabist blog, this is what Egypt's ruling military council has said on consititutional ammendments:

> The military does not want power and thinks a civilian government is the only path towards progress. They only want to safeguard the gains of the revolution … A constitutional committee will be formed during the next 10 days; a new constitution will be voted on in a referendum in 2 months.

TUESDAY 15 FEBRUARY

8.15am: Bahrain's interior ministry has confirmed that "clashes" took place at the funeral of a protester today. According to an opposition MP, a second protester died today. Al-Jazeera reported he was killed in clashes at the funeral procession.

10.35am: In Egypt, The Muslim Brotherhood said they had no plans to put up a candidate for the presidential elections in Egypt, but today they said they plan to set up a political party.

In a statement on their English-language website, the Brotherhood said they would become a political party when the time is right.

11.14am: A crowd of up to 20,000 people have gathered in Bahrain at the funeral of Ali Abdulhadi Mushaima, who was killed in yesterday's protests, according to an eyewitness in an audio interview.

The witness, who did not wish to give her full name, said:

> The scene is just unbelievable. There are thousands upon thousands on the road … There were definitely chants against the regime. The crowd was getting angrier and angrier. A lot of signs said they are peaceful, and this is what we get in return.

11.42am: Pro- and anti-government protesters have clashed in Sana'a, Yemen, according to Reuters.

> Hundreds of anti-government demonstrators and government loyalists fought with rocks and batons in the Yemeni capital today in political unrest fuelled by the Egyptian uprising.
>
> About 1,000 protesters, marching down a street that leads to the presidential palace, were blocked by anti-riot police, a Reuters reporter said. As they dispersed into side streets, they were confronted by hundreds of government backers and both sides hurled rocks at each other.

1.17pm: Bahrain's King Hamad has appeared on state TV. This, according to Ahram Online, is what he said:

> There have been sadly two deaths. I express my deep condolences to their families. Everyone should know that I have assigned deputy prime minister Jawad Al-Orayedh to form a special committee to find out the reasons that led to such regrettable events.

2.16pm: A Facebook tribute group, modelling on a similar group in Egypt, has been set up for the protester killed in Bahrain yesterday.

"We are all Ali Abdulhadi Mushamai" deliberately echoes Egypt's "We are all Khaled Said", the group set up by Google executive and activist Wael Ghonim.

3.20pm: Bahrain's Pearl roundabout has been renamed the "Nation's Square" by protesters, says AP. It also reports – significantly, given that the protesters are largely Shia and some have even accused them of being supporters of Iran – that they have been shouting chants of solidarity with Sunni Muslims. "No Sunnis, no Shias, we are all Bahrainis," is the chant. People on the roundabout are putting up tents and settling down for the night in a sign that they want it to become their equivalent of Tahrir Square.

4.43pm: Iran has confirmed the arrest of 1,500 people during yesterday's protests.

9.00pm: Chilling news from the US television network CBS: its correspondent Lara Logan was beaten and sexually assaulted by a mob in Cairo's Tahrir

Square during the celebrations following Mubarak's resignation. From the CBS statement:

> On Friday February 11, the day Egyptian president Mubarak stepped down, CBS correspondent Lara Logan was covering the jubilation in Tahrir Square for a 60 Minutes story when she and her team and their security were surrounded by a dangerous element amidst the celebration. It was a mob of more than 200 people whipped into frenzy.
>
> In the crush of the mob, she was separated from her crew. She was surrounded and suffered a brutal and sustained sexual assault and beating before being saved by a group of women and an estimated 20 Egyptian soldiers. She reconnected with the CBS team, returned to her hotel and returned to the United States on the first flight the next morning. She is currently in the hospital recovering.

WEDNESDAY 16 FEBRUARY

8.50am: It appears that a big demonstration is planned for tomorrow in Libya – the hashtag #Feb17 is being used on Twitter.

11.30am: There is a sense of frustration among some Libyans that the protests in Benghazi, their second biggest city, have not caught on in the capital Tripoli, even though tomorrow is supposed to be the big day for demonstrations to commemorate the failed uprising against Gaddafi in 2006. From Twitter:

\# **ShababLibya** guys in Tripoli get out onto the streets, start with 100, or we will see a massacre in #Benghazi, its now or never #Feb17

\# **EEE_Libya** in Tripoli #libya. Nothing but staged [pro-Gaddafi] protest now going on here. Tripoli wake up!!!!!!

4.37pm: The Yemeni president has been on the phone to Bahrain's king to express support for the king, as both countries face protests. Saleh blamed people with "foreign agendas" for trying to spread chaos across the region, Reuters reports, citing Yemen's state news agency. Saleh reportedly said to King Hamad:

There are plans to try and sink the region into a fervour of chaos and violence, and they have targeted the security of the region and stability of our countries. The people creating these works of chaos and sabotage are only implementing suspicious foreign agendas.

12.39am: More reports are emerging about attacks by Bahrain security forces on protesters in Pearl Square on Manama. Police appear to have started by firing rubber bullets and teargas into the square at sometime around 3am local time, and then moved in towards the crowd.

There are numerous messages on Twitter and other social media of a large squad of police and security forces in the area. Earlier in the evening there were estimates of thousands of protesters camped on the roundabout, but numbers dwindled later in the night.

2.58am: An official response has come from the Bahraini government, with a statement by the ministry of the interior. It confirms that police have cleared Pearl Square "after trying full opportunities for dialogue".

5.10am: The Guardian's Martin Chulov has just been on the line from the SMC Hospital, Bahrain's largest, which he says is crowded with thousands of people who have gathered there since the police assault on Pearl roundabout:

Many were at the Pearl roundabout when the attack began shortly after 3.15am. The attack was co-ordinated from every direction, and the tent city they had set up was literally cut through with knives. The lead trauma surgeon at SMC hospital was tied up and assaulted, and he's now in intensive care at the hospital.

There was no official word on deaths or injuries so far, but hospitals in Bahrain have reported hundreds of people with serious gaping wounds, broken bones and breathing difficulties caused by heavy doses of teargas.

5.52am: The leader of Bahrain's main Shia opposition group says the storming of the Pearl roundabout site where protesters had camped out overnight was "real terrorism". Abdul Jalil Khalil tells Reuters: "Whoever took the decision to attack the protest was aiming to kill."

THURSDAY 17 FEBRUARY

12.47pm: Of the crackdown in Bahrain, Peter Beaumont writes:

> If the Bahrain government thought it was going to defuse the protests
> with such a show of force it obviously has not been paying much atten-
> tion to events that occurred in Tunisia and Egypt where the use of
> violence weakened not strengthened the government's position. Its use
> of the state media has easily been as clumsy as Mubarak and Ben Ali's
> with state TV showing a very partial account of what happened last night
> – notably injuries to police officers.

5.28pm: Issandr El Amrani on the Arabist blog has had consistently good
analysis of the situation across north Africa in the past month. He's posted
another good piece, this time about Libya. He writes:

> My gut feeling is that the most important protests now taking place in
> North Africa are those in Libya. I say this with no disrespect to those in
> Algeria, where the regime certainly deserves to be brought down, or my
> own native Morocco, where the palace and Makhzen need a wake-up
> call that the status quo is not acceptable.
>
> But Libya shares something important with Egypt and Tunisia: an
> ageing leader (41 years in power) faces a looming succession crisis in
> which the leading candidates are his own sons. I simply don't think that's
> an acceptable outcome for any republic in the 21st century, and was a key
> aspect to the revolt against Mubarak in Egypt, and to a lesser extent in
> Tunisia (with the rumored heir apparent being his nephew).

FRIDAY 18 FEBRUARY

10.13am: Al-Jazeera English is showing a huge crowd gathered in Tahrir
Square for the "day of victory" – the numbers look similar to those we saw
last Friday, when Mubarak finally made his exit. People are waving banners
and chanting, and Al-Jazeera reports that the army has been handing out
celebratory flags to protesters.

11.33am: AP is reporting tens of thousands of Yemenis demonstrating
across the country today in the eighth day of protests there. There were
riots overnight, with protesters in Aden setting fire to a local government

building and a demonstrator shot dead by police, according to local officials. The protesters are calling for President Saleh to step down after 32
years as president. On social media sites demonstrators are calling for a
"Friday of rage" today.

12.28pm: Eight people are reported to have been injured in Amman,
Jordan, in clashes between pro- and anti-government demonstrators, in the
seventh Friday in a row of unrest there. About 2,000 people protested,
according to AP, with students from the growing Jaayin – or I'm Coming –
movement chanting: "We want constitutional reforms; we want a complete
change to policies."

2.54pm: AP reports on the violent turn of events in Bahrain:

> Security forces have fired teargas on thousands of protest marchers in
> Bahrain's capital after angry calls to topple the gulf nation's monarchy.
> Some demonstrators are moving in the direction of Pearl Square today,
> a day after riot police swept into the area to destroy an Egypt-style protest
> encampment. At least five people were killed in that attack. Witnesses say
> they saw some casualties in the clashes today.

3.47pm: According the Guardian's Martin Chulov in Bahrain, the latest
outbreak of violence occurred when a few hundred people marched to Pearl
roundabout, prompting the security forces to fire shots into the air. But a
number of people were injured and have been taken to hospital; the hospital
was at one point surrounded by riot police, sparking a moment of panic.

5.30pm: Jack Shenker reports from Cairo on the massive turnout there:

> Hundreds of thousands of protesters returned to Tahrir Square in a mass
> rally to mark the downfall of Mubarak. Amid widespread speculation over
> the intentions of Egypt's army, who are currently governing the country
> through a Supreme Military Council but have promised a swift transition
> to democratic civilian rule, prominent Islamic cleric Yusuf al-Qaradawi
> used his midday sermon in the square to warn Egyptians that their strug-
> gle was not complete.
>   "Don't let anyone steal this revolution from you – those hypocrites
> who will put on a new face that suits them," he told the crowds.

9.13pm: Protesters are "committing suicide" according to the chilling statement from the Revolutionary Committees – an integral part of Gaddafi's regime – published on the Azzahf al-Akhdar website:

> The response of the people and the Revolutionary Forces to any adventure by these small groups will be sharp and violent. The power of the people, the Jamahiriya, the Revolution and the leader are all red lines, and anyone who tries to cross or approach them will be committing suicide and playing with fire.

SATURDAY 19 FEBRUARY

11.15am: Crown Prince Salman bin Hamad al-Khalifa has ordered the withdrawal of troops from the streets, AP reports. Bahrain's police will "continue to oversee law and order", the government has added in a statement.

11.23am: In Yemen, riot police have opened fire on thousands of protesters marching through the capital, Sana'a, according to AP, which says the shots killed one and injured five.

1.08pm: Clashes are continuing with anti-government protesters in Libya between Benghazi and Al Bayda, Reuters reports a security source as saying. The area was "80% under control … a lot of police stations have been set on fire or damaged", the source said.

Local people say security forces have killed dozens of people in the past 72 hours.

1.35pm: Now that the crown prince has ordered troops off the streets, thousands of protesters have retaken Pearl Square, which is where demonstrations in the country kicked off, AP is reporting.

SUNDAY 20 FEBRUARY

11.36am: Martin Chulov reports from Pearl roundabout in the Bahraini capital Manama:

> The hub of Bahrain's anti-government revolt resembles a folk festival today, with tents pitched, candy and juice being handed out and

thousands of people continuing to stream to and from the site. Blood from the last battle to be fought here on Saturday afternoon between government forces and Bahraini youth still stains the ground in parts. But the razor wire that had barricaded the central Bahrain site has been taken away and the roundabout is again being used by traffic.

12.01pm: Associated Press is reporting that the death toll is Benghazi may be much higher than first thought:

A doctor in the Libyan city of Benghazi says his hospital has seen the bodies of at least 200 protesters killed by Gaddafi's forces over the last few days. The official spoke on condition of anonymity because he fears reprisal.

Witnesses told AP that a mixture of special commandos, foreign mercenaries and Gadhafi loyalists went after demonstrators on Saturday with knives, assault rifles and heavy-caliber weapons.

MONDAY 21 FEBRUARY

9.11am: In Yemen, President Saleh has rejected demands that he step down and described demonstrations against his regime as unacceptable acts of provocation, though he renewed calls for talks with the protesters. Meanwhile, a Yemeni teenager was killed and four people were wounded in a clash with soldiers in the southern port of Aden. The death brings to 12 the number of people killed in unrest in Yemen since Thursday.

3.43pm: AP reports that in Benghazi protesters have been celebrating in the streets claiming control of the city. In Tripoli, a fire was raging at the People's Hall, where Libya's equivalent of a parliament meets several times a year, and demonstrators were planning new marches in Green Square and Gaddafi's residence for tonight.

4.34pm: ABC News reports that an Egyptian father has named his daughter Facebook, as a way of thanking the social networking site for its role in helping protesters organise the demonstrations that forced Mubarak to quit. The baby's full name is Facebook Jamal Ibrihim.

TUESDAY 22 FEBRUARY

8.45am: Gaddafi appeared briefly on Libyan state TV last night to deny reports that he had fled the country, as key diplomats continued to disown his regime. "I want to show that I'm in Tripoli and not in Venezuela. Do not believe the channels belonging to stray dogs," Gaddafi said.

5.06pm: Gaddafi has insisted he is not standing down or leaving the country. He said he would die in Libya "as a martyr".

In a long speech, he called upon his supporters to take back the streets from those who have been rebelling against his rule, saying they should go out tonight and "chase them", and railed against the rebels, threatening them with the death penalty and calling them "rats" and drug addicts.

10.51pm: The UN security council has condemned the crackdown in Libya and demanded an "immediate end to the violence". It has called for those responsible for attacks on civilians to be held to account. The call came in a statement agreed by the 15-nation council expressing "grave concern".

11.30pm: Martin Chulov, the Guardian's Iraq correspondent, is now inside Libya and tweeting from there as one of the few reporters to have crossed the border since the uprising started. It reminds him of somewhere:

\# Brutalised and stagnant. Libya feels like Iraq.

WEDNESDAY 23 FEBRUARY

10.55am: France, which was slow off the mark when protests swept its former colony of Tunisia, is taking a more pro-active approach towards Libya. In a statement after a weekly meeting with ministers President Nicolas Sarkozy urged the EU to suspend all economic ties with Tripoli.

12.42pm: The BBC, Sky and al-Jazeera have all been showing the first live protest pictures from Libya. Protesters in the centre of Tobruk, one of the eastern cities no longer controlled by the regime, are waving the pre-Gaddafi green, black and red Libyan flag and holding posters proclaiming "Free Libya" and "Oil for the west". That the posters are in English seem to be an appeal for outside for help as Gaddafi has expressed his determination to fight to "the last bullet".

12.45pm: Martin Chulov has just texted us the following from Benghazi:

\# It seems impossible to imagine Gaddafi winning Benghazi back. His military has defected, or fled. His mercenaries have been routed and the flag of the monarch he ousted 42 years ago is now flying in many places. The mood here is switching between vehemence and one of victory. People are convinced that the dictator that many here have known for all their lives has just days left in office.

1.07pm: The Guardian's Ghaith Abdul-Ahad has just been on the phone from the Tunisia-Libya border. He says there are hundreds of people coming through, mainly Tunisians. Some have been harassed and some beaten up by Libyans who blame them for stirring up trouble. They are scared.

On the Libyan side the border is manned by plainclothes police who are "very, very, very loyal to Gaddafi, and very aggressive", Ghaith says.

1.56pm: Associated Press says militiamen loyal to Gaddafi have "clamped down" on Tripoli today, "with the sound of gunfire ringing in the air". The military has also moved heavy forces into the town of Sabratha, west of the capital, to try to put down protesters who have overwhelmed security head-quarters and government buildings, a news website close to the government reported.

One woman who lives near the centre of Tripoli told AP: "Mercenaries are everywhere with weapons. You can't open a window or door. Snipers hunt people. We are under siege, at the mercy of a man who is not a Muslim."

11.00pm: Obama has delivered a statement on Libya. The strongest passage:

The American people extend our deepest condolences to the families and loved ones of all who've been killed and injured. The suffering and bloodshed is outrageous and it is unacceptable. So are threats and orders to shoot peaceful protesters and further punish the people of Libya. These actions violate international norms and every standard of common decency. This violence must stop.

FRIDAY 25 FEBRUARY

11.46am: Libya's rebel movement has launched a new push against Gaddafi, AP reports, calling for mass demonstrations in Tripoli today as it seeks to solidify its gains and loosen the longtime leader's grip on the capital.

3.30pm: Six demonstrators have been killed in Iraq on the country's "day of rage", according to Associated Press. The news agency said that three people were killed in the northern city of Hawija, 150 miles north of Baghdad, after a crowd tried to break into the city's municipal building. Three more were killed in Mosul, also in the north of Iraq, when guards opened fire on hundreds of protesters gathered in front of the provincial council building, AP said, quoting police and hospital officials.

3.32pm: The entire Libyan mission to the UN in Geneva has quit, reports AP. Its second secretary asked the human rights council – discussing the possible suspension of his country for Gaddafi's war on its citizens – to stand for a moment of silence to "honour this revolution".

Most of Libya's delegation at the UN in New York abandoned the regime and called on Gaddafi to step down on Monday.

The Libyan delegation to the Arab League has changed its name to "the representative of Libyan people to the Arab League", Ahmed Nassouf, deputy director of protocol, told Reuters.

5.06pm: Our diplomatic editor, Julian Borger, reports that at the UN security council in New York, the British and French delegations are drafting a strong resolution under chapter seven provisions, which would identify the situation in Libya as "a threat to peace" and make mandatory "strictly nonmilitary" measures including "targeted sanctions … and an arms embargo".

9.00pm: The Guardian's Jack Shenker reports from Cairo on another massive demonstration there and increased unease at the country's military rulers:

> After a major rally in Tahrir Square to mark the one-month anniversary of the 25 January protests that launched Egypt's revolution, several hundred demonstrators are now camping outside parliament in an effort to force out Ahmed Shafiq, an old member of the Mubarak-era cabinet who has improbably clung on to the post of prime minister.

4.54pm: Gaddafi's son Saif al-Islam has been on a media blitz today. Earlier he told Turkey's CNN Turk television:

> We have plans A, B and C. Plan A is to live and die in Libya. Plan B is to live and die in Libya. Plan C is to live and die in Libya.

SATURDAY 26 FEBRUARY

2.58pm: In Libya Gaddafi's security forces have abandoned parts of Tripoli, where protesters now openly defy the regime, Reuters reports. The withdrawal of security forces from the working-class Tajoura district after five days of anti-government demonstrations leaves Gaddafi's grip on power looking tenuous, says the news agency.

8.13pm: Libya's former justice minister, Mustafa Mohamed Abud al-Jeleil, has led the formation of an interim government based in Benghazi, the online edition of the Quryna newspaper reported, according to Reuters. Quryna quoted him as saying that Gaddafi "alone" bore responsibility "for the crimes that have occurred" in Libya and that his tribe, Gaddadfa, were forgiven.

9.39pm: President Barack Obama has for the first time called on Gaddafi to step down, AP reports. Obama made the comments to German chancellor Angela Merkel in a telephone conversation today. The White House says Obama told Merkel that when a leader's only means of holding power is to use violence against his people, then he has lost the legitimacy to rule and needs to do what's right for his country by "leaving now".

10.03pm: Three people have been killed in clashes between Tunisian security forces and youths rioting in central Tunis, an interior ministry official told Reuters. The official, who declined to be named, said another 12 had been injured in the clashes, which he said occurred after a riot orchestrated by loyalists of the ousted President Ben Ali. He said about 100 people had been arrested.

SUNDAY 27 FEBRUARY

10.42am: Overnight, the UN security council voted unanimously to impose sanctions on Libya. It has imposed an arms embargo and asset freeze while referring Gaddafi to the international criminal court for alleged crimes against humanity.

11.06am: The Libyan regime has allowed a number of international journalists into the country, including the Observer's Peter Beaumont. Speaking by phone a few moments ago, he said:

> We arrived last night to chaotic scenes at the airport; there are a lot of people trying to flee, people sleeping on rugs outside. In fact at the hotel most of the staff have fled and that goes for some of the other big hotels. We're here at the invitation of the Libyan government to show that Tripoli is safe and not as bad as reported. The traffic is moving freely and it is relatively calm, but there are queues for food and there are queues for banks.

11.52am: Anti-government protests have now spread to Oman, which Reuters describes as a normally sleepy Gulf state. Al-Jazeera reports that two people have been killed in demonstrations today.

12.05pm: Reuters has conformed that the city of Zawiyah is in rebel hands.

> Armed men opposed to the rule of Gaddafi are in control of the city of Zawiyah, about 30 miles west of the capital, a Reuters reporter in the town said. The red, green and black flag of Libya's anti-Gaddafi rebellion was flying from a building in the centre of the town and a crowd of several hundred people was chanting "This is our revolution," the reporter said.

3.12pm: The Tunisian prime minister has resigned. From AP:

> The Tunisian prime minister, Mohamed Ghannouchi, has announced his resignation after a renewed outbreak of street violence. Ghannouchi was a longtime ally of President Ben Ali, and had pledged to guide the country until elections can be held this summer.

MONDAY 28 FEBRUARY

12.22pm: Yemen's President Saleh is to announce a new national unity government with the opposition within the next 24 hours, according to wire services. It is the latest attempt by Saleh to quell anti-government protests in the country, which show no signs of abating despite the demonstrations often having been met with violence by the security forces.

12.32pm: Yemen's opposition has swiftly rejected the offer, and will not join Saleh's unity government. "The opposition decided to stand with the people's demand for the fall of the regime, and there is no going back from that," said Mohammed al-Sabry, a spokesman for Yemen's umbrella opposition coalition.

1.11pm: A bizarre development: pop singer Nelly Furtado has taken to Twitter to reveal that in 2007 she was paid £1m by "the Gaddafi clan" to perform at a hotel in Italy. Furtado says she is now going to donate the money. No word on whether she'll factor in inflation.

1.33pm: The European Union has agreed sanctions against the Gaddafi regime. The measures include an arms embargo, asset freeze and visa ban, AP reports.

3.04pm: Nelly Furtado might have been wracked by guilt to return the proceeds from a gig she performed for Gaddafi, but will others, asks @libyansrevolt on Twitter:

\#   @NellyFurtado has led the way – will @beyonce @enrique305
@MariahCarey @Lionel_richie follow suit?

3.41pm: British forces have been asked to develop plans to impose a no-fly zone on Libya, David Cameron has just told the British parliament. Cameron has not ruled out the use of force.

7.19pm: The US appears to be intensifying efforts to turn the screws on the Gaddafi regime. In the last hour the US Treasury has said that $30bn in Libyan assets have been blocked. The US military has meanwhile said that ships and planes are being moved closer to Libya in case they are needed.

9.56pm: As political leaders in Europe and the US begin to crank up the push for more concrete action against the Gaddafi regime, including a possible no-fly zone, the Guardian's Simon Tisdall strikes a note of caution:

Criticised for reacting too slowly to the Libyan crisis, Britain and its allies now risk a dangerous, ill-thought-out over-reaction in raising the prospect of direct western military intervention. If any lesson has been learned from Iraq and Afghanistan, it is that while it is very easy to get into a war in the Middle East, it is difficult to control events once engaged, and harder still to find a way out.

TUESDAY 1 MARCH

8.18am: Libyan forces have been launching counterattacks against rebel-held territory. Air force jets bombed Ajdabiya, south of Benghazi, and witnesses have told AP pro-Gaddafi troops supported by tanks tried but failed to retake Zawiyah, west of Tripoli, overnight. Al-Arabiya is reporting a build-up of forces loyal to the Libyan leader near the border with Tunisia.

10.28am: The "Feb 17 Voices" project has sent through a translation of a statement from a group referring to itself as the "Youth of the February 17th Uprising" in Tripoli, which calls for peaceful demonstrations in the capital on Friday. "We pray for the souls of our honourable martyrs, who have fallen in every corner of our beloved nation," it reads. "We vow to continue the struggle until we achieve a clear victory, bringing down the regime and liberating the entirety of our homeland from the tyranny and oppression that it has suffered over 41 dark years."

The statement also backs the interim national council being formed in eastern Libya, and rules out "any form of negotiation" with Gaddafi's "criminal regime".

12.06pm: At Comment Is Free, Brian Whitaker has assessed the seriousness of Saudi protests. While initiatives such as petitions may seem tame compared to others in the region, "in a Saudi context they are momentous", he writes.

12.39pm: Russia's top diplomat has ruled out the idea of creating a no-fly zone over Libya, AP reports. Russian foreign minister Sergey Lavrov described the idea of imposing limits on Libyan air space as "superfluous" and said world powers must instead focus on fully using the sanctions that the UN security council approved over the weekend, says AP.

8.49pm: The UN general assembly has unanimously suspended Libya's membership of the UN human rights council because of violence by Libyan forces against protesters. It is the first time that a member state has been suspended from the council.

WEDNESDAY 2 MARCH

9.44am: A report in the New York Times that says rebel leaders in Benghazi are debating whether to ask for western airstrikes under the UN banner. One of the people quoted as possibly supporting airstrikes is Abdel-Hafidh Ghoga, a spokesman for the Libyan National Transitional Council, who, on Monday, said the council was "against any foreign intervention or military intervention". But the Times says Ghoga made clear, "if it is with the United Nations, it is not a foreign intervention".

9.57am: An important tweet from Martin Chulov:

\# Benghazi's organising committee has just formally asked UN to help end Gaddafi's airstrikes in eastern Libya.

3.17pm: Peter Beaumont has just returned from listening to Gaddafi's three-hour speech to the Libyan People's Congress. Peter says that the Libyan leader's tone was more conciliatory today than in his previous speeches, Gaddafi offering an amnesty for those who took up arms and promising that they'll be forgiven. He also said "we are sorry" for the deaths on both sides and said he believes there should be an investigation.

4.38pm: Martin Chulov, who was in Brega earlier when it was bombed, has called in. He said:

The battle is still raging, particularly in the area around the university, which is a giant area in the industrial zone there. Gaddafi forces had brought in jets, there was a lot of heavy weaponry being used, and by sunset who was actually in control of Brega was not clear.

THURSDAY 3 MARCH

7.59am: A Venezuelan peace plan for Libya that would involve "friendly countries" mediating between Gaddafi and his opponents is being mooted as providing a possible way out of the conflict this morning. Al-Jazeera's Dima

Khatib is reporting that Gaddafi has accepted the offer from Hugo Chávez. But details are vague.

9.37am: In Egypt, the under-pressure prime minister, Ahmed Shafiq, has resigned. His departure was announced on the Facebook page of the Egyptian military. Another million-man march was planned for tomorrow to force out Shafiq and other members of the cabinet linked to Mubarak.

6.39pm: Barack Obama says Gaddafi has lost his legitimacy to lead and "must leave". The White House news conference is the first time that the US president has appeared in person to demand the Libyan leader step down. He said:

> We will continue to send a clear message: the violence must stop. Gaddafi has lost the legitimacy to lead and he must leave. Those who perpetrate violence against the Libyan people will be held accountable.

8.42pm: The director of the London School of Economics, Sir Howard Davies, has resigned over fresh revelations that the institution had been involved in a deal to train hundreds of young Libyans to become part of the country's future elite.

10.14pm: US officials have expressed little enthusiasm for Venezuelan President Hugo Chávez's proposal to mediate a peace settlement between Gaddafi and the rebels, Reuters reports. "It's uncertain to me what an international commission is going to accomplish. Colonel Gaddafi needs to step down," state department spokesman PJ Crowley said.

FRIDAY 4 MARCH

11.33am: In a historic moment, Egypt's new prime minister Essam Sharaf has been addressing protesters in Tahrir Square. In a short speech, he told them he would do all he can "to realise their demands". He also said, to a rapturous reception, the security forces "should work for the good of the people".

11.56am: The head of Libya's rebel national council, Mustafa Abdul Jalil, has been addressing crowds in Benghazi, vowing "victory or death", Reuters reports. The former justice minister said:

We are people who fight, we don't surrender. Victory or death. We will not stop till we liberate all this country ... The time of hypocrisy is over.

2.05pm: Several people have been killed and dozens injured after the army opened fire on anti-government protesters in the Libyan city of Zawiyah, 30 miles west of Tripoli, according to Sky News. The news channel says that the army opened fire as protesters made their way towards the military lines on the outskirts of the city. It said that at least 10 anti-regime fighters had earlier been killed as Gaddafi's forces tried to take control.

6.49pm: Pro-Gaddafi forces appear to have fought their way into the centre of the disputed town of Zawiyah, the focal point of today's fighting, according to Reuters.

8.15pm: A huge explosion has been reported near the city of Benghazi, killing at least 17 people according to multiple reports. A sample tweet:

 # ShababLibya Confirmed 16 killed in Rajma (just outside Benina), Benghazi from the bombing of the weapon depot.

It remains unclear what caused the blast.

SATURDAY 5 MARCH

10.36am: Fighting continues in the western city of Zawiyah, where rebels claim to have repelled a major assault by pro-Gaddafi forces. The battle, which began at dawn, could prove significant to the regime's defence of Tripoli, which lies 30 miles to the east.

"They entered Zawiyah at six in the morning with heavy forces, hundreds of soldiers with tanks. Our people fought back ... We have won for now and civilians are gathering in the square," Youssef Shagan, the rebel force spokesman in Zawiyah, told Reuters.

4.05pm: More from Reuters in Zawiyah:

"The fighting has intensified and the [loyalist army's] tanks are shelling everything on their way. They have shelled houses. Now they are shelling a mosque where hundreds of people are hiding, said local resident Abu Akeel. "We can't rescue anyone because the shelling is so heavy."

Another resident in the main square said: "The attack has started. I see more than 20 tanks."

SUNDAY 6 MARCH

11.37am: Martin Chulov says an SAS team has been caught about 19 miles west of Benghazi and appear to be part of a British diplomatic mission to make contact with the opposition. A senior member of Benghazi's revolutionary council told Martin: "they were carrying espionage equipment, reconnaissance equipment, multiple passports and weapons. This is no way to conduct yourself during an uprising ... How do we know who these people are?"

12.22pm: The defence secretary, Liam Fox, has confirmed that a "small diplomatic team" is in Benghazi to talk to Libyan rebels but refused to confirm reports that any British nationals had been detained.

12.39pm: While Zawiyah and Ras Lanuf remain in the hands of the opposition, reports indicate that loyalist forces supported by aircraft have pushed rebels away from the coastal town of Bin Jawad to stop their advance on Gaddafi's home town, Sirte. Peter Beaumont writes:

> What is clear is that a large military deployment appears to be under way in Tripoli and the surrounding areas, with ever more tanks visible both inside the city and in the countryside and more missile launchers seen on the roads.

4.39pm: A doctor at Misrata hospital has told Reuters that at least 18 people have been killed in fighting between government and rebel forces, with many wounded. Earlier, the news agency quoted residents as saying that rebels repelled a government attack backed by tanks and artillery.

5.15pm: The British special forces men are on their way out of Libya. According to the Guardian's national security expert, Richard Norton-Taylor, the team of six SAS troops and two MI6 officers are now on HMS Cumberland in the Mediterranean.

MONDAY 7 MARCH

10.15am: Forces loyal to Gaddafi have reportedly retaken the previously rebel held town of Bin Jawad and are advancing on the oil refinery town of Ras Lanuf. The taking of Ras Lanuf had represented a major victory for the rebels on Friday but their advance towards Gaddafi's hometown of Sirte on the road to Tripoli was stopped in its tracks at Bin Jawad where rebels retreated under fire.

11.41am: Rebels in eastern Libya have called for the west to intervene with airstrikes to prevent Gaddafi acting "like a wounded wolf" and attacking oilfields in the country. "If the west does not intervene with tactical airstrikes he could put the oilfields out of commission for a long time," Mustafa Gheriani, a media officer for the rebel movement in Benghazi has told Reuters.

TUESDAY 8 MARCH

3.42pm: In Egypt, there are signs that a "million woman march" being held in Cairo to coincide with International Women's Day is turning ugly. Women are demanding female input on the drafting of Egypt's constitution (the committee drawing up amendments is all male) and legislative changes that will guarantee complete gender equality but there is a counterprotest. Twitter user @pakinammer is tweeting from the protest:

\# A guy now is schooling us on how women should stay home and raise men who can become presidents =)

\# A physical scuffle broke out now now. I think I'm leaving. This can get disgusting, easily.

\# One man, carried on shoulders, shouting: "A woman's place is her house." Some women arguing back. No point if you ask me.

5.13pm: Sky News is broadcasting a special report on Zawiyah. Sky is one of the few media organisations to have had a correspondent in the disputed city, Alex Crawford. In her accompanying web report, Crawford writes:

We saw ambulances being driven at high speed to pick up the first casualties and they too were fired on. It was mayhem at the Zawiyah teaching hospital, as dozens of people were stretchered in by friends, colleagues and strangers. The injuries were appalling.

She quotes a doctor at the hospital who said there was a "shoot-to-kill" policy. Crawford, who was in Zawiaya from midday on Friday to Sunday afternoon, says "the people were under almost constant attack" in that time. "We have seen with our own eyes Gaddafi's forces firing on peaceful protesters," she writes.

WEDNESDAY 9 MARCH

11.25am: Chris McGreal, in Benghazi, has been gauging the mood of the opposition forces. He says the bombardment over recent days has convinced the Libyan National Transitional Council that its forces are in for a protracted battle and of the need for foreign intervention.

> Certainly the euphoria of the early days when the rebels pushed hundreds of miles towards Tripoli and they thought that Gaddafi might fall within days, those days have gone. They realise that he's going to fight on if he can and not only has the push towards Tripoli stalled, but it's been reversed. They realise it's going to be a long struggle. They're looking increasingly to foreign governments to support them with no-fly zones.

5.54pm: Libyan state television is now broadcasting images of Zawiyah apparently firmly in the hands of the pro-Gaddafi government forces. The images appear to show a crowd of several hundred people in Zawiyah, with many waving green flags and carrying images of Gaddafi, chanting: "We want Colonel Gaddafi!"

6.18pm: Libya's National Transitional Council now has a website that it launched today, in both English and Arabic. It says:

> The council derives it legitimacy from the decisions of local councils set up by the revolutionary people of Libya on the 17th of February. These local councils facilitated a mechanism to manage daily life in the liberated cities and villages. The council consists of 31 members representing the various cities of Libya from the east to the west and from the north to the

south. The aim of the NTC is to steer Libya during the interim period that will come after its complete liberation.

11.14pm: Reuters reports from Marrakesh that Morocco's King Mohamed has offered a series of political reforms including a referendum on constitutional changes, greater freedom for political parties and a freely elected parliament and prime minister.

THURSDAY 10 MARCH

10.12am: France has just become the first major European power to recognise the Libyan National Transitional Council in Benghazi as the legitimate representative of Libyan people. It is to open an embassy in Benghazi and will allow the Libyan embassy in Paris to reopen.

10.27am: Libya is in a civil war, according to the International committee of the Red Cross. ICRC President Jakob Kellenberger said in Misrata 40 patients were treated for serious injuries and 22 dead were taken there. He said the Red Cross surgical team in Ajdabiya operated on 55 wounded this past week and "civilians are bearing the brunt of the violence", adding:

> We have now a non-international armed conflict, or what you would call civil war. We see increasing numbers of wounded arriving at hospitals in the east and we are extremely worried.

10.48am: The Guardian's Chris McGreal, in Benghazi, says there has been a shake-up in the opposition forces amid the bombardment by Gaddafi's forces of other rebel-held territory in recent days:

> One of the things that has happened is that the military leadership is clearing out all of the hundreds upon hundreds of young men who simply grabbed weapons in Benghazi and around from military bases and headed towards the front to fight. They have been very poorly disciplined, they have no experience, they have shot at the slightest provocation and they have become a danger to themselves, and to the rebel cause in some way. They are now being replaced by more experienced soldiers, people who have served with Gaddafi's army, in an effort to give some co-ordination and discipline.

11.44am: There is some worrying news from Libya about the Guardian correspondent Ghaith Abdul-Ahad. He is missing, having not been in touch with the paper since Sunday, when he was on the outskirts of Zawiyah.

3.16pm: Chris McGreal in Benghazi says the National Transitional Council (NTC) there is concentrating its diplomatic effort on three countries in its attempts to get a no-fly zone implemented, amid dismay at the US failure to act:

> They are pursuing a diplomatic approach with three countries. France is one of them, Britain and Turkey are the others. They seem to have largely given up on the US for the moment.

3.39pm: The EU has voted to recognise the Libyan NTC in Benghazi, al-Arabiya is reporting.

5.39pm: ITV News international editor Bill Neely was the first journalist into Zawiyah today after its recapture by pro-Gaddafi forces, and he has provided the following summary to the Guardian:

> It is certainly the worst devastation I've seen in any town centre. Mix a huge IRA bomb with a tank battle and add the aftermath of an artillery barrage and you get some idea of the damage to the centre of this town of a quarter of a million people.

6.58pm: Some good news regarding the Guardian correspondent Ghaith Abdul-Ahad – Libyan government officials have confirmed that he is in custody.

7.26pm: Nato has said imposing a no-fly zone over Libya would need "demonstrable need" as well as UN approval and support from other countries in the region, after a meeting of ministers from member states in Brussels.

FRIDAY 11 MARCH

9.32am: The focus may be on Libya, but Saudi Arabia is today bracing itself for a "day of rage". A coalition of liberals, rights activists, moderate Sunni Islamists and Shia Muslims have called for reform and set up a Facebook page that has attracted more than 30,000 people. The government, however, forbids protests and the big Saudi cities are already flooded with police.

10.10am: Things are also growing heated again in Bahrain, Reuters reports:

> Hardline Bahraini opposition and youth groups are preparing for a march on the royal court that is expected to spark fighting on the Gulf island where the majority is Shia but the ruling family is Sunni.

11.16am: This is the latest Reuters take on things in Yemen, where demonstrators are holding what they term a "Friday of no return":

> Tens of thousands of protesters took to the streets across Yemen today, trying to draw record crowds to show President Saleh his offers of reform would not soften their demand for his resignation.
>
> The demonstrations followed Thursday's proposal by Saleh, a US ally against al-Qaida's Yemen-based wing, for a new constitution to be put to referendum within the year and new electoral laws to ensure equal representation. Opposition figures rejected the offer, calling it "too little, too late".

2.10pm: A planned protest in Riyadh appears to have been squashed before it could begin, reports AP:

> Hundreds of police were deployed in the Saudi capital today and prevented protests calling for democratic reforms inspired by the wave of unrest sweeping the Arab world ... By midday, no protesters had shown up in the capital and the police presence significantly decreased.

3.50pm: A startling statistic from the International Organisation for Migration: A quarter of a million people have fled Libya since the uprising against Gaddafi's regime began last month.

SATURDAY 12 MARCH

10am: The Arab League, meeting in Cairo, has called on the UN security council to impose a no fly-zone on Libya.

6.14pm: Chris McGreal has filed from Benghazi:

> The rebels have admitted retreating from the oil town of Ras Lanuf – captured a week ago – after two days of intense fighting and that the nearby town of Brega was now threatened.
>
> The revolutionary army has been forced back by a sustained artillery, tank and air bombardment about 20 miles along the road to the rebel capital of Benghazi. The head of Libya's revolutionary council, Mustafa Abdul Jalil, claimed that if Gaddafi's forces were to reach the country's second-largest city it would result in "the death of half a million" people.

8.39pm: Yemeni security forces have killed four people and wounded hundreds more in the second day of a harsh crackdown on anti-government protests, witnesses said, according to AP.

SUNDAY 13 MARCH

1.53pm: Chris McGreal is in Brega. He writes:

> Gaddafi's forces have routed rebels in the east of the country, driving them into retreat from the town of Brega under a rain of rockets and shells, and opening up the road to the principal opposition stronghold, Benghazi. On Saturday night the exhausted and terrified rebel army piled into pickup trucks with machine-guns mounted on the back or towing anti-aircraft guns and raced away from a sustained assault by rocket launchers and artillery.

MONDAY 14 MARCH

3.44pm: Analysis just published by the Guardian's Brian Whitaker cautions observers not to be too gloomy at the apparent setbacks to opposition causes in Libya, Bahrain and elsewhere. He writes:

> Even if Gaddafi does succeed in quelling the Libyan uprising, it will be no more than a temporary setback for the wider Arab revolution: battles are being fought in too many places and on too many different fronts for anyone to stop it now.

TUESDAY 15 MARCH

12.33pm: A state of emergency has been declared in Bahrain, where fresh violence has broken out. A 1,000-strong force from Saudi Arabia and other members of the Gulf Cooperation Council arrived in Bahrain yesterday.

2.29pm: Gaddafi forces have started their attack on Ajdarbia, the last major town before Benghazi, 90 miles away. Libyan State TV says government troops are "in total control" of the eastern part of the town. Chris McGreal, who is in Benghazi, says government troops have entered the town but it is unclear who has the upper hand.

3.50pm: Reports from Bahrain say at least two people have died and some 200 have been injured. An opposition politician said a man was killed in Sitra and state television said a Bahraini policeman was also killed in clashes.

WEDNESDAY 16 MARCH

8.58am: Overnight an increasingly confident Muammar Gaddafi has mocked the west, particularly France, as his troops attacked Ajdabiya, the last rebel stronghold before Benghazi, where the unrest started. "France now raises its head and says that it will strike Libya," he told supporters at his Bab al-Azizia fortified compound in central Tripoli. "Strike Libya? We'll be the ones who strike you! We struck you in Algeria, in Vietnam. You want to strike us? Come and give it a try."

9.50am: At least four people have been killed in a crackdown in Bahrain, AP reports. Here's an extract of its account of the "full-scale assault on Pearl Square at daybreak":

> Stinging clouds of teargas filled streets and black smoke rose from the square from the protesters' tents set ablaze. Witnesses said at least two protesters were killed. Bahrain state TV also reported that two policemen died when they were hit by a vehicle after hundreds of anti-government protesters were driven out.

10.26am: Reuters brings news of a rare demonstration in Syria. It says security forces dispersed about 150 people who had been demanding the release of political prisoners in front of the interior ministry in central Damascus.

12.59pm: Ian Black, the Guardian's Middle East correspondent, has called from Tripoli.

> The mood music is one of increasing confidence. There were fireworks in the streets last night and lots of shooting in the air in praise of Gaddafi. There is a sense that the military side of this story is drawing to a close.

1.49pm: In Damascus, @razaniyat has been tweeting from the demonstration outside the interior ministry. Her tweets make grim reading.

\# i was taking a video of security forces hitting protersters and that's when five of them captured me and took my mobile.

\# they took a man and his child. hit a 80 year old woman and were hitting elderly.

\# the sit-in did not last more than 3 minutes and 2000, not exaggerating, were surrounding the protersters and started arresting ppl.

5.35pm: Some good news. The Guardian reporter Ghaith Abdul-Ahad, who was detained by the Libyan authorities two weeks ago, has been freed.

\# **petersbeaumont** Ghaith abdul ahad released. He is safe well and unharmed after his two week ordeal in libyan jail. Thin but in good spirits.

THURSDAY 17 MARCH

7.29am: Hillary Clinton has told CBS the Arab League's call last Saturday for a no-fly zone had caused a "sea change" in thinking. Supporters of a no-fly zone UN draft resolution, which include Britain and France, are pushing for a vote today, but China, Russia and India are lukewarm or doubtful that a no-fly zone could be enforced and whether it would make a difference at such a late stage.

9.45pm: The UN security council vote on a resolution supporting military action against the Gaddafi regime is being put to the vote now.

10.33pm: Here's the result: 10 in favour, zero against, five abstentions – including Russia, China and Germany. "The resolution 1973/2011 is adopted," says the chairman.

10.55pm: A Dubai-based blogger is watching the scenes of celebration in Benghazi.

\# **iyad_elbaghdadi** Benghazi now throwing what's probably the biggest party in its recent history.

11.00pm: From the first Guardian report on the security council vote:

> British, French and US military aircraft are preparing to protect the Libyan rebel stronghold of Benghazi after the United Nations security council voted in favour of a no-fly zone and airstrikes against Gaddafi's forces.
>
> With Gaddafi's troops closing in on Benghazi, the French prime minister, Francois Fillon, said "time is of the essence" and that France would support military action set to take place within hours.

11.25pm: The UN resolution is eight pages long but the key part is point four, "Protection of civilians", which "authorises member states that have notified the secretary general, acting nationally or through regional organisations or arrangements, and acting in cooperation with the secretary general, to take all necessary measures … to protect civilians and civilian populated areas under threat of attack in the Libyan Arab Jamahiriya, including Benghazi, while excluding a foreign occupation force of any form on any part of Libyan territory".

The phrase "take all necessary measures" means this is more than a no-fly zone: it allows airstrikes and any military action short of landing troops.

1.15am: The official Libyan state news agency JANA has issued a response to the UN vote, with dire warnings of military reprisals:

> Any foreign military act against Libya will expose all air and maritime traffic in the Mediterranean Sea to danger and civilian and military facilities will become targets of Libya's counter attack. The Mediterranean basin will face danger not just in the short term, but also in the long term.

FRIDAY 18 MARCH

8.37am: Reuters is reporting that Misrata, the last rebel-held city in the west, is coming under heavy bombardment.

8.54am: The Guardian's Paris correspondent, Angelique Chrisafis, tweets:

\# French airstrikes on Libya to begin imminently, according to government spokesman.

12.12pm: More unrest in Yemen, where citizens in Sana'a have been shot dead. The Guardian's Tom Finn is at a mosque in the city, and says he has counted 17 dead people being brought into the building wrapped in blankets. "The doctor says [there are] double that in the hospital," he says.

Al-Jazeera English is meanwhile reporting that up to 30 people have been killed and 200 injured after security forces opened fire in Sana'a.

12.54pm: Libya has declared "an immediate ceasefire", but has criticised the UN resolution, saying the use of military power would "violate" the UN charter. Moussa Koussa, the foreign minister, has just announced the "stoppage of all military operations" at a press conference in Tripoli. Koussa said Libya encourages the "opening of all dialogue channels" with the international community, but that this "unreasonable" resolution would "increase the suffering of the Libyan people".

1.49pm: The rebels do not plan to give up the fight against Gaddafi despite his declaration of an immediate ceasefire, writes Chris McGreal from Benghazi.

> The rebels say they don't trust Gaddafi. They see it as a reflection of his desperation to try and stave off the air attacks by France and Britain and that what he intends to do is to divide up the country and for that reason they are not going to call a ceasefire themselves. They plan to call for uprisings across the country to get rid of Gaddafi.

2.19pm: Despite the ceasefire announcement, Gaddafi forces are not only attacking in Misrata but also in Ajdabiya, according to al-Jazeera, which reports "gunfire and heavy artillery clashes" at the southern entrance to the eastern city.

3.55pm: Yemen's president has declared a state of emergency after "at least 25 protesters" were killed at an anti-government rally, according to Reuters.

9.23pm: Libya's deputy foreign minister, Khaled Kaim, has been holding another press conference, insisting that pro-Gaddafi forces have conducted no military operations since starting a ceasefire today.

9.41pm: Appearing on CNN just now, the US ambassador to the UN, Susan Rice, said Gaddafi's forces were in violation of the UN security council resolution through their advance upon Benghazi, and warned of "swift and sure consequences including military action".

SATURDAY 19 MARCH

8.57am: Overnight there were patchy reports of shelling and explosions around Benghazi and confirmation that a fighter plane has been shot down over the city. The Libyan regime has denied any involvement, saying its entire air force has been grounded and it is respecting its self-imposed ceasefire.

The next stage of the international response is to be co-ordinated at an emergency conference in Paris within a few hours. David Cameron, Nicolas Sarkozy, Hillary Clinton and Arab leaders are among those gathering to give final approval for a no-fly zone. There is a sense that jets will be streaking out to Libya as soon as the group gives the nod.

10.19am: Chris McGreal has called in from Benghazi. Rebels have now conceded, he says, that the plane shot down over the city was theirs – their only plane. He says there is currently "sporadic but fairly intense fighting" in the south-west of the city where Gaddafi's forces have broken through. There are also reports of fighting in the north of the city.

12.44pm: Al-Jazeera reports that 26 dead and more than 40 wounded are in Jala hospital in Benghazi after the city was bombarded by pro-Gaddafi forces.

2.25pm: French TV station BFM reports that French fighter jets are over Benghazi enforcing the no-fly zone. AFP also reports that several French fighter jets overflew "all Libyan territory" on reconnaissance missions.

2.48pm: Sarkozy has confirmed that French fighter planes are already enforcing the no-fly zone over Libya, particularly Benghazi. Speaking at a press conference after the emergency Paris summit, he said: "As of now our aircraft are preventing [Gaddafi's] planes from attacking the town."

3.22pm: The communique on enforcing the UN resolution agreed by world leaders at the Paris summit reads:

> Our commitment is for the long term: we will not let Colonel Gaddafi and his regime go on defying the will of the international community and scorning that of his people. We will continue our aid to the Libyans so that they can rebuild their country, fully respecting Libya's sovereignty and territorial integrity.

4.35pm: Chris McGreal has called in from Benghazi, where rebel forces have pushed back Gaddafi's forces from the city after intense fighting in which scores of civilians and fighters were killed. He says there is a real wariness among the rebels that Gaddafi's forces were able to penetrate the city's defences and take over areas of what has been the main rebel stronghold in Libya since the uprising began.

6.20pm: The death has been announced of Mohammad Nabbous, described as the "face of citizen journalism in Libya". Nabbous was apparently shot dead by Gaddafi forces in Benghazi on Saturday. Andy Carvin, social media strategist at NPR, said on Twitter:

> \# Mohammad Nabbous was my primary contact in Libya, and the face of Libyan citizen journalism. And now he's dead, killed in a firefight.

8.39pm: The Pentagon has issued a statement that Operation Odyssey Dawn is under way, with the launching of 110 Tomahawk missiles by US and British ships and submarines at strategic targets in Libya.

9.13pm: Libyan state television reports that the "crusader enemy", a reference to western forces, has bombarded civilian areas of several cities, including the capital Tripoli, Gaddafi's hometown Sirte and the rebel stronghold of Benghazi.

9.20pm: David Cameron has given a statement confirming that "British forces are in action over Libya", adding: "What we are doing is necessary, it is legal, and it is right."

10.25pm: Gaddafi has spoked by phone to Libyan television, saying he will arm civilians to defend Libya from what he called "crusader aggression" by western forces that have launched airstrikes against him:

> It is now necessary to open the stores and arm all the masses with all types of weapons to defend the independence, unity and honour of Libya.

12.12am: The rebel-held city of Misrata has been under siege by Gaddafi's forces for several days – and appears to have been one of the first beneficiaries of western aerial attacks. Reuters reports:

> Two residents said Gaddafi's forces appeared to have retreated from their positions, denying state TV reports that civilian areas and fuel depots were hit by the western warplanes.
>
> "The international forces struck Gaddafi battalions in the air military college, but some of the [government] forces fled shortly before the attack," resident Abdulbasset told Reuters by phone.

12.40am: Reuters reports:

> Sustained bursts of anti-aircraft gunfire rattled the Libyan capital Tripoli in the early hours of Sunday. Anti-aircraft fire was followed by explosions and machine gun fire, and shouts of "God is greatest". The night sky was lit up by tracer arcs.

1.35am: In the midst of all tonight's action, the bigger picture tweeted:

> \# **jstrevino** Closing thought for the evening, as the Allies pound Libya: to think it all began a few weeks back with a desperate Tunisian fruit vendor.

SUNDAY 20 MARCH

8.22am: Guardian Middle East editor Ian Black has just filed from Tripoli:

> Tripoli is quiet though understandably tense this morning after last night's attacks. But there is confusion about exactly where and what was hit. Heavy anti-aircraft fire erupted around 2.30am, not far from

Gaddafi's Bab al-Aziziya compound. One photographer distinctly saw the silhouette of a fighter jet.

Libyan TV, now broadcasting in full crisis mode, is reporting 48 dead and 150 injured. Government minders are preparing to take journalists to visit hospitals, though the hotel that houses the press centre is now full of demonstrators chanting pro-Gaddafi slogans.

10.15am: From a windy open field just outside Benghazi, Chris McGreal has called to report that the power of the rockets launched by the French was significant and had ripped through tanks being used by Libyan forces which now stand burning. He says military vehicles were "the principal advantage Gaddafi has over the rebels" and the attacks were likely to demoralise the Libyan forces.

3.16pm: Amr Moussa, head of the Arab League, has criticised the strikes carried out on Libya, saying there had been civilian casualties. Although the league supported a no-fly zone over Libya, Moussa said the UN resolution also agreed to protect civilians which it has failed to do. The US has said the airstrikes targeted mainly air defence systems in order to enforce the no-fly zone.

6.23pm: As the second night of airstrikes begin, the International Committee of the Red Cross has said it is "deeply concerned about the intensification in recent days of the fighting in and around densely populated centres in Libya, with the consequent risk to civilian lives."

It called on "all parties" to "abide strictly by the rules and principles of international humanitarian law".

8.59pm: Nick Hopkins, the Guardian's defence and security correspondent, has filed some detail on last night's airstrikes and on how the military campaign is likely to shape up:

> One hope is that the use of overwhelming force and the systematic destruction of Gaddafi's military capability might encourage his closest advisers to leave him. That, say analysts, may still not be enough to get rid of him.
>
> "I don't think that Gaddafi will ever stand down unilaterally," said Barak Seener of the Royal United Services Institute. "He thinks he has a natural right to be there."

With no obvious finish line to run towards, the military campaign against Gaddafi is likely to continue in the coming days with further sorties against specific targets – and commanders stepping up efforts to get Arab involvement in new missions, probably with aircraft from Qatar or the United Arab Emirates.

12.04am: The US defence secretary, Robert Gates, has said the US expects to turn control of the mission over to a coalition headed either by the French and British or by Nato "in a matter of days". Nato ambassadors approved a plan for the alliance to help enforce a UN arms embargo on Libya but officials said more discussion was needed on possible Nato involvement in enforcing the no-fly zone.

MONDAY 21 MARCH

9.12am: The Guardian's Chris McGreal is at "what is now the front line", just over five miles outside Ajdabiya, having travelled with rejuvenated rebel forces from Benghazi. He says rebel forces have gained 100 miles, and a substantial amount of morale, since coalition airstrikes began on Saturday morning.

> There definitely is continuing resistance. There have been a number of incoming tank rounds from Gaddafi's forces, which suggests that they've still got tanks, they may still have some rockets. But above us now we can hear planes, which we have to assume are coalition planes, and we have heard a number of very deep explosions in the past few minutes which suggests those are attacks by coalition forces, possibly on those same tanks which were shelling us just a few minutes earlier.

11.55am: Vladimir Putin, the Russian prime minister, has said the UN resolution resembles "medieval calls for crusades".

7.51pm: The Libyan regime is claiming that "many were killed" by airstrikes against targets including the airport at Gaddafi's home town of Sirte, Reuters is reporting.

10.01pm: Witnesses have told Reuters that the western Libyan town of Zintan faced heavy shelling earlier today from forces loyal to Gaddafi, forcing residents to flee, including to caves in the mountainous region. "Several houses have been destroyed and a mosque minaret was also brought down," Abdulrhamane Daw told the news agency by phone from the town. "New forces were sent today to besiege the city. There are now at least 40 tanks at the foothills of the mountains near Zintan."

TUESDAY 22 MARCH

8.31am: China has called for an immediate ceasefire in Libya, AP is reporting. China was one of five countries that abstained from last week's vote on the UN resolution.

8.43am: Ian Black has called London from Tripoli. He said:

> Libyan officials have admitted privately – it's not the kind of thing they say in public – that, yes, [the military action] has been effective, their air defence system has been demolished. They say – and of course there's no way of checking this – that there have been no flights inside Libya since last Thursday night when the UN security council passed its resolution. They like to portray themselves as being obedient and accepting the writ of the UN, at the same time as complaining that what the UN authorised was the protection of civilians and the complaint in Tripoli is what's happening is going far beyond that.

9.16am: There have been fresh airstrikes on Ajdabiya, the Guardian's Chris McGreal reports. He saw four large plumes of smoke coming from Ajdabiya, which is under control of Gaddafi's forces, a short while after hearing aircraft overhead.

1.11pm: In this Reuters dispatch, alarming accounts of scenes in Misrata.

> Doctors in Libya's rebel-held city of Misrata are operating on people with bullet and shrapnel wounds in hospital corridors after attacks by government forces killed dozens and wounded many more, residents said.
> "There is a catastrophic situation here," a resident, called Mohammed, told Reuters by telephone. "We call on humanitarian organisations to intervene as soon as possible to provide food and medical help."

11.30pm: Airstrikes on Libya will soon achieve the objectives of establishing a no-fly zone and averting a massacre of civilians by Gaddafi's troops, Barack

Obama has said in a press conference as he nears the end of his tour of Latin America.

Speaking at a news conference in El Salvador, he said he has "absolutely no doubt" that a non-US command entity can run the operation. The president said that Nato, which is the most obvious candidate to take on the role, was meeting to "work out some of the mechanisms."

12.53am: At least five people have been killed by gunfire around the Omari mosque in the southern Syrian city of Deraa, where hundreds of protesters have gathered for the past six days, according to reports filtering through tonight.

1.25am: Britain, France and the US have agreed that Nato will take over the military command of the no-fly zone over Libya in a move which represents a setback for Nicolas Sarkozy, who is believed to have wanted to diminish the role of the alliance.

The agreement, which will have to be put be to all 28 members of Nato, indicates that the alliance has resolved one of its most serious disagreements. Countries had been splintering as they tried to comply with Obama's demand that Washington be relieved of command of the air campaign.

WEDNESDAY 23 MARCH

9.45am: Nato warships will begin patrolling off Libya's coast today to enforce the UN arms embargo on the country, a spokesman said. The naval mission initially will consist of two Nato naval flotillas that routinely patrol the Mediterranean, AP says. The flotillas are made up of two frigates, six minesweepers and a supply ship.

3.39pm: Some very bullish comments from Ali Zeidan, one of 31 members of the NTC, who has told reporters in Paris that the rebels could overcome Gaddafi's forces in 10 days if the coalition continued its airstrikes. He also said he wanted the international community to train and arm the rebel fighters.

3.51pm: Chris McGreal has just emailed on the situation in Misrata.

Nearly 12 hours of allied airstrikes have virtually wiped out Gaddafi's forces that were attacking the rebel-held town of Misrata and ended five days of bloody assault that cost nearly 100 lives. Mohammed Ali, an IT engineer at the town's main hospital, said that waves of airstrikes which began shortly after midnight destroyed tanks and artillery that Gaddafi's army had been using to shell the heart of Misrata.

"The airstrikes went on until 11.30 this morning. After that there was no shelling. We are very relieved. We are very grateful. We want to thank the world. The Gaddafi forces are scattered around. All that is left is the snipers and our fighters can take care of them," he said.

6.51pm: The US defence secretary Robert Gates has acknowledged that there is no clear end to the international military enforcement of a no-fly zone over Libya. "I think there are any number of possible outcomes here and no one is in a position to predict them," Gates told reporters in Egypt.

12.36am: The attempt at a Nato show of unity in policing a UN arms embargo has been undermined by a third day of squabbling over who should be in charge of the air campaign. Amid arguments over the scope and command of the air campaign against Tripoli, Turkey has both blocked Nato planning on the no-fly zone and insisted that Nato be put in control of it, in order to be granted a veto over its operations, senior Nato officials said.

THURSDAY 24 MARCH

10.28am: Ian Black reports from Tripoli that Libyan TV has been showing images of civilian victims of the overnight bombing in Tajoura, east of Tripoli, which was apparently hit in an attack on a military base in the town.

In the small hours of the morning foreign news agency reporters were taken to a hospital and shown 18 charred corpses, which were said to be casualties of the latest attacks.

11.23am: Snippets of news are dribbling out of Syria following yesterday's protests in the southern city of Deraa. An official in the main hospital there has told Reuters that it has received the bodies of at least 25 protesters killed in the clashes. "They all had bullet holes," the official said.

4.32pm: France has confirmed that its air force has shot down a Libyan plane. This from Reuters:

A French warplane fired an air-to-ground missile at a Libyan military plane and destroyed it just after it landed at Misrata air force base, a French armed forces spokesman said. "The French patrol carried out an air-to-ground strike with an AASM weapon just after the plane had landed at the Misrata airbase," the spokesman said, adding that the plane had breached the UN-imposed no-fly zone.

4.50pm: Katherine Marsh (a pseudonym) in Damascus has just told us that Syria has announced major concessions ahead of planned protests tomorrow. The government says it will look at removing emergency laws, prepare new laws for political parties and media and respond to "legitimate demands".

6.27pm: Interesting breaking news from CBS News via Twitter:

\# Turkish foreign minister quoted as saying NATO will take command of Libya operation.

6.49pm: Command of military operations in Libya will be transferred from the US to Nato within a day or two, Reuters is quoting the Turkish foreign minister Ahmet Davutoglu as saying. "Compromise has been reached in principle in a very short time," Davutoglu told reporters. "The operation will be handed over to Nato completely."

8.31pm: Reuters has this from Syria:

Syrian security forces have pulled out from the main Omari mosque in the centre of the city of Deraa where six people were killed, a Reuters witness said.

Several thousand people later converged on the mosque to celebrate its "liberation", setting off fireworks and honking car horns.

FRIDAY 25 MARCH

8.47am: Overnight there has been a flurry of diplomatic activity over who should run the no-fly zone and other missions in Libya, as the US wants minimal involvement, preferring to hand things over to Nato. After six days' wrangling, agreement has been reached that Nato will take over the job of enforcing the no-fly zone over Libya.

From Ian Traynor and Nicholas Watt:

The US, Britain, France and Turkey agreed to put the three-pronged offensive – a no-fly zone, an arms embargo, and airstrikes – under a Nato command umbrella, in a climbdown by France that accommodates strong Turkish complaints about the scope and control of the campaign.

5.33pm: President Saleh of Yemen has said on national television that he is willing to hand over power, but did not specify when or to whom. Separate demonstrations both for and against the government have been held in different parts of the capital today.

MONDAY 28 MARCH

8.00am: Libyan rebels have been pushing west towards Gaddafi's home city of Sirte. Revolutionary forces have taken a number of government-held oil towns including Brega, Ras Lanuf and Bin Jawad. There have been rumours that the outskirts of Gaddafi's home city have been mined.

Turkey has offered to broker a ceasefire. The Turkish prime minister Recep Tayyip said the country was ready to act as a mediator to prevent a drawn out conflict that would become a "second Iraq".

9.11am: North African migrants have been arriving en masse into Italy as the Italian government declares a humanitarian emergency. More than 5,000 migrants are thought to have arrived on the Italian island of Lampedusa from Tunisia and North Africa, believed to be mostly Ethiopians, Somalians and Eritreans.

1.41pm: Chris McGreal is with rebels who are heading from Ajdabiya to Sirte. He says:

They just drive on as Gaddafi's forces retreat. Once there was the breakthrough at Ajdabiya, which came on Saturday after concerted coalition airstrikes against Gaddafi's tanks and armour there, after which Gaddafi's troops turned and fled, essentially the rebels have just been following them down the road. It's not been a fighting pursuit, it's just been following them as they retreat.

There does seem to be some kind of defence about 50 miles out of [Sirte]. It's not clear how large that is, but it's large enough to hold up the rebels now for the first time in a couple of days.

Chris says that if Sirte was to fall to the rebels it would be a "huge political and psychological blow to Gaddafi's government".

9.08pm: The coalition has flown 178 sorties in the skies over Libya in the last 24 hours, according to a Pentagon briefing.

1.20am: Barack Obama has been speaking in Washington. He said the US intervened in Libya to prevent a slaughter of civilians that would have stained the world's conscience and "been a betrayal of who we are".

Here's the instant take from the Guardian's Richard Adams in DC:

Call it the "Obama doctrine" if you like but President Obama tonight presented his case for limited US military involvement in Libya, while attempting to rebut the "false choices", in his words, of staying on the sidelines or more aggressive attempts to bring regime change directly targeted against Gaddafi.

This speech won't shut his critics up but it will shape the terms of debate in favour of Obama's policy. In the end, though, it's Gaddafi's fate that dictates the success or failure of Obama's policy, and no speech can change that.

TUESDAY 29 MARCH

8.15am: Gaddafi has called for an end to the "barbaric offensive" against Libya in a letter addressed to international powers meeting in London today. AFP reports that in the letter, Gaddafi likened the Nato-led airstrikes to military campaigns launched by Adolf Hitler during the second world war.

9.07am: Ian Black, speaking from Sirte, warns against any hopes of an imminent rebel victory. "The idea that Gaddafi's forces would simply collapse in the face of a rebel advance is a delusion," Ian said, in response to a rebel fighter who stated yesterday that Gaddafi will be gone "before the week ends".

12.15pm: More than 40 foreign ministers are meeting in London this afternoon to discuss the situation in Libya. It will focus on co-ordinating assistance in the face of a possible humanitarian disaster and building a unified international front in condemnation of the Gaddafi regime and in support of Nato-led military action in Libya.

1.49pm: Chris McGreal is in Bin Jawad, where he reports that the rebels have been forced back from their previous position outside Sirte.

> It's the repeating pattern that we have seen in the past with Gaddafi's forces, which is the rebels advance in a vacuum created by airstrikes, and then they over extend themselves, are not able to defend themselves, and then what happens is that Gaddafi's forces bring up artillery, their tanks, and they just lay down a line of explosive shells that force the rebels back and the rebels retreat, usually almost in panic.

1.51pm: The Syrian president Bashar al-Assad has accepted the resignation of his entire cabinet, Syrian state TV is reporting.

WEDNESDAY 30 MARCH

9.15am: In a call from Ajdabiya, Chris McGreal has spoken of a sense of anger, betrayal and weariness among the rebels after they were driven back by Gaddafi's troops.

> Just a few days ago the rebels were announcing they were marching to Tripoli and they'd be there by the end of the week. Yesterday as they were retreating they were angrily demanding to know where Sarkozy was … they feel betrayed when the airstrikes are not there to protect them.

11.30am: Ian Black, who is in Tripoli, says that even if the rebels were to be armed by coalition forces, "it would be a very long haul to lick them into shape, [to turn] this disorganised and rather chaotic group of people into a fighting force and a coherent movement strong enough to overthrow the regime".

12.53pm: Syria's President Assad, who sacked his cabinet yesterday, has been speaking in Damascus. He said what is happening in Syria should not be called a revolution. Syria is the victim of a worldwide conspiracy, which began weeks ago, through the satellite channels. These people aim to weaken the last stronghold in the Arab world, Assad said, according to reports. The situation, he added, has "returned to normality".

3.34pm: President Assad's speech has gone down badly in Syria. Residents in Deraa have told the Guardian that the address was met with fury: "The speech was nonsense and has given security forces the green light to continue its oppression on our people," said one man speaking by telephone from the city.

5.00pm: Chris McGreal has just called to report that Brega has fallen to pro-Gaddafi forces. He says they are now advancing towards Ajdabiya and the rebels are retreating there. That returns the situation to where it was on Saturday – before the rebels pushed forward with the help of coalition airstrikes.

9.30pm: There is uncertainty over the status of Libya's foreign minister Moussa Koussa, who, Reuters say, has flown to London from Tunisia and defected. The Libyan government said he was travelling on a diplomatic mission. Britain's Foreign Office said it did not know anything about the reported journey, and no meeting was scheduled.

10.07pm: The British foreign office has confirmed that foreign minister Moussa Koussa has fled to Britain, according to PA. The Foreign Office said foreign minister Moussa Koussa had arrived on a plane from Tunisia and was "no longer willing" to represent the dictator's regime.

THURSDAY 31 MARCH

8.23am: News of CIA operations in Libya are all over the US papers this morning after Reuters broke the story overnight. Obama reportedly signed a secret order several weeks ago authorising the CIA to carry out a clandestine effort to provide arms and other support to Libyan opposition groups.

The New York Times says in addition to the CIA presence, dozens of British special forces and MI6 intelligence officers are working inside Libya. US officials told the paper that British forces have been directing airstrikes from British jets and gathering intelligence about the whereabouts of Libyan government tank columns, artillery pieces and missile installations.

The Washington Post notes that such operations are risky.

The CIA's history is replete with efforts that backfired against US interests in unexpected ways. In perhaps the most fateful example, the CIA's backing of Islamic fighters in Afghanistan succeeded in driving out the Soviets in the 1980s, but it also presaged the emergence of militant groups, including al-Qaida, that the United States is now struggling to contain.

9.40am: Nato is now officially in command of all air operations over Libya, having taken over from the US at 6am. The operation, codenamed Unified Protector, includes enforcement of the no-fly zone, maintaining the arms embargo on Libya, and the protection of civilians.

11.48am: Brian Whitaker has analysed Assad's speech to the Syrian government yesterday:

Contrary to the impression given in some of the news reports, Assad did talk about reform, and talked about it rather a lot. Syria is already reforming, he said, and will continue to do so. But just when it seemed that he might be on the point of announcing some specific new reforms, he stopped speaking and the parliament gave him a final round of applause ...

There will be no hasty concessions to protesters as happened in Tunisia and Egypt; that would be a sign of weakness and would only encourage further demands. Instead, the relevant ministries will announce their plans in due course, after full and careful consideration, etc. That is certainly a bold strategy, but in the midst of growing turmoil it's either a sign of supreme confidence or extreme recklessness.

4.13pm: At a press conference with the Turkish prime minister Recep Tayyip Erdogan, David Cameron has said the Libyan defector Moussa Koussa has no immunity from prosecution and he would be happy for the Scottish authorities to interview him over the Lockerbie bombing.

It is unclear what role, if any, Koussa played in the blowing up of Pan Am flight 103 over Lockerbie in December 1988, which killed 270 passengers, crew and townspeople. Koussa later emerged as head of Libyan intelligence services. In 2003, Gaddafi accepted Libya's responsibility for the attack and paid compensation to victims' families.

4.31pm: US defence secretary Robert Gates has told members of Congress that there will be no US ground forces deployed in Libya "as long as I am in this job" during what appears to have been a testy appearance before a congressional committee.

SUNDAY 3 APRIL

10.00am: Chris McGreal writes from Benghazi on discord in the rebel movement:

> The revolutionary leadership is split over competing claims to command its armed campaign as the rebels attempt to shore up their credibility in the west after losing almost all the territory gained by foreign airstrikes.
>
> The dispute comes as the military leadership continues to struggle with the lack of discipline that has been so damaging to its campaign and which led to the death of 13 rebel fighters and medics at the weekend after one of them indiscriminately fired an anti-aircraft gun and provoked a western airstrike. Four vehicles were destroyed including an ambulance. The revolutionary council described the incident near the town of Brega as a "terrible mistake" for which it took responsibility.

MONDAY 4 APRIL

9.56am: Libyan rebels have regained control of the strategic oil town of Brega, Associated Press reports.

11.07pm: Some breaking news from AP: Scottish authorities responsible for the investigation into the Lockerbie bombing are expected to meet Libyan defector Moussa Koussa in the coming days.

Scottish police and prosecutors spoke to Foreign Office officials today, and made a formal request to speak to the Libyan former minister, who arrived in the UK last week.

TUESDAY 5 APRIL

12.40pm: In Yemen, Fresh clashes have broken out in Taiz in southern Yemen. It has been reported that 15 people were killed after security forces and armed men in civilian clothes opened fire on protesters yesterday.

THURSDAY 7 APRIL

10.43am: The prospects for Libyan refugees whose boat sank of Italy yesterday are fading, reports Reuters.

> Italian rescue vessels have resumed their search for survivors from the boat carrying refugees from Libya that sank south of Sicily on Wednesday but hopes of finding anyone alive are fading. The interior minister, Roberto Maroni, said 51 people, most from central Africa, had been picked up by rescue vessels responding to a distress signal sent via Maltese authorities ...
>
> Many smaller boats carrying migrants have sunk while attempting to reach southern Europe from Africa, killing unknown numbers of refugees and migrants.

FRIDAY 8 APRIL

11.39am: Protests have resumed in Syria, according to reports from activists on Twitter:

\# **Razaniyat** Just now: more than 1500 protest in Qamishli now following Friday prayers in Qasimlo mosque marching towards Hilaliya square.

\# **wissamtarif** Qamishli is uprising! Chanting "Freedom Freedom".

\# **Mohammad_Syria** Hundreds of Kurds are protesting in Amodah Hasaka chanting for Freedom for all Syrians.

1.23pm: More details have emerged of a Turkish peace plan for Libya. It envisages a ceasefire, a humanitarian corridor and "a comprehensive democratic change and transformation process that takes into consideration the legitimate interests of all Libyan people", says Turkish prime minister Recep Tayyip Erdogan. He defended Turkey's stance towards foreign military intervention and insisted his country had "no hidden agenda".

1.58pm: The Guardian correspondent in Damascus, Katherine Marsh (a pseudonym), has just sent this update:

There are reports of security forces opening fire and using teargas to disperse protesters in Deraa. Activists say four were killed and that ambulances were prevented from reaching the injured, but the Guardian has so far been unable to independently confirm that.

It seems that today is going to see as many, if not more, people on the streets than last Friday in a growing challenge to Assad who has so far not met the protesters' demands. But with information taking a while to leak out and be verified through amateur footage and calls to eyewitnesses, the full picture will not be clear until later.

3.53pm: Al-Jazeera's Rula Amin, reporting from Douma, a Damascus suburb, says the breadth of the protests marks a step change.

It's a new situation in Syria. We saw thousands of people taking to the streets after Friday prayers, from all walks of life: young and old, professionals and not professionals, educated, not educated, there were some Islamists, some nationalists.

SATURDAY 9 APRIL

10.39am: Overnight, the death toll in Syria has risen to at least 32, making it the bloodiest day of demonstrations in the country's three-week uprising. Activists have called for daily protests.

1.10pm: In Libya, forces loyal to Gaddafi have been shelling retreating rebels west of Ajdabiya. AP has more:

The government attacks on Ajdabiya quickly changed the fortunes of rebels who had earlier sent units deeper toward the strategic oil port of Brega, and captured two soldiers loyal to Gaddafi. Earlier, rebels had pushed deeper toward Brega, a key prize in the back-and-forth battles with government forces.

1.26pm: As many as 100,000 people marched earlier today in the Yemeni city of Taiz, where about 400 were injured in previous protests, according to reports.

3.34pm: Reuters quotes witnesses as saying that Syrian security forces have opened fire today on mourners near a mosque in the flashpoint city of Deraa after a mass funeral for pro-democracy protesters.

MONDAY 11 APRIL

9.57am: The African Union says Gaddafi has accepted a peace plan for ending the conflict in Libya, which includes an immediate ceasefire. It has called on Nato to halt air raids. Representatives are travelling to Benghazi today to present the Libyan peace plan to the opposition leadership. Opposition spokesman Mustafa Gheriani told Reuters the rebels would respond to the plan but it could only work if Gaddafi stands down.

12.06pm: After attacking protesters in Tahrir Square on Saturday, the military have dealt another blow to hopes that post-Mubarak Egypt would be characterised by freedom of speech. The military court has jailed blogger Maikel Nabil for three years for accusing the army of deception over its role in the revolution, al-Ahram reports. The blogpost in question was titled "The army and the people were never one hand." Nabil was accused of "insulting the military" and "disturbing public security".

12.59pm: There are unconfirmed reports from Syria circulating on Twitter that a student has been killed at a protest at Damascus University's faculty of science.

\# **FreeSoria** Thousands of students protest in Damascus University and security forces use live bullets, one killed so far.

\# **SyrianJasmine** First martyr in the demo of University of Damascus science faculty Fadi Alasmi may his soul rest in peace

1.09pm: Chris McGreal, in Benghazi, reports that the African Union representatives were treated to a frosty reception on their arrival in the city:

> The delegation of five Africans, three presidents and two foreign ministers were greeted by a sea of demonstrators waving their revolutionary flags – the old Libyan flag – chanting "Gaddafi must go now", "No solution with Gaddafi" and "Stop Gaddafi's war machine".

TUESDAY 12 APRIL

9.00am: Libya's revolutionary leadership has flatly rejected an African Union peace initiative because it does not require Gaddafi to immediately relinquish power. Mustafa Abdul Jalil, the revolutionary council chairman, said the rebels had told the AU its proposal had been overtaken by events, including the UN security council resolution authorising airstrikes, and was in any case unacceptable because it left Gaddafi in power while both sides negotiated. Gaddafi himself had previously endorsed the AU's "road to peace".

9.20am: The former Libyan foreign minister, Moussa Koussa, who defected to the UK last month, has warned his country risks becoming the "new Somalia". In a statement Koussa said he "couldn't continue" serving Gaddafi after recent events in the country, despite acknowledging that "what I did to resign will cause me problems". "I ask everybody to avoid taking Libya into civil war," Koussa said. "This would lead to so much blood and Libya would be a new Somalia."

11.05am: In Bahrain, the daughter of a prominent activist has gone on hunger strike in protest after the arrest of her father, husband and other relatives who took part in pro-democracy action. Zainab al-Khawaja, known on Twitter as angryarabiya, demanded the immediate release of the men in an open letter to US president Barack Obama, posted on her blog.

> Our wonderful memories have all been replaced by horrible ones. Our staircase still has traces of my father's blood. I sit in my living room and can see where my father and husband were thrown face down and beaten. I see their shoes by the door and remember they were taken barefoot. As a daughter and as a wife I refuse to stay silent while my father and husband are probably being tortured in Bahraini prisons.

11.48am: Moussa Koussa, the former Libyan foreign minister who defected to Britain, is being allowed to leave the UK. Ian Black writes that the former Libyan foreign minister has been questioned by Scottish police about his role in the Lockerbie affair.

> Koussa is expected in the Qatari capital of Doha on Wednesday where an international conference on the future of Libya is being held with representatives from the Benghazi-based opposition. Koussa is said to be

seeking to establish whether he has a role to play in the rebel movement along with other senior defectors from the Gaddafi regime – perhaps by brokering a deal between Tripoli and Benghazi.

It is understood Koussa spent a week being debriefed by officials from MI6 at a safe house before being allowed to go free. He was questioned by Dumfries and Galloway police about the 1988 bombing of Pan Am flight 103 in which 270 people died, though was he was not a suspect.

WEDNESDAY 13 APRIL

1.33pm: Ian Black has filed from Doha.

Arab and western leaders are discussing creating an international fund to help the Libyan opposition in the east of the country, amid renewed demands that Gaddafi step down at once.

In the Qatari capital, Doha, William Hague, Britain's foreign secretary, and the Qatari prime minister, Hamed bin Jassem, chaired a first session of the international Libya "contact group" to explore ways ahead in the face of military impasse between the Gaddafi regime and the rebels – and a sense that the crisis has turned into a long haul. Diplomats said the group would meet once a month, with the next session due in Italy.

Ian notes that "the most conspicuous absentee from the conference" was Moussa Koussa, the former Libyan foreign minister and most high-profile defector from the regime.

THURSDAY 14 APRIL

9.13am: A group of five big emerging powers has expressed misgivings about the Nato-led airstrikes in Libya and called for an end to the fighting, Reuters reports. The leaders of Brazil, Russia, India, China and South Africa met today for a one-day summit of the Brics group in China. In a joint statement, they said:

We share the principle that the use of force should be avoided. We are of the view that all the parties should resolve their differences through peaceful means and dialogue.

11.44am: As the Nato meeting opens in Berlin there has been criticism of the alliance from the Libyan opposition, which is now saying that 23 people were killed in Misrata today, many of them civilians, after 80 Russian-made Grad rockets were fired into a residential area. A rebel spokesman in Misrata told Reuters by telephone: "A massacre … will take place here if Nato does not intervene strongly."

FRIDAY 15 APRIL

7.52am: Barack Obama has signalled the return of America to the forefront of the international effort in Libya. In a joint article written with David Cameron and Nicolas Sarkozy, the three leaders commit their countries to pursue military action until Gaddafi has been removed. They write:

> Our duty and our mandate under UN security council resolution 1973 is to protect civilians, and we are doing that. It is not to remove Gaddafi by force. But it is impossible to imagine a future for Libya with Gaddafi in power. The international criminal court is rightly investigating the crimes committed against civilians and the grievous violations of international law. It is unthinkable that someone who has tried to massacre his own people can play a part in their future government.

In their article the three leaders call the attack on Misrata a "medieval siege … to strangle its population into submission".

TUESDAY 19 APRIL

8.30am: The Syrian government is under renewed pressure as clashes break out between security forces and protesters in Homs, Syria's third largest city. AP says more than 5,000 anti-government protesters took over the main square overnight. Reuters quotes witnesses saying security forces fired shots and teargas at the demonstrators early this morning after instructing them to leave.

12.31pm: The Washington Post's Leila Fadel is one of the few journalists to report from inside Misrata. Fadel says the question for residents is how long they can survive as Gaddafi escalates his attacks and supplies become ever more scarce.

Overhead, snipers eyed their targets while camped out in the insurance building – the tallest on the block – and in an adjacent bank. Rebels said the snipers are remarkably efficient, picking off their marks with shots to the head and chest. Rebels don't bother to operate at night, because the snipers use night-vision goggles to target anything that moves.

3.00pm: The Syrian cabinet has approved a bill lifting the 50-year-old emergency law, AP reports. It still requires the signature of President Assad before it can come into effect.

3.36pm: A decision to repeal emergency laws would be the president's "biggest concession yet to the protest movement", writes Ian Black:

Opposition activists have warned in advance that new laws will maintain severe curbs on political freedoms. But the symbolic value of the change is enormous. The emergency law has been in force since 1963 – the year of Syria's first Ba'ath coup. It restricts public gatherings and the free movement of individuals, allows government agents to arrest "suspects or people who threaten security", authorises the monitoring of personal communications and legalises media censorship.

WEDNESDAY 20 APRIL

2.55pm: Katherine Marsh has emailed from Damascus to say that there are few signs protests will abate. Moves to lift the emergency law have been greeted sceptically, she says.

One Syrian points out that the government's decision to lift emergency law sits uncomfortably with its claim the day before that the country is facing a "Salafist [fundamentalist Sunni] insurrection". "Why lift emergency law at the time we are supposedly facing an unprecedented terrorist threat?" said Mahmoud. "If you want to have policy of disinformation, it needs to be more credible that this."

3.55pm: In Bahrain, Zainab al-Khawaja, the activist known on Twitter as angryarabiya, has ended her hunger strike after 10 days, her mother said. This message, attributed to her mother, appears on her blog:

In the past few days Zainab's health has deteriorated and she has had trouble breathing with fast heart beat. In the last two days she was having trouble standing up or sitting straight and I had to give her water using a spoon.

In such circumstances she was visited by people from human rights organisations who promised to do all they can for her detained family and requested that Zainab ends her hunger strike especially since she could not speak on behalf of her loved ones in detention due to the hunger strike.

7.17pm: Two photojournalists have been killed in Misrata, Xan Rice reports.

Oscar-nominated British documentary-maker Tim Hetherington, 40, co-creator of the Sundance-winning documentary Restrepo, was killed covering fighting between Gaddafi's forces and the opposition. Chris Hondros, 41, a US Pulitzer finalist who works for Getty Images, was also killed …

Hetherington wrote in his last post on Twitter on Tuesday: "In besieged Libyan city of Misrata. Indiscriminate shelling by Gaddafi forces. No sign of Nato."

THURSDAY 21 APRIL

4.13pm: Syrian's President Assad has fulfilled last week's promise to lift a 48-year-old state of emergency. It seems unlikely it will halt activists's plans for a "Great Friday" tomorrow – mass demonstrations in several Syrian cities after weekly Muslim prayers.

FRIDAY 22 APRIL

12.03pm: From Katherine Marsh in Damascus:

Thousands have started to protest in the following places: Douma, close to Damascus, and the suburbs of Zabadani and Midan – people in the latter have not taken to the streets before. There are also breaking reports of protests in Deir Ezzor, Latakia and towns in Idleb province … The fear barrier seems to have come down in Syria in a spectacular fashion. Concessions seem to be failing to quell unrest.

4.45pm: The death toll in Syria has risen rapidly. Katherine Marsh now reports that at least 88 people have been killed, according to activists, after troops opened fire with live rounds in a number of cities.

SATURDAY 23 APRIL

1.30pm: The violence continues in Syria, where security forces have opened fire on mourners at mass funerals for pro-democracy protesters killed yesterday, the bloodiest day of uprising against President Assad's regime. About 100 people are now believed to have died.

SUNDAY 24 APRIL

10.37am: Yemen's President Saleh has agreed to a proposal by Gulf Arab mediators to step down within 30 days and hand power to his deputy in exchange for immunity from prosecution. A coalition of seven opposition parties said they also accepted the deal but with reservations.

11.23am: At least 12 mourners are thought to have been killed in Syria yesterday as pro-democracy protesters buried their dead from Friday's protests.

MONDAY 25 APRIL

9.27am: Syrian troops in armoured vehicles entered Deraa, where the protests began, and opened fire overnight, residents said. A resident named Mohsen told al-Jazeera there have been five deaths so far.

10.24am: The author and Sunday Times correspondent Hala Jaber has been tweeting chilling details of the continued assault on Misrata overnight, based on phone calls from the western city.

\# "Gaddafi toops bombing misrata heavily with rockets from the periphery of city," reported by doctor there.

\# doctor reporting "Family arrived – carbonized babies, mother, father. They were in their car."

\# "Doctors amputating an arm and a leg of a man now in hospital, another surgery carried out on a child."

2.38pm: This from Ian Traynor, the Guardian's Europe editor, on an overnight attack in Tripoli:

> Nato headquarters in Brussels confirmed the attack on the Gaddafi compound, describing the buildings as a legitimate target under the terms of the UN mandate empowering the military alliance to hit regime facilities deemed to be threatening the safety of Libyan civilians.
>
> "We can confirm that the alliance carried out a precision airstrike in central Tripoli last night," said a Nato official. The target was "a communication headquarters used to co-ordinate attacks against the civilian population ... We have no evidence of any civilian casualties."

4.57pm: Some breaking news from Libya on Reuters: Three people died in the Nato attack on Gaddafi's compound, according to a Libyan government spokesman, who said the Libyan leader is safe and in high spirits. He claimed the airstrikes were an attempt on Gaddafi's life.

TUESDAY 26 APRIL

10.02am: A Human Rights Watch Syria researcher, Nadim Houry, has been monitoring the crackdown from Beirut. The situation is especially dire in Deraa, he says.

> Between Friday and Saturday over 100 people were killed. The deployment of the army in full gear encircling a city and cutting it off, is very worrisome when you know the fatal history of the 1980s when the city of Hama paid a very heavy price for opposition to Assad's father.

12.50pm: Amina, a gay rights activists and blogger from Damascus, gives an account of how two members of the Syrian security forces came to arrest her early in the morning. She claims her father saw the men off through the force of his argument. "My father is a hero," she writes in the latest post on her blog A Gay Girl in Damascus. "In the night we celebrated this little victory; they may come back but maybe not."

THURSDAY 28 APRIL

7.28am: Reports are emerging of a mass resignation in Syria. Katherine Marsh has this:

More than 200 members of President Assad's ruling Ba'ath party have resigned in protest at an increasingly bloody crackdown on pro-democracy protesters that is believed to have claimed at least 500 lives.

"Considering the breakdown of values and emblems that we were instilled with by the party and which were destroyed at the hand of the security forces ... we announce our withdrawal from the party without regret," 30 party members from the coastal city of Banias said in a letter.

Meanwhile, the UN security council overnight failed to agree on a statement condemning Syrian violence. Russia said security forces were also killed and the actions don't threaten international peace. China and India called for political dialogue and peaceful resolution of the crisis, with no mention of condemnation.

1.21pm: Tribal leaders in Libya have issued a joint statement calling on Gaddafi to step down. The statement, from 61 tribal chiefs or representatives, came as the rebels claimed to be gaining ground in Misrata. It was released via the French writer Bernard-Henri Levy. It says:

Faced with the threats weighing on the unity of our country, faced with the manoeuvres and propaganda of the dictator and his family, we solemnly declare: Nothing will divide us. We share the same ideal of a free, democratic and united Libya.

FRIDAY 29 APRIL

7.54am: CBS correspondent Lara Logan has given an interview. This from Reuters:

Logan felt sure she would die while being sexually assaulted by a mob when covering the jubilation in Cairo's Tahrir Square after Egyptian president Mubarak stepped down, she says in an interview to be broadcast on Sunday. "There was no doubt in my mind that I was in the process of dying," she says in a transcript released by CBS's 60 Minutes programme.

11.17am: The Guardian's Xan Rice has interviewed the leader of the rebellion in Misrata, the only rebel-held city in western Libya. The rebel leader makes an urgent plea to the international community for weapons.

Khalifa al-Zwawi, an appeal court judge who heads Misrata's transitional council, said that after weeks of fierce fighting, rebel forces would eject the last of Gaddafi's troops from the city "very soon".

"Once we have done that our target is to eliminate the Gaddafi regime," he said. "We want to go to Tripoli and set it free, and Libya free. We want to move from defence to attack … The most important thing for us now is arms. We need weapons that are suitable to take on Gaddafi. As soon as our freedom fighters reach people in other cities they will join our revolt."

7.54pm: Julian Borger has this on events in Syria:

Thousands of Syrians have defied their government's bloody attempts to suppress protests, braving gunfire from security forces to demonstrate in Damascus and across the country. At least 42 people were killed, most of them in the opposition stronghold of Deraa, where villagers tried to break through the security cordon to relieve its besieged population.

Further deaths were reported in Latakia and Homs after the security forces opened fire on demonstrators. There was news of protests in 50 towns and villages. Despite the government crackdown, the demonstrations, many starting as Friday worshippers left mosques, appeared to be at least as big as last week.

SATURDAY 30 APRIL

10.00pm: Alarming news from Syria and the besieged southern city of Deraa. Troops have stormed the Omari mosque, a hub for protesters, killing four people, according to AP. The assault lasted 90 minutes, during which troops fired tank shells and heavy machine guns, resident Abdullah Abazeid told the agency. Three helicopters participated in the operation, dropping paratroopers on top of the mosque itself, he said.

SUNDAY 1 MAY

10.40am: A Nato airstrike has killed Muammar Gaddafi's youngest son and three of his grandchildren, a Libyan official in Tripoli has said, while accusing the alliance of trying to assassinate the Libyan leader. It would be the first time someone from Gaddafi's inner circle has been killed in six weeks of Nato airstrikes.

Government spokesman Moussa Ibrahim said Gaddafi's son, Saif al-Arab Gaddafi, 29, was "martyred" in the attack on his villa in Tripoli, where his father had been staying the night. Saif, described by Ibrahim as a student who had studied in Germany, is said to have had only a minor role in the country's power structure.

10.54pm: The fallout from the killing of Gaddafi's son is summed up in a front-page report from tomorrow's Guardian:

> The British embassy in Tripoli was set on fire and other western missions were ransacked by angry Libyan crowds yesterday in retaliation for a Nato airstrike that killed members of Muammar Gaddafi's family.
>
> Britain responded to the burning of its chancellery and official residence by expelling Libya's ambassador to London, Omar Jelban, who was given 24 hours to leave the country.
>
> The UN announced it was withdrawing its last international staff from Tripoli, as security degenerated.

MONDAY 2 MAY

8.40pm: While global attention today has been absorbed by the news of the killing of Osama bin Laden in Pakistan, the conflict continues in Libya. Xan Rice has this from Misrata:

> Gaddafi's forces have bombarded Misrata with missiles and tank fire, preventing ships carrying humanitarian aid from entering the port for a fourth straight day …
>
> In Misrata, where more than 1,000 people have been killed since late February, there is increasing anger that Nato is not doing enough to destroy Gaddafi's missile launchers that continue to pummel the city.

WEDNESDAY 4 MAY

10.43am: News comes from Bahrain that more than 40 doctors and nurses who treated anti-government protesters injured during recent demonstrations have been charged with "acts against the state". The medical staff are accused of "promoting efforts to bring down the government" and "harming the public by spreading false news", the Independent reports.

3.00pm: The Guardian's diplomatic editor, Julian Borger, has breaking news on war crimes charges against Gaddafi.

> The Gaddafi regime committed war crimes against Libyan pro-democracy protesters, opening fire "systematically" on peaceful demonstrations, according to a report to be issued today by the prosecutor for the international criminal court, who will seek arrest warrants against top members of the regime later this month.

FRIDAY 6 MAY

10.18am: Amina, a Syrian-American who has been documenting various brushes with the security forces on her blog A Gay Girl in Damascus, writes:

> It's Friday morning; I'm in Damascus. Today may be the big day of the National Uprising that we have been working for. This might be the last post on this blog. Or the next one may be triumphant.

2.07pm: Hundreds of thousands of Yemenis have taken to the streets of the capital Sana'a to demand that Saleh step down. Rival rallies by both Saleh's supporters and opponents have become a fixture in the capital Sana'a on Fridays, but the anti-Saleh crowds far outnumber those of his backers, says AP.

2.54pm: Our correspondent in Damascus emails having spoken with Wissam Tarif of the human rights group Insan.

> Tarif told the Guardian he has counted protests in 68 towns and villages so far today. He says at this time last week they had 43 … He says eyewitnesses have told him that snipers are on rooftops in several towns and that live ammunition has been used in al-Tel and Hajr al-Aswad, both close to Damascus. He is unable to get information from the outskirts of Homs, although tanks are confirmed as inside the city.

4.30pm: There are reports that at least 12 people have been killed in today's crackdown in Syria. Reuters reports that the number killed in Hama has risen to six, and Avaaz claims a further six were killed in Homs. Some of the latest YouTube videos to emerge from Syria are too gruesome to even link to.

SUNDAY 8 MAY

7.16pm: Ian Black writes with disturbing news from Cairo:

> Egypt's transitional government moved quickly to defuse tensions after Muslim-Christian clashes in Cairo left 12 dead and cast a cloud over hopes for peaceful post-revolutionary change.
>
> Angry demonstrations erupted in the capital after a Coptic church in the Imbaba neighbourhood was burned down on Saturday night. Military police separated opposing camps at one protest reminiscent of the dramatic events that overthrew the regime in February.
>
> Fighting broke out over rumours, which turned out to be false, that a Christian woman was being held inside a church and prevented from converting to Islam.

MONDAY 9 MAY

8.39pm: The European Union has imposed an arms embargo on Syria, reports AP.

TUESDAY 10 MAY

9.00am: Nato warplanes struck Tripoli this morning in the heaviest bombing of the Libyan capital in weeks. Overnight, Nato warplanes struck at least four sites in Tripoli, setting off crackling explosions that thundered through the Libyan capital, AP reports.

WEDNESDAY 11 MAY

2.03pm: The EU is to open an office in Benghazi, its foreign policy chief Catherine Ashton has told the European parliament. She said the office will help the flow of humanitarian aid and support to the Interim National Transitional Council, according to a BBC report.

5.27pm: Tom Finn, who is in Sana'a, Yemen, reports that around 2,000 protesters marching from Change Square towards the Ministerial Council headquarters have been shot at by men in military uniforms:

> So far two teenagers have been killed and around 60 people – among them women and children – have sustained bullet wounds … The march was part of new efforts by Sana'a protesters to put more pressure on President Saleh. Other measures include blocking roads and carrying out acts of civil disobedience.

11.51pm: Nato says it has carried out more than 2,400 airstrikes in Libya since March 31, as part of its effort to assist the rebels.

12.10am: At least 18 people have been killed and hundreds wounded in Yemen, reports Reuters. Troops opened fire on demonstrators in three cities.

THURSDAY 12 MAY

11.44am: In Bahrain, the head of the military has confirmed that Saudi-led Gulf forces sent to the kingdom to crush dissent will remain in place even after emergency rule is lifted next month. The move is likely to further irritate Iran, which has labelled the 1,500-strong force an "occupation" by Sunni states to shore up the Sunni monarchy against a Shia-majority population.

FRIDAY 13 MAY

11.24am: The first reports of protests after Friday prayers in Syria are beginning to come in from credible sources on Twitter. From the founder of the human rights group Insan:

> \# **wissamtarif** Demos in #AienArab #Amouda #Derbasieh #Qamishli #Amouda Chanting "people want to topple the regime"

4.31pm: Six people have been killed in today's protests, the Damascus-based human rights lawyer Razan Zeitouneh has told the Guardian via Skype.

> The regime felt that they could scare people enough to stop people coming on to the streets – they have arrested thousands of people. But

today it was as usual – more and more went on to the street – so they started shooting people. Today was clear proof that nothing will stop the protests. No kind of violence will stop them.

6.44pm: Martin Chulov in Tripoli reports that Libyan officials are claiming a Nato bombing raid last night resulted in heavy civilian casualties.

The Libyan government has shown video of what it claims to be an attack on a guest house in the city of Al-Brega in eastern Libya where dozens of Islamic imams or sheikhs were staying as part of a peace march to the east.

The gruesome images showed 11 dead imams and 45 wounded Muslim holy men – five of them in a coma – according to Libyan government officials speaking in the courtyard of a Tripoli mosque where Islamic elders and Christian Coptic priests had gathered to condemn the attack.

WEDNESDAY 18 MAY

2.09pm: In Yemen, a deal that would end the rule of Ali Abduallah Saleh within a month is due to be signed by the Yemeni president and the opposition today, Reuters reports.

The deal, intended to end three months of protests against the president that have paralysed Yemen's economy, will give Saleh immunity from prosecution. But Shadi Hamid, analyst at the Brookings Doha Centre, cast doubt that it will be struck. Two previous near-deals fell through at the last minute. He said: "I won't believe it until I see it, that's what we learned in Yemen … Everyone thought that the deal was done a few weeks ago but Saleh found a way to back out in final hours and days."

THURSDAY 19 MAY

1.57pm: The human rights campaign Avaaz has a grim update on the besieged town of Talkalakh on Syria's border with Lebanon.

The number of protesters killed in Talkalakh has risen to 35 since the beginning of the invasion last Sunday. We have their names to verify this. Water and electricity have been cut in the entire town and residents have told us they will run out of food in a matter of days. Shooting and shelling by the army continues day and night. The neighbourhood Hay al-Borj was entirely destroyed yesterday, without a single house left standing. The neighbourhood is completely deserted.

3.31pm: The refusal of Yemen's President Saleh to sign a Gulf council deal for him to step down has provoked new protests. Gulf foreign ministers are to hold an emergency meeting to discuss the crisis.

5.14pm: Obama has taken the podium in Washington for what is being billed as a key speech on the Middle East. He begins:

For six months, we have witnessed an extraordinary change take place in the Middle East and North Africa. Square by square; town by town; country by country; the people have risen up to demand their basic human rights. Two leaders have stepped aside. More may follow. And though these countries may be a great distance from our shores, we know that our own future is bound to this region by the forces of economics and security, history and faith.

6.42pm: An early take on the Obama speech by Ewen MacAskill:

"The status quo is not sustainable," Obama said in a major speech at the state department in Washington on Thursday, the first on the Middle East since he spoke in Cairo in 2009.

In a speech dubbed Cairo Two, he threw US weight behind the protesters, saying: "We face a historic opportunity. We have embraced the chance to show that America values the dignity of the street vendor in Tunisia more than the raw power of the dictator … After decades of accepting the world as it is in the region, we have a chance to pursue the world as it should be."

FRIDAY 20 MAY

8.19am: It sounded bold, but the substance was more cautious, says the Guardian's Middle East editor Ian Black of Obama's speech:

The complete omission of Saudi Arabia was a glaring oversight … Strikingly, Saudi Arabia, one of the most repressive countries in the Arab world and a key US ally and oil supplier, got not a single mention in the 5,400-word speech.

Nor did Obama offer any really new ideas on the Israeli-Palestinian impasse, reiterating the "unshakeable" US commitment to Israel's security.

10.10am: Patience is running out with Yemen's President Saleh, reports Tom Finn from the capital Sana'a. He continues to prevaricate on whether he will sign a Gulf council deal to stand down with immunity from prosecution. One of the hitches is that he wants opposition leaders to sign up to the deal, Tom reports.

> This is maybe his last chance. People have become so disillusioned with these negotiations. If he isn't willing to put his name on paper on Sunday we could see a serious escalation of protests … It has reached the stage of complete disillusionment.

6.40pm: Just a day after Obama told Syria's Bahsir al-Assad that he should accept reforms or "get out of the way," Assad sent his reply. From AP:

> At least 23 people were reported killed in several different locations, activists said, but with the protests continuing, the toll could rise. Troops opened fire on demonstrations in the protest flash points of Homs, Hama, Baniyas and Damascus, as tens of thousands of Syrians took to the streets in towns across the country.

SUNDAY 22 MAY

5.11pm: In a piece for tomorrow's Guardian, a former Royal Navy admiral has warned that Nato's military campaign in Libya "defies strategic logic" and needs to be completely rethought. Rear Admiral Chris Parry said the conflict is becoming all too reminiscent of the campaigns in Iraq and Afghanistan, and a "classic example of how to act in haste and repent at leisure".

According to the Guardian's defence correspondent, Nick Hopkins, "Parry's analysis is understood to be shared by many senior strategists at the Ministry of Defence, who cannot speak out despite growing frustration at the limits of Nato's activity."

MONDAY 23 MAY

10.08am: Despite a large number of online videos continuing to emerge from Syria, Assad's regime is cracking down on use of social media, just three months after allowing citizens to have open access to Facebook and YouTube, the New York Times reports.

> Security officials are moving on multiple fronts – demanding dissidents turn over their Facebook passwords and switching off the 3G mobile network at times, sharply limiting the ability of dissidents to upload videos of protests to YouTube, according to several activists in Syria. And supporters of President Assad, calling themselves the Syrian Electronic Army, are using the same tools to try to discredit dissidents.

TUESDAY 24 MAY

10.06am: Camille Otrakji is a rarity – a dissident Syrian blogger who broadly backs the regime. In a provocative appearance on Bloggingheads TV he has claimed that only 1% of the Syrian population have actively taken part in the protests and around 70% of Syrians would support President Assad's regime if it adopted reform. He also claims the protest movement risks plunging Syria into a civil war.

11.27am: There are reports of renewed fighting in the Yemeni capital, Sana'a. From Reuters:

> "Gunmen and soldiers spread out everywhere and the sound of gunfire can be heard from time to time," one witness told Reuters. Fighting in the same area yesterday killed seven people including a civilian bystander.
>
> The clashes, in the sandbagged streets surrounding a fortified mansion belonging to the wealthy and politically powerful al-Ahmar clan, pitted loyalist forces against guards of Sadiq al-Ahmar, head of the Hashed tribal federation.

Meanwhile Tom Finn, the Guardian's stringer in Sana'a, tweets:

\# I can't tell which is louder, the mortar fire in Sana'a right now or the media's beating of the civil war drum

2.17pm: Breaking news from Egypt: Hosni Mubarak is to stand trial, according to prosecutors.

From AP:

> Mubarak will stand trial on charges of conspiring in the deadly shootings of protesters during the uprising that ousted him, the prosecutor-general said.
>
> The 83-year-old leader, his two sons and a close business associate also have been charged with abusing their power to amass wealth, the prosecutor-general's office said in a statement. A trial date has not yet been set.

THURSDAY 26 MAY

8.56am: The fighting in Yemen appears to have escalated overnight. This is the latest from Tom Finn:

> I'm still hearing shelling now after more than 12 hours of continuous fighting in Sana'a. The local hospitals are filled with the injured. A doctor said that 26 tribesmen were killed last night, mostly from sniper fire.

9.38am: Syrian dissidents and opposition groups are to gather in Turkey next week to plot the overthrow of Assad's regime and set up a transitional council to represent the Syrian revolution on the international stage. Leading US-based dissident Ammar Abdulhamid will be attending the three days of talks in the city of Antalya. Writing on his blog, he says:

> This will be a major test for the Syrian opposition groups and their ability to remain relevant to the current goings-on in the country. Success will be premised on their ability to court the support of protest leaders and committees acting inside the country ... This is the dawn of a new age in Syrian politics.

FRIDAY 27 MAY

9.18am: Human Rights Watch has written to Formula One urging it to reconsider rescheduling the Grand Prix in Bahrain. F1 bosses are meeting next week to decide a new date for the Bahrain Grand Prix after the event was postponed in March due to security concerns.

9.38am: The Yemeni capital Sana'a is now a city divided, Reuters reports. It says that the north of the city is controlled not by the militia leader Sadeq al-Ahmar, but by a general who until now has stayed out of the conflict.

South Sana'a is under the control of Saleh's security forces, and the north is mainly controlled by General Ali Mohsen al-Ahmar, one of Yemen's most powerful military leaders, who defected in March to protesters demanding the end of Saleh's nearly 33-year-old rule.

11.37am: Reuters correspondent Suleiman al-Khalidi, who spent several days reporting from the southern protest hub of Deraa in March and was later detained by the Syrian security forces, has written an account of the scenes of torture he witnessed during his detention.

Mostly I was blindfolded, but the blindfold was removed for a few minutes. That allowed me – despite orders to keep my head down so that my interrogators should remain out of view – to see a hooded man screaming in pain in front of me.

When they told him to take down his pants, I could see his swollen genitals, tied tight with a plastic cable. "I have nothing to tell, but I am neither a traitor and activist. I am just a trader," said the man, who said he was from Idlib province in the north-west of Syria. To my horror, a masked man took a pair of wires from a household power socket and gave him electric shocks to the head.

12.04pm: Tribal leader Sadeq al-Ahmar has addressed a crowd of thousands after Friday prayers and announced a ceasefire in the fighting with government, Tom Finn reports from the Yemeni capital during Friday prayers.

Al-Ahmar came on to the microphone briefly to loud cheers to announce they have signed a ceasefire. He said he was fully backing the protest movement here. There was deafening applause when he announced that he wanted the revolution to be peaceful.

MONDAY 30 MAY

10.13am: Hundreds of soldiers loyal to Yemen's embattled President Saleh have stormed a protest camp in the southern city of Taiz killing at least 20 people, according to medical official and witnesses. Witnesses said that troops fired on the crowds indiscriminately, AP reports. The city of Taiz has been a hotbed of anti-government protests since crowds began calling for Saleh to stand down in early February.

1.25pm: The South African president, Jacob Zuma, has arrived in Tripol for what is being seen as a last-ditch attempt to broker a diplomatic end to the fighting in Libya. Gaddafi has reportedly told confidantes that it would betray the memory of his son Saif al-Arab, who was killed by a Nato airstrike, to surrender power, and instead wants to assume a background role while civil institutions are allowed to emerge from his four-decade rule.

TUESDAY 31 MAY

1.04pm: Activists and bloggers are pressing Egypt's military rulers to investigate growing accusations of abuses against protesters, including claims that soldiers subjected female detainees to so-called "virginity tests". Bloggers say they will hold a day of online protest on Wednesday to voice their outrage.

3.04pm: The independent Yemeni news site Al-Masdar Online says 11 people have been killed in the southern city of Taiz, citing local sources. The same website says 57 people were killed and 1,000 injured when Yemeni troops stormed a protest camp in the city on Sunday and Monday.

WEDNESDAY 1 JUNE

10.00am: The US secretary of state, Hillary Clinton, has said Syria's alleged torture and killing of a 13-year-old boy, Hamza al-Khatib, who is becoming a symbol for the revolution, illustrates that the government is making no effort to institute real reform.

10.15am: Yemeni medical officials say at least 41 people were killed in overnight shelling and street battles between government forces and rival tribal fighters in the capital, Sana'a, AP reports.

11.47am: Here's more on Hamza al-Khatib, fast becoming the symbol of the Syrian revolution, from this morning's Guardian:

The boy, from a village called al-Jizah near the southern city of Deraa, has become the most famous victim yet of Syria's bloody chapter of the Arab Spring. Hamza was picked up by security forces on 29 April. On 27 May his badly mutilated corpse was released to his horrified family, who were warned to keep silent.

According to a YouTube video and human rights activists, Hamza was tortured and his swollen body showed bullet wounds on his arms, black eyes, cuts, marks consistent with electric shock devices, bruises and whip marks. His neck had been broken and his penis cut off.

Like Neda Agha-Soltan, the young woman who was shot dead in street protests after Iran's disputed presidential elections two years ago, Hamza has come to symbolise the innocent victims in a struggle for freedom against tyranny and repression.

Several Facebook pages have been started, including one with more than 61,000 followers called "We are all Hamza al-Khatib".

THURSDAY 2 JUNE

8.35am: The crisis in Yemen is escalating, with at least 41 people killed yesterday during clashes between President Saleh's troops and forces loyal to Sadeq al-Ahmar, the influential tribal leader. Hillary Clinton last night increased US pressure on Saleh to step down, telling reporters that he and his regime should "move out of the way to permit the opposition and civil society to begin a transition to political and economic reform".

9.25am: The Financial Times has an interesting article about yesterday's meeting in Turkey during which Syrian opposition activists sought to agree a united front.

Some activists have questioned what the meeting in Antalya can achieve, given the difficulty of representing an inchoate and still-evolving protest movement inside Syria. There are no high-profile leaders, and the movement is apparently driven by young, non-affiliated people – different from the traditional opposition made up of the Muslim Brotherhood, leftwingers and Kurdish nationalists …

Some also voiced distrust of the motives of those outside Syria campaigning for change.

11.34am: Brian Whitaker has the following useful context for the situation in Yemen:

> With many erstwhile supporters – both civil and military – abandoning him, it's clear that Saleh can never regain the authority he once had. But there's still the question of how, exactly, he can be ousted from office.
>
> One thing to keep in mind is that armed conflict in Yemen is not unusual; in fact it's almost routine. The regime has fought an on-off war with Houthi rebels in the north for years, as well as a separatist insurrection in the south which sprang up more recently.

4.45pm: A two-day meeting in Turkey of Syrian opposition figures has concluded with a call from the 300 delegates for Assad to resign immediately, handing power to the vice president until a council is formed to manage the transition to democracy.

FRIDAY 3 JUNE

10.15am: About 250 people are feared to have drowned after their attempt to flee the violence in Libya apparently ended in tragedy off the Tunisian coast, reports the Guardian's John Hooper. Coastguards and military personnel are reported to have saved at least 570 people, all from sub-Saharan Africa, during a rescue operation in rough seas and shallow waters off the Kerkennah islands east of the Tunisian coast.

11.33am: Associated Press is reporting that Bahraini police have fired teargas and rubber bullets at protesters marching toward Pearl Square in the country's capital.

> The downtown square was the centre of weeks of Shia-led protests against Sunni rulers earlier this year in the Gulf kingdom. Today's march in Manama comes two days after authorities lifted emergency rule. It was imposed in March to quell demonstrations by Bahrain's Shia majority demanding greater freedoms and inspired by uprisings across the Arab world.

1.31pm: President Saleh has been injured in the shell attack on the presidential palace, al-Arabiya TV has reported.

3.21pm: The Syrian Observatory for Human Rights has said that Syrian security forces have now killed 27 protesters in the city of Hama. "There are also scores of wounded and the death toll may rise," the Observatory's Rami Abdulrahman told Reuters.

5.39pm: The Guardian's Brian Whitaker ponders what the rocket attack on Saleh's presidential palace means for the unrest in the country, and considers the different scenarios:

> In what might be the best scenario for Yemen's future, Saleh would be seriously injured but not dead. In fact, sufficiently injured for the doctors to decide that he needs urgent treatment abroad.
>
> Flying him out of the country for medical reasons would provide a near-perfect exit from the crisis. The vice president could take over and Yemen could begin to calm down. It's unlikely that anyone would want Saleh back if or when he recovered.

6.45pm: Formula One's governing body has ruled that the Bahrain Grand Prix in October can go ahead, despite the continuing unrest in the tiny state.

SUNDAY 5 JUNE

9.28am: Yemen's President Saleh has flown out of the country to Saudi Arabia, ostensibly to seek treatment for the wounds he suffered on Friday during a rocket attack on the presidential palace in Sana'a. There is now intense speculation as to whether he will ever return home to continue his authoritarian 33-year rule – and, if not, whether this will leave a power vacuum in the already chaotic nation.

10.15am: From Syria, Nidaa Hassan has sent us this:

> Despite the cutting of the internet across the majority of cities on Friday, Syria's regime has not been able to hide what was one of the bloodiest weekends in the uprising. At least 64 of 79 people killed on Friday were shot dead in Hama.
>
> Yesterday, the focus turned to Jisr al-Shaghour in the north-western province of Idleb where 11 were shot dead after activists said Syrian security forces and troops backed by tanks and helicopters opened fire in the city. Activists say the town is still surrounded today.

12.01pm: President Saleh will return to Yemen from Saudi Arabia within days, an official from his ruling party has told Reuters.

12.55pm: The UK foreign secretary, William Hague, has completed a visit of the rebel capital of Benghazi in a mark of support for those seeking to unseat Gaddafi. He has denied that the use of British Apache helicopters to attack targets in Libya amounts to "mission creep".

3.35pm: Syrian state TV, quoted by AP, is reporting that 11 people have been killed and 120 injured after Israeli troops fired on pro-Palestinian demonstrators trying to storm Syria's Golan Height border with Israel. There is no independent verification for the figures.

MONDAY 6 JUNE

8.22am: The US and Britain are reportedly urging Saudi Arabia to persuade Saleh to formally stand down. But diplomats are privately frustrated with Riyadh, writes Ian Black.

> "The Saudis put a lot of money into Yemen but like everyone else they have been puzzled about how to handle it," said a former diplomat. "It has tried to influence events but didn't take charge and seemed to lack strategic direction."

9.49am: The Saudi English-language daily, Arab News, carries a cautious editorial on Yemen which is characteristically grovelling about Saudi Arabia's role.

> Because it shares a border with Yemen, it is imperative that the Kingdom use its good offices, which it has, with the Yemeni government and the opposition to stop the fighting. Now that Saleh is in Saudi territory, perhaps he can be persuaded to sign a deal brokered by the Gulf states which he thrice reneged on but which allows him to leave office with dignity.

2.54pm: Nato secretary general Anders Fogh Rasmussen has given another upbeat progress report on the campaign against Gaddafi's regime. Speaking at his monthly press conference he said:

The figures speak for themselves. Since Nato first took action to protect Libya's people, we have kept up a high operational tempo, with over 10,000 sorties. We have damaged or destroyed almost 1,800 legimate military targets. That includes around 100 command and control sites – which Gaddafi used to organise attacks on civilians …

Our message to the Gaddafi regime is clear: we started this mission, and we will complete it.

3.26pm: A new report on Libya by the International Crisis Group provides a very different view from Rasmussen's upbeat assessment.

The longer Libya's military conflict persists, the more it risks undermining the anti-Gaddafi camp's avowed objectives. Yet, to date, the latter's leadership and their Nato supporters appear to be uninterested in resolving the conflict through negotiation. To insist, as they have done, on Gaddafi's departure as a precondition for any political initiative is to prolong the military conflict and deepen the crisis.

7.26pm: Reports from Syria suggest that 120 security forces personnel and policeman have been killed in the northern town of Jisr al-Shughour. The state news agency, Sana, initially said 28 personnel had been killed, including in an armed ambush and at the state security post. It revised the figure up to 43, 80 and then 120 within the space of an hour without an explanation.

TUESDAY 7 JUNE

8.26am: An online campaign is gaining momentum to free a prominent Syrian-American blogger who was kidnapped on Monday. Amina Arraf, author of the blog A Gay Girl in Damascus, was seized with a friend, according to a posting on the blog by her cousin, Rania. In an update Rania said the family suspected Amina had been deported.

10.20am: Yemen's president Saleh is suffering from a collapsed lung and 7cm-deep shrapnel wound, according to CNN. Activists think his return is unlikely despite claims by the acting president that Saleh will return from Saudi Arabia within days.

10.36am: Nato has again bombarded Tripoli, with nine attacks, and this time in daylight, AP reports.

11.48am: Egypt's official news agency says the long-banned Muslim Brotherhood has been recognised as the Freedom and Justice party, AP reports. The announcement would allow the group to run in parliamentary elections set for September.

4.52pm: Accounts continue to vary sharply on what happened in the northwestern Syrian town of Jisr al-Shughour, but witnesses in the town say protesters did fight back against the security forces. Activists fear that the regime is exaggerating reports of deaths among security forces as a pretext to a further crackdown against the town amid reports of tanks in the area.

WEDNESDAY 8 JUNE

10.36am: Tunisia's prime minister says the country is delaying its first elections since the ousting of Ben Ali until 23 October, to ensure they are fair and transparent. The elections had been planned for 24 July but Tunisia's electoral commission proposed last month that they be postponed until October to give nascent political parties more time to prepare.

11.39am: The Turkish prime minister, Recep Tayyip Erdogan, a warm ally of Assad, has called on Syria to rein in violence against its people. He said:

> Syria should change its attitude towards civilians and should take its attitude to a more tolerant level as soon as possible.

12.30pm: The Formula One boss, Bernie Ecclestone, has told the BBC the Bahrain Grand Prix cannot go ahead despite his intention, because the teams are opposed to it.

4.09pm: Reuters is reporting "dire scenes" in the town of Zinjibar, southern Yemen, with bodies in the street being eaten by wild dogs as government forces battle Islamist militants. The fighting has reduced Zinjibar, once home to more than 50,000 people, to a ghost town without power or running water, the news agency said.

6.16pm: US embassy officials in Syria are urgently seeking to establish further details about Amina Abdallah Araf al Omari, who writes the blog A Gay Girl in Damascus, write Esther Addley and Nidaa Hasan.

According to a post on the blog, Araf was abducted by security forces on Monday evening, as questions emerged over the identity of the author.

The blogger, who writes of her life as a lesbian feminist participating in the protests, has said that her mother is American and she is a joint US-Syrian citizen. But Angela Williams from the US embassy in Damascus told the Guardian officials had not been able to confirm any of the details in the blog, and had no records of someone of that name living in Damascus.

6.52pm: Andy Carvin, NPR's Twitter expert, has written about the Amina controversy:

I still have many more questions than answers, but I currently believe Amina is a real person, but one who is much more expressive about herself online than offline. It is possible that Amina Arraf is a pen name, to protect herself in Syria, but so far I can't prove it one way or another.

THURSDAY 9 JUNE

8.38am: Columns of Syrian tanks have surrounded Jisr al-Shughour, near the Turkish border, and most of the town's 41,000 people are reported to have fled after armed clashes at the weekend. Many of the troops were from the army's 4th division commanded by Assad's younger brother Maher.

9.00am: Gaddafi's regime in Libya is using rape as a weapon of conflict, according to new evidence submitted to the chief prosecutor of the international criminal court. Luis Moreno-Ocampo told reporters at the UN in New York that there was even evidence that the government had been handing out doses of Viagra to soldiers to encourage sexual attacks. US Ambassador to the UN Susan Rice made similar allegations in April.

10.17am: The Guardian's Martin Chulov is on the Turkish border with Syria. He tweets that Turkish authorities are blocking journalists from reaching refugees fleeing the besieged town of Jisr al-Shughour.

\# Turkish govt blocking access to fleeing Syrians here in southern town of Yayladagi. They clearly don't want to upset Damascus.

\# Columns of ambulances taking wounded syrians to hospitals in Turkey's Hatay province. Hundreds of syrian cars have fled north past us.

2.52pm: Russia has confirmed it will vote against France and Britain's attempt to secure a UN security council resolution condemning Syria.

FRIDAY 10 JUNE

8.23am: Ominously, the Syrian government says it has begun "restoring security" to Jisr al-Shughour. A violent crackdown in the town has been feared for days after the government claimed 120 security personnel were killed in the area by "armed gangs". Syrian refugees fleeing the town recall a very different series of events and say they fled to Turkey fearing a massacre.

9.51am: Refugees have told Martin Chulov that 5,000 troops have massed in the Jisr al-Shughour today and shooting has been heard. Martin said the Syrian revolution has "reached a potentially decisive stage, but the information is patchy and it does need a lot of collaboration".

SATURDAY 11 JUNE

10.09am: The besieged town of Jisr al-Shughour is almost deserted this morning, surrounded by tanks and heavy armour, AP reports:

> About 80% of the population has fled, with more than 4,000 Syrians taking sanctuary across the Turkish frontier. The town – normally inhabited by 41,000 people – has become a focal point of the Syrian revolution. Refugees who crossed the border into Turkey said the chaos had erupted as government forces and police mutinied and joined the local population against the forces loyal to Assad.

SUNDAY 12 JUNE

8.13pm: The Guardian's latest report on Syria:

Heavy shelling and gunfire has rocked the Syrian town of Jisr al-Shughour, two days into a military assault that has caused more than 5,000 refugees to flee into neighbouring Turkey.

The continued assault suggests some groups in the town are resisting the armed forces as the regime tries to crush a sustained challenge to President Assad.

The bombardment has reportedly left much of the city in ruins. Farmland to the north has been torched and residents hiding in the mountains say they have been joined by almost all who had remained behind.

MONDAY 13 JUNE

8.29am: The blogger behind A Gay Girl in Damascus turns out to be a straight middle-aged American based in Edinburgh. Tom MacMaster revealed that he was the sole author of the hoax blog. "The events [in the Middle East] are being shaped by the people living them on a daily basis. I have only tried to illuminate them for a western audience," he wrote.

Like many, the Guardian was taken in by the hoax. The Guardian readers' editor Chris Elliott has written that the episode has been a cautionary tale:

> When using social media – as we will continue to do as part of our journalism – the Guardian will have to redouble its efforts in establishing not just methods of verification, but of signalling to the reader the level of verification we think we can reasonably claim.

The hoax is a gift to the Syrian propaganda machine. The state news agency Sana has a rare "urgent" update. It says: "US citizen confesses participation in the misleading media campaign through creating personality of a virtual Blogger as a Syrian woman kidnapped by gunmen in Damascus."

3.49pm: Brian Whitaker, the Guardian's former Middle East editor, examines Tom MacMaster's stated justification for his Gay Girl in Damascus hoax, starting with his statement that he was trying to "illuminate" things "for a western audience".

> Living a fantasy life on your own blog is one thing, but giving an interview to CNN while posing as a representative of the region's gay people appears arrogant and offensive, and surely a prime example of the "liberal Orientalism" that MacMaster claims to decry.

TUESDAY 14 JUNE

9.00am: Turkey is setting up a fifth refugee camp in its southern border towns, but with the number of Syrians who have crossed the boundary topping 7,000, these camps may not be sufficient to deal with the fast-increasing number of people in need of help, one Jisr refugee, Abu Ali, told Martin Chulov:

> There are 7,000 people across the border; more and more women and children are coming towards the barbed wires. Jisr is finished, it is razed.

10.27am: Gaddafi's troops have fired rockets into neighbouring Tunisia, Reuters reports.

> Libyan troops fired Grad rockets from positions controlled by Gaddafi over the border into Tunisia on Tuesday, witnesses said, in an assault likely to raise already high tensions between the two countries. The explosions caused no damage or injuries.

11.58am: Turkey is considering changing its softly-softly approach to Syria, the Turkish daily Hurriyet reports.

> Only a day after its general elections [on Sunday], Turkey has begun a substantial re-evaluation of its Syrian policy, as more than 7,000 Syrians have now fled to Hatay while another 15,000 mass near the border, according to reports. "Turkey will keep engaging with Syria [to urge it to enact reforms and abstain from violence], but Syria's attitude will determine our position," a ministry official speaking on condition of anonymity told Hürriyet.

WEDNESDAY 15 JUNE

3.57pm: Nato is using Twitter to help it identify targets in Libya, Richard Norton-Taylor and Nick Hopkins report.

> Potentially relevant tweets are fed into an intelligence pool then filtered for relevance and authenticity, and are never passed on without proper corroboration. However, without "boots on the ground" to guide

commanders, officials admit that Twitter is now part of the overall "intelligence picture".

THURSDAY 16 JUNE

8.58am: The White House has defended the legality of the Libya conflict in a detailed report, and urged Congress not to send "mixed messages" about US commitment. In the face of growing doubts about the campaign the administration's report argues the president has the constitutional power to continue the US role against Gaddafi's forces even though Congress has not authorised it.

1.11pm: The Iranian embassy in London has emailed a statement denying British government claims that Iran is helping Syria implement its violent crackdown. It says:

> Recently, some of the British officials have made unfounded and baseless allegations against the Islamic Republic of Iran concerning the incidents in Syria. The Embassy of the Islamic Republic of Iran strongly condemns these inappropriate remarks and denies firmly these untrue allegations which aim to tarnish Iran's popular image in the region.

MONDAY 20 JUNE

8.50am: The eyes of the world will be on the Syrian president today, as he addresses the nation for the first time in two months. It will be only Assad's third such speech since the uprising began with protests in the southern Hauran Plain on 18 March.

9.05am: In Tunisia, the trial of Ben Ali in absentia begins, with a verdict possible today, AP reports. The Tunis Criminal Court is hearing embezzlement, money laundering and drug trafficking cases against the ousted dictator. The charges were brought after the discovery of around $27 million in jewels and cash plus drugs and weapons at two palaces outside Tunis after he fled the country. Saudi Arabia did not respond to an extradition request.

In the statement, Ben Ali "vigorously denies" accusations against him.

9.22am: Despite being largely overshadowed by events elsewhere, protests have been taking place in Morocco, where there were clashes on Sunday between pro-government demonstrators and pro-democracy activists protesting against the constitutional reforms unveiled by the king on Friday, which they believe do not go far enough.

9.59am: The Syrian president has begun speaking. He says this is a "defining moment in the country's history".

11.30: Assad's speech has come to an end after about an hour and a quarter. He promised a "national dialogue" to address central political and economic issues, including reform of the constitution, and sought to draw a distinction between people with legitimate demands and others he variously described as terrorists, wanted criminals, Muslim extremists and foreign conspirators, denouncing conspiracies against Syria as "germs". Assad urged refugees in Turkey and those waiting at the Turkish border to return home and said he was eager for the army and security forces to be able to return to base. But he said gunmen in the northern town of Jisr al-Shughour had "sophisticated weapons and communications".

11.43am: #assadspeech is trending on Twitter.

\#   **martinchulov** #assadspeech different tone from last 2. Wants people to think he's listening. But still sounding like old-school overlord.

\#   **Syrian84** The speech doesn't define our future, we define it with our unity. #AssadSpeech

\#   **RazanSpeaks** Demonstrations have started in Idlib, Homs, Hama, Aleppo and some Damascus suburbs in response to #AssadSpeech

12.44pm: Ian Black assesses the speech:

Assad's latest attempt to draw the sting from the Syrian uprising was replete with a drearily familiar litany of blame – foreign conspiracies, germs, fomentors of chaos, Muslim extremism – for the ills that have befallen his country.

But it is a measure of how much pressure he feels both at home and abroad that there were at least some admissions of the need for change

– to be considered through a "national dialogue" that will address central political and economic issues ... Talk of future elections was similarly vague, and there was no explicit commitment to change the constitutional role of the ruling Ba'ath party – vital to allow the emergence of a multi-party system.

TUESDAY 21 JUNE

8.54am: The former Tunisian president and his wife have been sentenced to 35 years in jail after being found guilty of theft in absentia by a Tunisian court. Ben Ali and his wife, Leila Trabelsi, were accused of theft and unlawful possession of large sums of foreign currency, jewellery, archaeological artefacts, drugs and weapons.

WEDNESDAY 22 JUNE

9.31am: The head of the Arab League, Amr Moussa, who played a central role in securing Arab support for bombing Libya, has told the Guardian he has had second thoughts about the campaign.

When I see children being killed, I must have misgivings. That's why I warned about the risk of civilian casualties ... You can't have a decisive ending. Now is the time to do whatever we can to reach a political solution. That has to start with a genuine ceasefire under international supervision.

9.52am: The official Bahrain news agency says that eight activists have been handed down life sentences after being charged with "organising and managing a terrorist group for the overthrow and the change of the country's constitution and the royal rule". A further nine activists were given 15 years.

12.07pm: The Italian foreign minister Franco Frattini has called for an immediate ceasefire in Libya and warned that Nato's campaign risks losing credibility over civilian casualties.

12.30pm: Maryam al-Khawaja, from the Bahrain Centre for Human Rights, whose father Abdulhadi was among the activists sentenced to life imprisonment today, has been speaking to the Guardian over the phone. She said:

These are civilians being tried in military courts … My father's defence officers were not even allowed to speak during the hearing which the judge had previously promised he would be allowed. This definitely wasn't even anything close to a fair trial. Bahrain has been using their anti-terrorism laws to put people in prison … Almost anything can be regarded as being terrorism in Bahrain if the government wishes to see it in that way.

3.23pm: Two thirds of people across the Middle East and North Africa believe the Arab Spring will produce more democratic governments, a new poll has found. The overall results of the poll conducted by YouGov for Doha Debates masked wide variations in different regions. Optimism was highest in North Africa where 85% believe the unrest would result in more democracy within the next five years.

THURSDAY 23 JUNE

12.12pm: Nato's secretary general Anders Fogh Rasmussen has rejected a call by the Italian foreign minster for a ceasefire in Libya. In an interview with the French newspaper Le Figaro Rasmussen said:

The allies are committed to making the necessary effort for a sustained operation. We will take the time needed until the military objective is reached: end all attacks against Libyan civilians, return armed forces to barracks and freedom of movement for humanitarian aid.

3.03pm: Hundreds more Syrians are reported to have fled to Turkey after the Syrian army moved in on a safe haven close to the Turkish border that the Turkish army had pledged to protect. There has been no word from Ankara on what is being seen as a provocative move.

FRIDAY 24 JUNE

3.23pm: So far seven people are confirmed to have been killed in the protests in Syria today as the government continues its crackdown, writes Nidaa Hassan in Damascus.

There are reports of deaths in Homs and the Damascus suburbs of Kesweh and Barzeh. Activists say the death toll is rising and that heavy violence was used in many areas, including Barzeh, close to Damascus. It's still too early to tell the full extent of Syria's protests today but numbers seem bigger than last week. And the widespread nature of the protest shows the failure of Assad's speech to dampen revolutionary fervour. This is the 15th Friday in which people have taken to the streets.

3.54pm: The United Nations human rights commission has described the long prison sentences handed out to 21 activists in Bahrain this week as a "political persecution".

4.14pm: Gaddafi has released dozens of rebel supporters and allowed them to sail back to Benghazi on Friday in a move that could mark the beginning of broader talks between the adversaries, Reuters reports. In a transfer facilitated by the Red Cross, a ship carrying about 50 men detained by Gaddafi's forces in western Libya docked in Benghazi's harbour alongside hundreds of other refugees.

Ostensibly separately, the rebels sent five of their prisoners back to Tripoli.

MONDAY 27 JUNE

1.05pm: Prospects of a negotiated solution to the Libyan crisis have in some eyes receded further after the ICC's decision to issue arrest warrants for Gaddafi, writes Ian Black:

> The ICC referral has been attacked by some for pursuing legal avenues at the expense of a possible political solution to the crisis. Critics argue that Gaddafi and his closest associates will have no incentive to relinquish power or go into voluntary exile if they know they are certain to end up in the dock in the Hague.

TUESDAY 28 JUNE

3.41pm: Saudi Arabia is to withdraw most of its security forces from Bahrain from next Monday, Reuters reports.

> "The Saudi troops will be withdrawn starting on Monday because their situation is getting much calmer," said a Bahrain government source. Another source confirmed the withdrawal and said not all the troops

would be withdrawn at once … Saudi Arabia is suspected of coming to an agreement with the United States to allow it to help crush the Bahrain unrest.

WEDNESDAY 29 JUNE

8.10am: Overnight Cairo's Tahrir Square has seen the worst clashes since the fall of Mubarak. Jack Shenker was on the spot last night to witness police showering the square with teargas canisters and fire bullets into the air.

> The Guardian witnessed successive volleys of teargas launched into the square and surrounding streets by government forces, including towards areas where ambulances had congregated to treat the wounded. Injured protesters, mostly with head wounds and gas inhalation, were carried to safety on the shoulders of fellow demonstrators.

9.14am: From AP:

> The military government has issued a statement on its Facebook page saying the clashes were designed to "destabilise the country" and drive a wedge between the groups behind the uprising and the security forces. It called on Egyptians not to join the protests.

AP says many of the protesters are believed to be relatives of some 850 people killed during the uprising that ousted Mubarak, and are frustrated over what they perceive as the slow pace of prosecution of police officers believed to be responsible for the deaths.

2.14pm: Bahrain's King Hamad has ordered an investigation into the unrest that his government violently suppressed. Activists have dismissed the move as meaningless. Zainab al-Khawaja, whose father Abdulhadi al-Khawaja was one of eight activist given a life sentence last week, tweeted:

> \# King Hamad and his games. I feel sorry for people who had high hopes that his speech wud be meaningful

2.56pm: The Reuters news agency has been expelled from Tripoli in the latest crackdown on media by the Libyan government.

THURSDAY 30 JUNE

8.24am: The tents are back in Cairo's Tahrir Square. Nabil Abdel Fattah, a political analyst at the al-Ahram Centre, explains why protesters have returned to the streets:

> These clashes are the result of Egypt's new regime trying to reproduce the authoritarian policies and brutal, unaccountable security apparatus that were the tools of dictatorship for the old regime, and they are a critical turning point for the revolution.

8.30am: France's decision to parachute weapons to Libyan rebels risks "Somalia-sation" of Libya, the African Union has warned. Jean Ping, head of the African Union Commission, told the BBC:

> The risk of civil war, risk of partition of the country, the risk of Somalia-sation of the country, risk of having arms everywhere, [of] terrorism.

10.32am: Syrian troops have withdrawn from the cities of Hama, Deir Ezzor and some Damascus suburbs, according to Wissam Tarif, from the human rights group Insan. He says the move is not tactical but a sign that the army is overstretched.

"It's exhaustion, it's an operation that is not sustainable," Tarif said in a Skype interview.

FRIDAY 1 JULY

2.27pm: Syria has seen its biggest demonstrations today after months of unrest, footage from activists appears to show. Video footage is circulating showing tens of thousands of people at an anti-government rally in the central city of Hama, today. Activists claim 200,000 people have rallied in a square in the city. The Syrian army left the town almost three weeks ago, residents claim.

SATURDAY 2 JULY

1.20pm: Assad has sacked the governor of the city of Hama. Although the state report gave no reason or detail for his sacking, video footage showed the huge crowds of protesters in a central square of the provincial capital calling for an end to Assad's rule.

Hama was the site of an armed Islamist revolt against Assad's father, Hafez al-Assad, in 1982. At least 10,000 people were killed and part of the old city was flattened when the army crushed the uprising

MONDAY 4 JULY

9.00am: Muammar Gaddafi has been told by the opposition he can live out his retirement in Libya if he surrenders all power. Mustafa Abdul Jalil, who heads the rebels' National Transitional Council, told Reuters: "As a peaceful solution we offered that he can resign and order his soldiers to withdraw from their barracks and positions, and then he can decide either to stay in Libya or abroad."

4.40pm: David Smith has just called from Tripoli with a report from a press conference with Khaled Kaim, the Libyan deputy foreign minister. Kaim said that talks between the government and the rebels had been going for about two months, outside Libya and over the phone. He said Italy had helped with visas, but refused to say whether meetings had been held in Italy (Rome denies they have), and said some were held at the sidelines of a recent African Union summit in Equatorial Guinea. Nato was the main problem in the whole conflict, Kaim said; without the alliance's involvement the Libyan people would just be able to sort it out among themselves.

TUESDAY 5 JULY

8.15am: Ominous news continues to emerge from the central Syrian city of Hama. The army has re-entered the city to enforce a crackdown on dissent. The latest reports suggest that three civilians were shot dead in the city.

9.00am: Tunisia's ousted President Ben Ali has been convicted in absentia on charges of possessing illegal drugs and weapons after a one-day trial in Tunis. He was sentenced to 15 years in jail, the BBC reports.

WEDNESDAY 6 JULY

8.24am: The death toll in the crackdown on the central Syrian city of Hama has risen to 22, according to the National Organisation for Human Rights. The New York Times sees the city as a bellwether of the unrest in Syria.

Since the uprising erupted in mid-March, the government has wavered between harsh crackdown and tentative reform. Hama has emerged as a microcosm of this shifting strategy, which has befuddled even some of the government's supporters.

The crackdown has raised fears of a repeat of a notorious massacre in Hama in 1982. But observers say that activists are hoping to prevent a bloodbath by documenting the assault on YouTube and social networking sites. The Independent's Robert Fisk, who covered the 1982 crackdown in Hama, writes:

> In 1982, there was no YouTube, no Twitter, there were no mobile phones. Not a single photograph of the dead was ever published. Some of Syria's tanks now appear to be brand-new imports from Russia. The problem is that the people's technology is new too.

FRIDAY 8 JULY

8.15am: The Syrian government has reacted with fury to a trip by the US ambassador to the rebellious city of Hama. Robert Ford travelled to Hama to show solidarity with residents who are refusing to allow the army to enter the city – scene of the largest demonstrations so far. A Syrian foreign ministry official accused Ford of aggravating the situation.

8.30am: Tens of thousands of Egyptians are returning to Tahrir Square on what looks set to be the biggest challenge yet to the military backed transitional government. Protesters are angry at the slow pace of change and lack of accountability of the police under Mubarak.

8.40am: In Yemen, President Saleh has appeared on state TV for the first time since an attack on his compound forced him to seek medical treatment in Saudi Arabia more than a month ago. In a defiant seven minute prerecorded address he called for "dialogue" to end Yemen's unrest and revealed he had undergone eight operations.

2.26pm: David Smith, the Guardian's man in Tripoli for the last few weeks, has been thrown out of Libya, after writing about dissent in the capital. He explains:

On Wednesday, I was ordered to pack my bags and leave the country because officials objected to an article in which I interviewed critics of Gaddafi. The government demanded that the Guardian publish an apology "to the Libyan people", which it had itself prepared. The paper refused.

Guardian journalist Xan Rice's spell in Tripoli ended similarly abruptly last month. Reporters from the Daily Telegraph, CNN and Reuters have also been expelled in recent days.

SUNDAY 10 JULY

4.52pm: This from Jack Shenker in Cairo:

The interim prime minister, Essam Sharaf, took to the airwaves late on Saturday pledging to "meet the people's demands", following mass rallies across the country in which Egyptians accused the ruling council of army generals of betraying the revolution that toppled Mubarak this year.

In a short and strained address to the nation, Sharaf said all police officers accused of killing protesters would be stopped from working, and promised that the trials of former Mubarak ministers and other regime officials would proceed "as soon as possible". Activists dismissed the announcement as empty rhetoric and claimed it contained nothing substantive.

MONDAY 11 JULY

9.31am: The US ambassador to Syria, Robert Ford, has condemned pro-regime protests outside the US embassy after his visit to Friday protests in Hama provoked anger from the regime. Writing on the embassy Facebook page, Ford said:

On July 9 a *mnhebak* [pro-Assad] group threw rocks at our embassy, causing some damage. They resorted to violence, unlike the people in Hama, who have stayed peaceful ... How ironic that the Syrian government lets an anti-US demonstration proceed freely while their security thugs beat down olive branch-carrying peaceful protesters elsewhere.

TUESDAY 12 JULY

8.31am: Last night, the US edged very close to calling for Assad to go. Hillary Clinton accused Syria of either allowing or inciting "mobs" to attack the French and US embassies to deflect attention from the violent crackdown against protesters. She said:

> President Assad is not indispensable and we have absolutely nothing invested in him remaining in power ... From our perspective, he has lost legitimacy, he has failed to deliver on the promises he's made, he has sought and accepted aid from the Iranians as to how to repress his own people, and there's a laundry list of actions that have been concerning.

WEDNESDAY 13 JULY

8.30am: Efforts to find a political solution to the Libyan crisis are intensifying as France, Britain and the US acknowledge that Nato military action alone is unlikely to force Gaddafi to step down. The UN and western countries are urging formal talks between the Benghazi-based rebels and the Gaddafi regime amid new signs that Tripoli might agree to discuss a transition of power.

8.57am: Egypt's elections could be delayed – a key demand of many opposition activists. Reuters reports:

> Parliamentary elections may not be held until November, about two months later than originally planned, an army source said on Wednesday. But the source said the registration of candidates would start in September, which he said meant the army was sticking to its commitment to start the handover of power to civilians then.

THURSDAY 14 JULY

8.47am: Libya says it plans to charge Nato secretary general Anders Fogh Rasmussen with war crimes. AFP quotes Libyan prosecutor general Mohamed Zekri Mahjubi as saying:

> As Nato secretary general, Rasmussen is responsible for the actions of this organisation which has attacked an unarmed people, killing 1,108

civilians and wounding 4,537 others in the bombardment of Tripoli and other cities and villages.

2.25pm: Turkey is drafting a "road map" for resolving the Libya crisis, which will be discussed by foreign ministers at tomorrow's contact group meeting in Istanbul. The German news site Deutsche Welle notes Turkey's shifting stance towards Libya:

> Ankara's plan aims to secure an immediate ceasefire and a deal between Tripoli and Benghazi that would include full access to humanitarian assistance and the Libyan military's withdrawal from major cities. But Turkey's policy zigzags in the last three months have called into question the successful outcome of Ankara's efforts.

FRIDAY 15 JULY

10.02am: Robert Ford plans to ignore Syrian government warnings against travelling to more protest hotspots. An embassy official told the Guardian that the US ambassador will continue to highlight the regime's brutal repression of the demonstrations, but would not be travelling to a protest today.

SUNDAY 17 JULY

9.47am: Egypt's prime minister, Essam Sharaf, is expected to announce a cabinet reshuffle today, following a fresh protest on Friday. He has accepted the resignation of his foreign minister Mohammed El-Orabi, Reuters reports.

3.13pm: Hundreds of thousands of protesters have taken to the streets of Yemen to demand the resignation of President Saleh on the 33rd anniversary of his rule. AP reports:

> Activist Nouh al-Wafi says demonstrators in the southern city of Taiz on Sunday carried black flags and placards that read "today is the fateful day." Similar protests also were taking place in several other major cities including Amran, Saada and al-Bayda.

MONDAY 18 JULY

10.22am: More than 30 people were killed in Homs over the weekend as a result of the first sectarian violence to be reported in Syria, a source with links to the city has told the Guardian.

The Syrian opposition has been keen to downplay any reports of tensions between majority Sunnis and the ruling Allawite minority. But the source said violence between the two groups resulted in at least 31 deaths, with the security forces failing to intervene.

TUESDAY 19 JULY

8.19am: The US and Libya have held their first face-to-face talks since the conflict in Libya began, but the two sides disagreed about what was discussed – and what happens next. The Libyan government spokesman, Moussa Ibrahim, described it as a first step, while a US official said it was a "one-time thing".

2.48pm: Al-Jazeera's Rula Amin tweets:

\# Eyewitnesses in Homs now say at least 13 people were killed today , situation remains very tense

\# just spoke to an eyewitness from Homs, he says shabiha and security sprayed at the funeral with a machine gun

WEDNESDAY 20 JULY

1.03pm: More than 50 rebels have been killed in six days of fighting with Libyan government forces over the strategic eastern oil town of Brega, AP reports:

The new toll comes after Mohammed Idris, a doctor at the Ajdabiya hospital where the casualties were taken, raised the number killed in Tuesday's fighting to 27, with 83 wounded. Idris said on Wednesday that most had been shot in the head and chest.

THURSDAY 21 JULY

12.42pm: Qatar has broken ranks in the Arab world when it comes to Syria, writes Ian Black:

> Qatar has lived up to its reputation for being a maverick in Middle Eastern politics by suspending the operations of its embassy in Damascus. The emir of the small but fabulously wealthy Gulf state has already gone far beyond the Arab consensus by supporting the Libyan rebels, sending cash and weapons to help them in their fight against Gaddafi ...
>
> Qatar was not reacting directly to Syrian repression but to attacks on its diplomatic mission in the leafy Damascus suburb of Ein Rummaneh. That was pelted with stones, eggs and tomatoes in protest at coverage of the unrest by Al-Jazeera TV – the satellite channel owned by Qatar, based in Doha and watched by millions of Arabs.

FRIDAY 22 JULY

9.21am: The Syrian opposition is so keen to play down reports of sectarian violence that it has named today's planned protests the Friday of National Unity, Lebanon's Daily Star repots.

3.09pm: Activists have claimed as many as 1.2 million Syrians are protesting in Deir Alzour and Hama, reports al-Aribya.

4.14pm: In his latest audio address, Gaddafi has ruled out talks with the rebels. "There will be no talks between me and them until Judgment Day," he said.

TUESDAY 26 JULY

8.18am: Amnesty International's website has been blocked in Saudi Arabia after it accused the kingdom of using anti-terrorism proposals to quash political dissent. The Saudi embassy in London described as "baseless" Amnesty's criticisms which can now be read in Arabic on a British-hosted Amnesty blog in an attempt to circumvent the Saudi censors.

11.16am: There was a marked increase in Nato airstrikes in the last 24 hours. In its latest update on the campaign Nato said there were 54 strike sorties on

Monday with 36 targets hit. Nato has insisted that the bombing campaign will continue during the Islamic holy month of Ramadan, which begins next Monday, if there is a threat to civilians.

WEDNESDAY 27 JULY

10.00am: Syrian opposition groups say targeted assassinations of protest leaders and mass arrests signal a tactic change by the Syrian state in attempts to stamp out dissent ahead of an anticipated escalation in nightly demonstrations during Ramadan, Lebanon's Daily Star reports.

Meanwhile Syrian activists are meeting in Turkey for what they claim is the first meeting of its kind since the uprising began, AFP reports. Bahiya Mardini, who heads the Cairo-based Arab Free Speech Committee, said the Istanbul meeting will focus on "developing the co-ordination between activists and working groups of the revolution".

3.44pm: Britain has expelled all eight remaining Libyan embassy staff in London to make way for representatives from the National Transitional Council as the "sole governmental authority" of the country.

FRIDAY 29 JULY

8.11am: The Libyan rebels' chief of army staff, Abdul Fatah Younis, has been killed after being called back from the the front for questioning about secret trips to Tripoli.

The circumstances of his death are unclear; the president of the NTC, Mustafa Abdul Jalil, suggested Younis, a former Libyan interior minister before his defection, had been killed by "pro-Gaddafi" forces. But there are many other theories about the murder.

8.20am: Islamists in Egypt, including the Muslim Brotherhood, have called for a "Million-strong Demonstration of Islamic Identity" today. According to the Egyptian daily al-Masry al-Youm groups distributed fliers denouncing "American funding of liberal parties" and rejected the postponement of parliamentary elections (it is thought that having elections more quickly would benefit the Muslim Brotherhood because it is the best organised political outfit). They stressed that Egypt is "a civil state based on Islamic principles and not an American secular state".

11.12am: Doug Saunders of Canada's Globe and Mail tweets:

\# The killing of Younis surprised nobody who's spent time among the
rebels. But also shows why Nato countries don't want to arm them.

12.56pm: Chris Stephen, in Misrata, writes that Libya's opposition has serious questions to answer about the death of its army chief of staff:

> The credibility of Libya's opposition regime, and perhaps of those
> governments like the UK who have supported it, will suffer a heavy blow
> unless a fuller explanation can be given for the death of rebel army
> commander Abdel Fatah Younis.
>
> Mustafa Abdul Jalil, president of the NTC, insisted that Younis was
> killed as he headed back from the frontline at Brega on Thursday to
> answer questions in the rebel capital, Benghazi. But Jalil – who took no
> questions and left quickly – was unable to say where they general was
> killed, or when, or even how assassins could kill a general known for travelling in a bullet-proof jeep in a heavily-armed convoy.

1.09pm: A quick guide to Friday protest nomenclature: in Syria it's the
"Friday of Your Silence is Killing Us"; in Egypt it's the "Friday of Unity and
the People's Will"; in Yemen it's the "Friday of Patience and Perseverance".

MONDAY 1 AUGUST

8.25am: Up to 100 people are believed to have been killed in Hama when
President Assad sent in tanks to crush protests in a brutal display of force yesterday. Armoured vehicles smashed through makeshift barricades and, although
the international media are banned from Syria, video clips apparently show
unarmed civilians taking cover from shelling and heavy machine gun fire.

10.22am: Last night Barack Obama spoke about the attack on Hama:

> The reports out of Hama are horrifying and demonstrate the true character of the Syrian regime … In the days ahead, the United States will
> continue to increase our pressure on the Syrian regime, and work with
> others around the world to isolate the Assad government and stand with
> the Syrian people.

1.09pm: At least four civilians have died in today's attack on Hama, Reuters reports. The killings were in the residential district of Hamidiyah, according to the agency, bringing to 84 the number of civilians reported killed since the crackdown began yesterday.

4.23pm: The Egyptian army has violently retaken Tahrir Square from protesters. Jack Shenker reports:

> Armed riot police and soldiers fired into the air as tanks moved in on Tahrir, where an occupation by demonstrators had been ongoing for over three weeks. Eyewitnesses reported swarms of security personnel storming the square from several directions, smashing tents and stalls before dragging away some protesters into military detention. Egypt's cabinet office said that "thugs" had been arrested.

WEDNESDAY 3 AUGUST

8.19am: It is a historic day in Egypt where Mubarak, who ruled Egypt with an iron fist for 30 years, goes on trial to face charges of corruption and unlawful killing.

An ambulance believed to be carrying Mubarak has arrived outside the court, where crowds are gathering to witness this momentous event.

9.03am: Hosni Mubarak's two sons, Gamal and Alaa, have arrived in the metal cage in the Egyptian courtroom, live television pictures show. A glimpse can be seen of the former dictator in a holding cell, lying on a stretcher.

9.26am: The appearance of Mubarak behind bars on a stretcher has not won any sympathy for him from participants in the Egyptian revolution which toppled him, judging by the reaction on Twitter.

\# **mosaaberizing** Even on a bed in a cage, Mubarak's eye seem to be filled with arrogance, hands resting on chin. Unbelievable.

\# **lilianwagdy** mubarak is obviously faking sorry you get zero sympathy from me dude

9.54am: Hosni Mubarak stands charged with corruption and the unlawful killing of protesters in the uprising against him earlier this year. He faces the death penalty if convicted. His sons Alaa and Gamal are charged with corruption, while Habib el-Adly, the former interior minister, is charged with murder and attempted murder in connection with the deaths of those killed during the uprising.

Six others described as senior police officers or former interior ministry officials are also charged with murder and attempted murder in connection with the uprising.

12.37pm: Events in the Cairo court today have been chaotic and even bizarre. One lawyer claimed it was not Mubarak in the dock, but a clone, the real president having died in 2004. He asked for a DNA test to be carried out. Mubarak's lawyer, Ferid el-Deeb, has asked for 1,631 witnesses to be called. Another lawyer requested compensation from Mubarak for damage to Egypt's security because "God said in the Qur'an that Egypt is a safe place". A lawyer from the Egyptian treasury asked for a billion Egyptian pounds in compensation from Mubarak. There were 30 lawyers in the courtroom and the judge was asked to admit another 130 waiting outside.

The trial has now been adjourned and it is unclear when it will restart.

1.03pm: Jack Shenker confirms from Cairo that Mubarak's trial has been adjourned and will continue on 15 August. Former interior minister Habib El-Adly's case will continue tomorrow.

4.36pm: In Syria, tanks are occupying the main central square in Hama in the fourth day of attacks on the city. There are reports that tanks are heavily shelling houses, security forces throwing bombs into residences, and there is heavy gunfire. The government has been accused of taking the opportunity of the distraction of the Mubarak trial to continue its attacks.

THURSDAY 4 AUGUST

8.58am: The United Nations security council has adopted a statement condemning attacks on civilians and widespread human rights abuses by the Syrian regime. In the statement, 14 of the 15 members of the security council expressed their "profound regret at the death of many hundreds of people" and called for an immediate end to all violence. Only Syria's neighbour Lebanon dissociated itself from the text.

12.05pm: The trial of Mubarak's former interior minister, Habib El-Adly, has been adjourned until 14 August.

3.53pm: Al-Jazeera's Rula Amin has been tweeting updates on Hama, based on conversations with eyewitnesses. Although communications are down in the Syrian city some people are managing to get information out using satellite phone.

\# Activist in Hama says snipers are taking positions on rooftops, almost dividing city into 4 sections, still no electricity

\# Activist in Hama says there was shelling between 4-5am, then from 12-2 pm. Security seems to be positioning itself for control

\# activists in Hama says all shops, banks, govt offices all shut down, no water in some neighborhoods and mobile & landlines down

4.38pm: Activist group Avaaz has issued a statement saying 109 people have been killed today in Hama, Syria, as the crackdown continues there, citing a "medical source". The bodies that have come to al-Hourani hospital were shot at close range and mostly in the head, Avaaz says.

Meanwhile, Amnesty International has given a scathing response to the UN security council statement condemning the Syrian government's violent crackdown on protesters, calling it "completely inadequate".

FRIDAY 5 AUGUST

4.50pm: Tanks have been attacking the besieged city of Hama for a sixth day, videos and reports from activists and residents show. Nevertheless protests against the regime have continued today. Ten people have been killed across Syria today as security forces fired on protesters in several cities, including Damascus, activists report.

MONDAY 8 AUGUST

1.34pm: Pressure is mounting on the Syrian government from its neighbours following over a week of bloody attacks on anti-government protesters in cities across the country. Kuwait has recalled its ambassador. Jordan's foreign minister called the violence "disturbing". The Arab League has said it is "alarmed" by what has happened. Most significantly, Saudi Arabia's King Abdullah recalled his ambassador, called the violence in Syria "not acceptable", and told Assad to stop the attacks and introduce meaningful reforms "before it's too late".

THURSDAY 11 AUGUST

12.44pm: The BBC's Matthew Price has been to Zlitan with the Libyan government, which claims 85 civilians were killed by an airstrike there (Nato says there were mercenaries and military casualties).

On Nato's response that the Libyan claims are uncorroborated, Price writes:

> Try telling that however to 15-year-old Salwa Jawoo. Her name was on some of the school books at the scene – I found her in Zliten hospital. Her face was scarred – she had a broken shoulder. She said she was sitting outside her home when the first missile struck. It was the second one that injured her. "There was no military camp. We were just living there. Why did they attack us?" she asked …
>
> We will likely never know precisely how many died at Majar or who they were. The front line is not far away. From the site plumes of white smoke can be seen rising from where the fighting is taking place. It would make sense that soldiers would need somewhere to rest in the area. Most of the bodies in the mortuary were men of fighting age.

FRIDAY 12 AUGUST

9.51am: Rania Abouzeid, a journalist from Time, entered Hama clandestinely and has penned a harrowing account of the restive Syrian city:

> Residents speak of being unable to reach bodies in the streets, of snipers targeting people in their homes, of house-to-house searches, mass indiscriminate detentions, looting and even rape. There are cars in the streets that have been shot up, several with bullet holes that pierced the windscreens on the driver's side, at head level. It's unclear how many people were killed, although residents speak of hundreds dead. In the coming days, there will be an accounting, as families slowly return and the numbers of missing, detained and dead are ascertained.

3.19pm: Syrian security forces have opened fire in cities across the country. The Local Co-ordination Committees says that 13 people have been killed, including five in Aleppo. It says there have also been deaths in Deir el-Zour, Hama, Homs, Idlib and the Damascus suburbs of Douma and Saqba.

MONDAY 15 AUGUST

7.40am: Syria has used gunboats for the first time to crush the uprising. At least 19 people were shot dead in the Syrian port city of Latakia on Sunday morning as the Assad regime's aggressive military campaign to quell protests during the holy month of Ramadan continued.

8.46am: There are reports of clashes between supporters and opponents of Mubarak outside the courtroom where the former president's trial is scheduled to resume today. And al-Jazeera Arabic's crew have reportedly been attacked by pro-Mubarak protesters.

12.04pm: Following unruly scenes in court, the judge has announced that Mubarak's case is to be adjourned until 5 September.

He also said there would be no more live television broadcasts of the proceedings for the sake of the public interest. There was applause from some sections of the court but evident discord from other people in the courtroom.

5.07pm: In Syria, the western port city of Latakia has come under attack from government forces for a third day. Many people have been trying to flee the city, with some reportedly being arrested as they did so. Around 30 people are estimated to have been killed in the city since Saturday, including at least two today. There are also reports a Palestinian refugee camp has been targeted by Syrian forces in Latakia.

THURSDAY 18 AUGUST

11.06am: Libyan rebels in Misrata are saying the Zawiyah oil refinery has been taken, according to reports. Martin Chulov gives this assessment of its strategic importance.

> Without petrol in the tanks of his military, Gaddafi can no longer launch
> ambitious offensives. Unless he can somehow secure some other supply

line (an unlikely prospect), his positions from now on will largely be defensive. The rebels now appear to have an upper hand for an assault on the capital where urban fighting likely awaits.

12.28pm: Luke Harding has arrived at the oil refinery in Zawiyah, where Libyan rebels are celebrating. He says:

> I am standing in it looking at the Mediterranean in front of me …There are a lot of excited rebels here. They took the refinery yesterday after a five-hour firefight. They said a couple of Gaddafi people were killed. A few others tried to flee by sea and they were then taken out by a Nato airstrike. I can't confirm that but what's absolutely clear is that this oil refinery, which is the largest in Libya and significant to the post-Gaddafi Libya future, is in rebel hands.

1.38pm: A series of attacks have been carried out in southern Israel, close to the border with Egypt's Sinai Peninsula. The number of people killed and injured is unclear but the Israeli ambulance service said six people have been killed. Defence minister Ehud Barak blamed a Palestinian faction from Gaza but also hit out at Egypt for the total loss of "security control" in the Sinai. A Hamas leader has denied responsibility for the attacks.

2.56pm: As was widely expected, Barack Obama has finally said Syrian President Assad must resign "for the sake of the Syrian people".

The Obama administration has also imposed fresh sanctions on Syria's government, freezing any of its assets in the United States as well as banning petroleum products of Syrian origin.

From Obama's statement:

> The future of Syria must be determined by its people, but President Assad is standing in their way. His calls for dialogue and reform have rung hollow while he is imprisoning, torturing, and slaughtering his own people. For the sake of the Syrian people, the time has come for President Assad to step aside.

3.00pm: The European Union has also urged Assad to resign as Syrian leader amid the crackdown, while the leaders of Britain, France and Germany have issued a statement that echoes the call for Assad to go, saying he "has lost all legitimacy and can no longer claim to lead the country".

FRIDAY 19 AUGUST

11.58am: More than 40 Syrian "revolution blocs" have forged a coalition to unite their efforts against the regime of Assad, according to a statement received Friday by AFP, the Daily Star (Lebanon) reports. It says 44 groups have signed up to join the Syrian Revolution General Commission, calling for "a democratic and civil state of institutions that grants freedom, equality, dignity and respect of human rights to all citizens".

1.01pm: Syrian security forces have reportedly opened fire on people protesting after Friday prayers. Al-Jazeera says six people have been killed in the southern city of Daraa, according to activists. One person was reported killed in a Damascus suburb and another in the central city of Homs.

SUNDAY 21 AUGUST

9.40am: In Libya, rebel forces have made a swift advance towards the capital, Tripoli. It is, the rebels claim with a dramatic flourish, "zero hour" for Gaddafi, according to various reports.

2.37pm: The Guardian's Luke Harding, who is just west of the Libyan capital, has called in.

> Having been at the front line it's clear to me, I think, the regime in Tripoli – it's a matter of days, or even hours, before it collapses. The rebels are advancing, they're more or less at the gates of Tripoli ... My sense is that Tripoli will fall in the next day or two, possibly as early as tomorrow.

7.58pm: In a lengthy interview on state TV, President Assad has warned there will be "repercussions" for any country interfering in Syria's affairs. He tells his interviewers the situation "may seem dangerous ... but in fact we are able to deal with it".

8.14pm: AP reports that hundreds of euphoric Libyan rebels have pushed to the western outskirts of Tripoli without meeting any resistance.

Associated Press reporters with the rebels said they reached the Tripoli suburb of Janzour around nightfall Sunday. They were greeted by civilians lining the streets and waving rebel flags. Hours earlier, the same rebel force of hundreds drove out elite forces led by Gaddafi's son Khamis in a brief gun battle.

The elated fighters danced and cheered, hauling off truckloads of weapons and advanced full speed toward the capital in pickup trucks.

10.54pm: Speaking from an unknown location, Gaddafi has called on Libyans to save Tripoli and says Libya is being destroyed, Sky News reports. In a rallying call made in an audio message played on state television, Gaddafi says:

Beautiful Tripoli, they will make it into a destroyed city. The imams of the mosques, you must leave now and march. Go out with your weapons. All of you. There should be no fear.

12.09am: The Libyan rebels have reached Green Square in the centre of Tripoli, Sky News reports.

1.04am: Libyan rebels say they will rename central Libya's Green Square as Martyrs' Square, its original name, al-Jazeera reports. Jubilant opponents of Gaddafi are shooting at a poster of him.

MONDAY 22 AUGUST

6.32am: Gaddafi forces are still fighting in Tripoli, and are estimated to now have control of 15–20% of the city, a rebel spokesman tells al-Jazeera. This comes as AFP reports the sounds of heavy gunfire near Gaddafi's compound in Tripoli.

7.31am: The international criminal court has confirmed that Gaddafi's son, Saif al-Islam, has been arrested. Gaddafi's eldest son Mohammed is also believed to be under house arrest. A rebel spokesman has promised they would guarantee Gaddafi's safety and said they wanted to see him stand trial in Libya and nowhere else.

8.17am: Luke Harding has called from Tripoli after coming under fire while entering the city.

There are clearly some people who are extremely unhappy about the rebels. They are either trying to defend their property, as they see it, or just stop the advance. There are pockets of resistance all over the place – this fight is not over.

12.04pm: The rebel flag is flying over Green Square, Luke Harding reports from Tripoli.

From where I'm standing I can see the rebel flag – the red, black and green tricolour – hanging over the Ottoman place in the centre of Green Square, as well as three giant yellow cranes which were supposed to lift a giant portrait of Gaddafi, but never did so.

This morning it has been pretty tense, but here at least it is fairly calm. I haven't been all over the city so it would be premature to say it is all over. But it seems to be isolated groups of regime loyalists who are fighting rather than a co-ordinated offensive or counter attack by Gaddafi's forces.

1.49pm: Mustafa Abdul Jalil, leader of Libya's National Transitional Council, is giving a press conference in Benghazi. He thanks the international community for supporting Libyans and preventing casualties, and pays tribute to the "heroic efforts" of fighters in Misrata and the western mountains. Speaking through a translator, Jalil says:

God has chosen that Gaddafi's end should be at the hands of these youth, so that they may join the Arab uprising. I declare that Gaddafi's rule is at an end ... I call on all Libyans to act with responsibility and not take justice into their own hands ... treating prisoners of war well and kindly ... We all have the right to live with dignity in this nation.

Jalil confirms that the rebels do not have control of all of Tripoli and the surrounding areas. He also says Gaddafi's sons Mohammed and Saif al-Islam are being detained by the rebels.

12.46pm: Gaddafi's son Saif al-Islam has not been detained by rebels as earlier suggested. Journalists report seeing him in Gaddafi's residential compound in Tripoli and outside the Rixos hotel.

TUESDAY 23 AUGUST

10.55am: The international criminal court now denies that it ever confirmed Saif al-Islam had been arrested.

A blog by the Libyan activists Feb 17 quotes spokesman Fadi el-Abdallah, telling the BBC:

> What we said yesterday is that we received information about the arrest of Saif al-Islam and we were trying to confirm that by contacting the NTC in Libya, but Saif al-Islam Gaddafi was not under the custody of the ICC.

11.19am: Repressive regimes don't all stick together – Bahrain has declared its recognition of Libya's NTC. The kingdom's state news agency says:

> In light of recent developments in Libya, the Kingdom of Bahrain reiterates its recognition of Libya's National Transitional Council as the sole legitimate representative of the brotherly Libyan people, wishes Libya to achieve prosperity, progress and stability, development and reconstruction.

4.35pm: The Associated Press is reporting that "hundreds of Libyan rebels" have stormed Gaddafi's main military compound in Tripoli. An AP reporter saw the rebels enter the gates of the Bab al-Aziziya after hours of fierce gun battles.

5.29pm: Sky and the BBC are showing pictures of rebels climbing on the statue of a hand crushing an American aeroplane inside Gaddafi's compound. Gaddafi spoke in front of the statue when the conflict began in February.

5.39pm: Luke Harding describes the rebel attack on Gaddafi's compound today:

> The bombardment was furious. Mortars, rockets, small arms fire, a dark, rolling, continuous symphony. The noise reverberated across the city, sometimes coloured by rebel cheering and hooting.

WEDNESDAY 24 AUGUST

11.14am: In an audio report, Luke Harding describes a visit to a hospital where dead and wounded have been taken.

> It is a pretty ghastly scene. On the left as you come in there is a room full of dead fighters, who have been shot – a terrible smell. The doctors weren't sure how many they brought in yesterday but it is dozens … The hospital is lacking all sorts of medical supplies.

12.23pm: Libyan rebels are advancing on Sirte, the last major stronghold of pro-Gaddafi forces, reports Chris Stephen from Misrata, with opposition columns now 35 miles west of the city.

> Sirte is Gaddafi's birthplace but to the symbolic value of capturing this city is added the urgency of overrunning bases from which Scud missiles are now being launched against Misrata.
>
> These Soviet-era rockets are the heaviest weapons so far deployed by pro-Gaddafi forces. At least four have been aimed at the city, the latest exploding amid a flash of orange in a thunderous detonation in the early hours of this morning, causing momentary panic among hundreds of people gathered to greet relatives freed from captivity in Tripoli.

THURSDAY 25 AUGUST

4.29pm: Moussa Ibrahim, Gaddafi's spokesman, has phoned AP to say that the Libyan leader is safely in hiding and leading the battle against the Libyan rebels.

Ibrahim said Gaddafi's morale was high. He "is indeed leading the battle for our freedom and independence". Ibrahim refused to say where in Libya Gaddafi was hiding. "All of the leader's family are fine," he said.

FRIDAY 26 AUGUST

8.19am: In its first Tripoli press conference the National Transitional Council has said its cabinet will be moving from Benghazi to the capital. Al-Jazeera quoted Ali Tarhouni, the NTC's finance minister, as saying: "I declare the beginning and assumption of the executive committee's work in Tripoli."

1.38pm: Rebel units are massing in Misrata for an attack on Sirte, writes Chris Stephen.

Tanks, heavy artillery and rocket launchers abandoned by fleeing government forces, are being assembled for the attack, and hurriedly painted black, a precaution against being hit in friendly fire incidents.

Rebels told the Guardian on Thursday that a British and French special forces team is helping co-ordinate the assault, in which Misratan units will push eastwards to link up with forces from Benghazi which are this morning fighting their way westwards.

SATURDAY 27 AUGUST

4.11pm: Libyan rebels are reported to have taken Bin Jawad, a town about 100 miles from Sirte. Sam Kiley, Sky's security editor, is reporting from close to the town that the rebels have broken through much quicker than anticipated, after using rockets salvos to clear pro-Gaddafi forces out.

MONDAY 29 AUGUST

8.55am: Abdelbaset al-Megrahi, the man convicted of the Lockerbie bombing, has been found barely alive in Libya by CNN. Its correspondent Nic Robertson said: "He appears to be a shell of the man that he was, far sicker than he appeared before … at death's door." The network showed footage of al-Megrahi being kept alive on oxygen and an intravenous drip at his home.

1.58pm: The first cracks in Libya's rebel coalition have opened, with protests erupting in Misrata against the reported decision of the NTC to appoint a former Gaddafi henchman as security boss of Tripoli. Protests started in the early hours today in Misrata's Martyrs' Square, with about 500 protesters shouting that the "blood of the martyrs" would be betrayed.

6.28pm: Algeria's state news agency has reported that members of Gaddafi's family have entered Algeria. The report cited the foreign ministry as saying the family entered the neighbouring country, but it did not immediately provide additional details or say whether Gaddafi himself was with the family.

TUESDAY 30 AUGUST

9.30am: Celebrations to mark the end of Ramadan in Syria have been marred by the shooting dead of at least seven people this morning, writes Nour Ali.

> Four people were shot dead in the southern province of Deraa and another in Homs following demonstrations which came out across the country after morning prayers, activists from the Local Co-ordination Committees say.

11.46am: Gaddafi loyalists in Sirte must surrender peacefully by Saturday or face an invasion of the town, the rebels have just announced. The deadline was given at a press conference in Benghazi, by Mustafa Abdul Jalil, head of the NTC. He said there will be a pause in the fighting during the Eid celebration, which begins tonight.

THURSDAY 1 SEPTEMBER

1.06pm: One of Muammar Gaddafi's sons, Saadi, has offered to surrender while another, Saif al-Islam, has vowed to fight to the death. The NTC has confirmed it has been negotiating with Saadi. Meanwhile Gaddafi's foreign minister, Abdel Ati al-Obeidi, has handed himself in and urged Gaddafi loyalists to surrender.

4.38pm: In a new audio message, Gaddafi has vowed not to surrender and urged his supporters to fight on. He predicted that Libya would descend into "hell" as "heavily armed" followers would fight on. In the message, aired by Syria's Arrai TV, he claimed Nato was weak and was trying to censor his messages. "We won't surrender again; we are not women; we will keep fighting," he said.

MONDAY 5 SEPTEMBER

9.34am: The trial of Egypt's deposed leader Hosni Mubarak has resumed in Cairo, amid reported scuffles. This is the third session of the trial and will not be televised, the Egyptian daily al-Masry al-Youm reports.

The paper's site describes violence outside the the court:

Supporters of the 83-year-old Mubarak and the families of protesters killed in the revolution have gathered outside the heavily fortified police academy where the courtroom has been set up. The two sides scuffled and hurled stones at each other. Eyewitnesses said at least four members of the martyrs' families were injured after police forces tried to prevent them from accessing the police academy without permits.

4.00pm: The British prime minister, David Cameron, has asked Sir Peter Gibson to examine allegation of British involvement in the rendition of terrorist suspects to Libya, as part of his inquiry into the treatment of detainees. In a statement to parliament the prime minister said new guidance had been issued to security service personnel on the treatment of detainees.

TUESDAY 6 SEPTEMBER

1.46pm: There are conflicting reports about the size and composition of a convoy of Gaddafi loyalists said to have arrived in Niger overnight. Reports vary from 50 vehicles plus an escort from Niger, to 250 military vehicles, to more than a dozen pick-ups, to just 10 vehicles. Niger's foreign minister, Mohamed Bazoum, has denied that Gaddafi or his family were part of the convoy.

THURSDAY 8 SEPTEMBER

8.55am: Syria's violence has escalated sharply, with up to 28 people reportedly killed across the country yesterday. Homs has been the focus of the latest crackdown after reports of army defections in the city.

5.47pm: Mahmoud Jibril, the chairman of the Libyan rebel NTC, has given his first press conference from Tripoli. He emphasised that the war was not over, told Libyans they had to stay unified, and said it was too soon for the "political game" to start. He repeated an earlier promise to serve only in an interim capacity and not to stand in future elections.

FRIDAY 9 SEPTEMBER

1.24pm: Thousands of protesters have returned to Cairo's Tahrir Square today, in a protest called "correcting the path" designed to put pressure on

Egypt's ruling military council to end military trials of civilians and set a time-frame to transfer power to a civilian government, among other demands.

5.36pm: Interpol has issued red notices for the arrest of Muammar Gaddafi, his son Saif al-Islam and his intelligence chief, Abdullah Al-Senussi, following a request by the international criminal court. This means they are now on the organisation's most-wanted list. Niger has pledged to arrest the three wanted by the ICC if they cross into its territory.

SATURDAY 10 SEPTEMBER

10.24am: Egypt's ruling council has declared a state of alert following last night's storming of the Israeli embassy in Cairo. Egyptian prime minister Essam Sharaf is holding a crisis cabinet meeting to deal with the diplomatic crisis and civil unrest – the biggest challenge to face the interim regime since the overthrow of Mubarak.

Three people died during the street clashes between the protesters and the police outside the embassy, and more than 1,000 people were hurt, according to the Egyptian health minister. A total of 19 protesters were arrested.

11.12am: Peter Beaumont says the attack on the Israeli embassy appears to have resulted from a coincidence of two protests.

> The regular Friday demonstration outside the embassy – which had seen a protective wall recently erected outside it – appears to have been joined by a hardcore of "ultra" football fans from the usually arch-rival Zamalek and Ahly teams who had been marching to protest clashes with police and Ahly fans that had occurred earlier in the week.
>
> The Israeli embassy has been the focus of weekly protests, largely led by young secular pro-Palestinian Egyptians who have cast the relationship with Israel as emblematic of the failings of both the old Mubarak regime and the military. Anger with Israel increased in August with Israel's killing of Egyptian soldiers during its pursuit of gunmen who attacked Israeli civilians and military close to the shared border.

12.48pm: Libya's NTC has confirmed the truce with Gaddafi loyalists is in effect over, paving the way for fresh assaults on the last remaining strongholds loyal to the former regime.

MONDAY 12 SEPTEMBER

10.00am: Saadi Gaddafi has crossed into Niger. He is the most high-profile former regime member to flee to the neighbouring country. Saadi, 37, entered the country in a convoy with nine other people, Niger justice minister Amadou Morou said. Adamou said Saadi "has no status at all" in Niger, indicating that he has not been granted refugee status, which guarantees certain rights.

TUESDAY 13 SEPTEMBER

2.37pm: Saadi Gaddafi has been speaking to CNN's Nic Robertson. He says Saadi told him he was on a "humanitarian mission" in Niger. He said thousands of his tribesmen left their homes and travelled to Niger because of their fear of the Libyan rebels.

He said he wanted to negotiate with the NTC now ruling Libya and make sure his tribesmen are allowed safely back into the south of Libya.

WEDNESDAY 14 SEPTEMBER

11.03am: There is a growing suspicion in Cairo that Egypt's security forces allowed the Israeli embassy to be stormed last week for political reasons, writes Jack Shenker.

> According to some eyewitnesses on the ground, the "storming" of the embassy was nothing of the sort – rather the security forces deliberately allowed the so-called mob to enter the building, suggesting the entire event may have been orchestrated for political ends. Activist and blogger Wael Eskander directly contradicts the army's account of events …
>
> "The protesters that night couldn't have taken on the army, but the army were peaceful and welcoming," he said. "All this was a play, and only the most ardent of fools in denial will see it as something else. There was no storm. Mubarakism is still alive."

THURSDAY 15 SEPTEMBER

8.27am: Rumours that David Cameron and Nicolas Sarkozy plan to visit Libya first starting circulating yesterday. Downing Street is refusing to

confirm the trip, but it is being reported by al-Jazeera and other organisations that both men are expected in Tripoli and Benghazi.

The French president is said to be revelling in his new nickname "Sarkozy
the Libyan" and will be hoping that trip will revive his flagging poll ratings
and France's tarnished image in the Arab world.

9.03am: Reuters has more on Cameron and Sarkozy's trip to Libya, which
it describes as their "victory lap".

> Both leaders are hugely popular on the streets of Libya, where "Merci
> Sarkozy" and "Thank you Britain" are common graffiti slogans. Both
> may hope to earn political dividends back home from what now appears
> to have been a successful bet.

10.24am: Any satisfaction that Cameron and Sarkozy will draw from today's
visit may be tempered with anxiety about when exactly this war will finish,
writes Chris Stephen in Misrata.

> It is nearly four weeks since rebel forces entered Tripoli, yet pro-Gaddafi
> forces are still holding out in the coastal stronghold of Sirte and in the
> towns of Bani Walid and Sabha.
>
> On 27 September, Nato's mandate, already extended by three
> months in June, is due to run out. A further three months' extension
> can be agreed by the alliance, but Cameron is likely to want to bring
> down the curtain on what has proved a controversial mission without
> wanting to seek a further extension.

4.00pm: The two leaders are now getting a hero's welcome in Benghazi. "It
is great to be here in a free Benghazi. People in Britain salute your courage
... you showed the world you can get rid of dictator," Cameron tells the
cheering crowd.

Cameron says Gaddafi wanted to hunt the rebels down like rats, but they
showed the courage of lions.

5.50pm: Nour Ali sends this analysis of the attempt by Syrian opposition
forces to form a unified front today:

Syria's opposition has struggled to coalesce, creating numerous group-ings and initiatives in various cities over the past six months. Today's announcement, made in Istanbul, of a national council has left many onlookers underwhelmed. It is hard to assess the importance of the opposition grouping until all 140 members, including 70 dissidents in Syria, most of whom have not been named, are known and the reaction of protesters and other members of the opposition becomes clear. But this is very unlikely to be the final word on a body to repre-sent the opposition.

FRIDAY 16 SEPTEMBER

1.40pm: Libyan fighters loyal to the new rulers have launched a concerted push to capture two of Gaddafi's three remaining strongholds. Heavy clashes have been reported in Sirte, where 11 anti-Gaddafi fighters were reportedly killed on Thursday, and in Bani Walid. Anti-Gaddafi forces have reportedly taken control of the airport in Sirte and the western part of the town. A commander told AP forces loyal to the new rulers are about a mile from the heart of Bani Walid.

2.05pm: The deposed Egyptian dicator, Hosni Mubarak, is reported to have denied ordering the shooting of protesters, in his first testimony since the start of his high-profile trial in August.

"I want to clarify that the president's work is regulated by the constitu-tion, and that he cannot order the shooting of demonstrators," he told the court, according to the Egyptian daily al-Masry al-Youm.

5.03pm: Turkey's prime minister Recep Tayyip Erdogan has attended Friday prayers in Tripoli's Martyrs' Square on a visit to Libya. He said Libya belongs to the Libyan people and "must never turn into an Iraq". He also made reference to Syria, saying those who inflict repression on people will not survive.

5.10pm: Up to 28 people have been killed in today's protest in Syria, on the six-month anniversary of the Syrian uprising, according to activists.

MONDAY 19 SEPTEMBER

8.17am: Yemeni forces reportedly opened fire with anti-aircraft guns and automatic weapons on tens of thousands of anti-government protesters in the capital city, Sana'a, yesterday. At least 26 people were killed and dozens were wounded, witnesses said, in the deadliest attack for months in protest against the regime of President Saleh.

12.53pm: The unfolding horror of what is happening in Sana'a continues to be conveyed on Twitter.

Journalist and human rights activist Josh Shahryar:

\# Number of dead bodies being brought to hospital on the rise. I can count some 13 now. All male, some of them young children.

\# I was questioning RPG [rocket-propelled grenade] use yesterday, but there is one protester in the morgue with half his chest missing, can't be bullets.

New York Times stringer Laura Kasinof:

\# An rpg struck one block from me at Rabat st. A second one hit a nearby building 30 min later. Next to protest

3.59pm: The official Saudi press agency has released a photograph of King Abdullah meeting President Saleh in Riyadh today. Saleh's burnt hands, following the the June attack on his palace, are clearly visibly. The press agency reveals little about what was discussed. It says the king expressed his support for "a unified safe and stable" Yemen.

4.55pm: An exodus is under way from the town of Sirte, birthplace of deposed dictator Muammar Gaddafi, where a humanitarian crisis is looming. Reuters reports that hundreds of families have today fled the town as NTC forces edge closer with rocket launchers and artillery guns.

5.54pm: The death toll from the fighting in Sana'a continues to rise. The latest report from Reuters says 28 people have died in clashes today, while 187 have been wounded.

TUESDAY 20 SEPTEMBER

4.24pm: Barack Obama has congratulated the people of Libya for ousting Gaddafi, and defended Nato's intervention as an example of what the international community can achieve.

Speaking at the United Nations the US president said:

> Make no mistake, credit for the liberation of Libya belongs to the people of Libya. It was Libyan men and women and children who took to the streets in peaceful protests, who faced down the tanks and endured the sniper's bullets. It was Libyan fighters, often out-gunned and outnumbered, who fought pitched battles town by town, block by block. It was Libyan activists in chatrooms and mosques who kept the revolution alive even after some of the world had given up hope. It was Libyan women and girls who hung flags and smuggled weapons to the front.

But he added that Nato's intervention showed what the international community could achieve when it was united.

> Our international coalition stopped the regime in its tracks and saved countless lives and gave the Libyan people the time and the space to prevail ... This is how the international community should work in the 21st century.

WEDNESDAY 21 SEPTEMBER

12.46pm: A fragile ceasefire in Sana'a appears to be breaking with numerous of reports of gunfire and explosions. A doctor told Tom Finn that five people had been killed in the latest clashes. The violence followed an estimated 100,000 people attending the funeral of 83 people killed in three days of violence in Sana'a. A 10-month-old baby boy who was shot in the head was the focus of the event.

THURSDAY 22 SEPTEMBER

10.57am: Four people have been killed in Yemen today, al-Arabiya reports. It says two women were shot dead by snipers in Change Square, the heart of the protest movement in Sana'a, while two men were killed in shelling on the square as battles raged between rival military units.

3.30pm: Tom Finn in Sana'a has had an interesting chat with the UN envoy in Yemen, and sends this:

> With violence still raging on the streets of Sana'a, diplomats have been working desperately behind the scenes to negotiate a political way out of the fighting. Jamal Bin Omar, the UN envoy to Yemen, flew in to Sana'a on Monday and has been meeting with various people to try and bring an end to the violence and find a way out of the political crisis.

FRIDAY 23 SEPTEMBER

8.55am: President Saleh has flown back to Yemen after months recovering from injuries sustained in a June attack on his compound. The dramatic move comes at the end of a week which has seen the worst bout of violence in the eight-month uprising. Tom Finn writes:

> The timing of Saleh's return was described to me by a Yemeni analyst who did not wish to be named as "a characteristic Saleh move". He told me that Saleh's aim is to "suddenly emerge in a time of crisis so as to appear a saviour and peace keeper". He also speculated that Saleh would probably resign "within days" in an effort to excuse his surprise return and calm the situation.
>
> Others believe it will have the opposite effect. Faizah Suleiman, a female protester leader from the coordinating council at Change Square, said she expected the president's return to coincide with an even more brutal crackdown. "If we're still alive we'll march this afternoon," she said.

12.40pm: AP reports that Yemen's President Saleh has called for a ceasefire, saying the only way out of the crisis is through negotiations. In a statement from his office, Saleh also urged political and military figures to adopt a truce.

4.55pm: Hakim al-Masmari, the publisher and editor in chief of the Yemen Post, has the following observations about the return of Saleh:

> The arrival of the presidential jet has sharply escalated the interminable problems that now blight Yemen at every point. The security forces are fracturing daily and resentment continues to grow on the country's

seething streets, where homes have an hour of electricity each day and food prices have risen around 400% in the past seven months.

Yemen is a ticking time bomb. And Saleh's return has just shortened the fuse.

MONDAY 26 SEPTEMBER

8.48am: Women in Saudi Arabia will be given the right to vote and to stand for election within four years, King Abdullah announced yesterday, in a cultural shift that appears to mark a new era in the rigidly conservative Islamic kingdom. The right to vote in council elections will not take effect until 2015, and women will still be banned from casting ballots in elections this Thursday. But the king invited women to take part in the next shura council, a governing body that supervises legislation.

12.36pm: Online activists Anonymous and RevoluSec claim to have hacked into Syrian government websites to highlight the brutality of the crackdown against protesters. In a post on Tumblr Anonymous claimed to have redirected official city websites to a graphic showing the number of people killed in the uprising. Al-Jazeera reported that activists had "replaced the official sites with caricatures of Syrian President Assad and a message saying, "Don't let Bashar monitor you online", along with tips on how to avoid detection by Syria's online intelligence – known as the Syrian electronic army.

TUESDAY 27 SEPTEMBER

1.00pm: A Libyan commander has claimed that NTC forces are now in control of the port in Gaddafi's hometown of Sirte. But there were mixed messages from the revolutionary forces, with another commander claiming that they could take Sirte "whenever we choose," but were holding back to protect civilians. There are mounting concerns about the plight of civilians in Sirte. Some say that Gaddafi loyalists are preventing them from leaving.

1.10pm: The British ambassador in Damascus, Simon Collis, has begun a blog. In his first post, "The truth is what big brother says it is", he writes that he decided to start the blog after Syria "passed a terrible milestone … six months of unrest and violent suppression of mostly peaceful protests". He adds:

This is a regime that remains determined to control every significant aspect of political life in Syria. It is used to power. And it will do anything to keep it.

4.17pm: Tens of thousands of people have attended a peaceful but noisy rally in Sana'a demanding that Saleh stand down. The rally was lined by hundreds of troops loyal to the renegade general Ali Mohsen.

THURSDAY 29 SEPTEMBER

4.00pm: Twenty medical staff in Bahrain have been sentenced to jail for up to 15 years, after being convicted of taking part in demonstrations. Activists say they were simply treating injured protesters. The authorities accused them of spreading stories to foment terror and possession of unlicensed weapons. The sentences were widely condemned. Amnesty described them as "ludicrous".

FRIDAY 30 SEPTEMBER

8.31am: A draft UN resolution on Syria may have to be watered down further to remove even the threat of sanctions, AP reports.

The Europeans insist that if Syria doesn't comply with demands, including an immediate halt to violence and respect for human rights, the council should consider sanctions. But Russia's UN ambassador Vitaly Churkin said Moscow is totally opposed to even mentioning the possibility of sanctions.

8.49am: Yemen's President Saleh continues to play for time insisting he won't stand down if his opponents are allowed to stand for elections. In an interview with the Washington Post, he said: "If we transfer power and they are there, this will mean that we have given in to to a coup." He also claimed troops loyal to the defected general Ali Mohsen were shooting protesters.

TUESDAY 4 OCTOBER

8.33am: Three relatives of Syria's new opposition leader, Burhan Ghalioun, have been arrested in his home city of Homs, according to activists. The campaign group Avaaz claims that Ghalioun's brother, nephew and niece were all arrested after he spoke of plans to overthrow the Assad regime at a meeting of the Syrian National Council in Turkey.

WEDNESDAY 5 OCTOBER

8.40am: Russia and China have vetoed an already watered down UN security council resolution that threatened action against the Assad regime if it did not immediately halt its military crackdown against civilians. It would have been the first legally binding resolution adopted by the security council since the Syrian military began using tanks and soldiers against protesters in mid-March.

The US ambassador to the UN, Susan Rice, expressed "outrage" at the vote and walked out of the chamber as the Syrian ambassador was speaking. She said: "The United States is outraged that this council has utterly failed to address an urgent moral challenge and a growing threat to regional peace and security."

1.07pm: There have been heavy clashes between revolutionary forces and pro-Gaddafi forces in the centre of Sirte, al-Arabiya reports. Fighters loyal to the interim government have been promising a "final assault" on the city. The National Transitional Council says it will declare Libya liberated after the fall of Gaddafi's birthplace.

4.17pm: Nato has offered to help the new Libyan government after the completion of its current mission. Speaking after a meeting of defence ministers, secretary general Anders Fogh Rasmussen said:

> We have fulfilled the mandate of the United Nations. And we are close to completing our mission. Tomorrow, when we meet with our partners in the operation, we will discuss the prospects for ending our mission.

THURSDAY 6 OCTOBER

12.55pm: Two mass graves, which could contain as many as 1,000 bodies, have been found in Tripoli according to forces loyal to the interim government. They follow the reported discovery of two other mass graves in the capital last week.

2.07pm: The UN's human rights office has raised its tally of people killed during seven months of unrest in Syria to more than 2,900. The figure represents an increase of at least 200 since the beginning of September. Rupert Colville, a spokesman for the UN high commissioner for human rights Navi Pillay, says the figure is based on "reliable sources" inside and outside the country.

FRIDAY 7 OCTOBER

10.24am: The Nobel peace prize has gone to three women including Tawakkul Karman, a leading anti-government activist in Yemen.

1.38pm: An estimated 2,000 Gaddafi loyalists are putting up fierce resistance in Sirte after being surrounded on all sides. Most of the city residents have fled but hundreds of civilians are still thought to be trapped in the city.

MONDAY 10 OCTOBER

8.40am: Last night, Cairo erupted ino the worst violence since the 18-day uprising that ousted Mubarak as president of Egypt in February. At least 24 people were killed and more than 200 injured in the centre of Cairo after a demonstration over an attack on a Coptic Christian church was reportedly met by gunfire.

Egyptian troops are among the dead following the violence, which comes after several outbreaks of sectarian tensions this year.

10.02am: The horror of the violence in Cairo was captured on Twitter by people watching the events unfold before them. Here is a sample of Tweets, in no particular order:

\# **RawyaRageh** Sheer and utter chaos in downtown Cairo. Crew attacked, tapes smashed, ppl running in every direction

\# **mosaaberizing** Just saw a group of half naked "civilians" beat and drag an old protester then hand him to the army.

\# **Sarahcarr** Just awful scenes in the hospital. Women screaming men crying. A protester said "the army ran us over like we are animals"

11.05am: The Guardian's Jack Shenker is in Cairo. From his report:

> Coptic Christians make up approximately 10% of the Egyptian popula-
> tion, and some have been fearful that Egypt's ongoing political turmoil
> could allow ultra-conservative Islamists to flex their muscles and inspire
> a crackdown on social minorities. There has also been criticism of the
> army for being too lenient on previous attacks against Christians, with
> many witnesses accusing soldiers of being actively complicit in last night's
> bloodshed.
>
> Egyptian troops are among the dead following the violence, which
> comes after several outbreaks of sectarian tensions this year.

1.25pm: The official death toll from Sunday's violence stands at 25, with
272 injured, according to Egypt's health ministry. There has been fresh
violence in Cairo today, with several hundred Christians pelting police with
rocks outside the Coptic hospital where many of the Christian casualties of
Sunday's violence were taken.

5.21pm: The latest violence in Egypt is "a shocking reminder of the potential for deterioration" in the country, writes the Guardian's Ian Black:

> It is hard to imagine a worse blow than the killing of Coptic protesters
> by members of the security forces, but all too easy to gauge the bitter
> disappointment as the great hopes of Tahrir Square fade.
>
> Far beyond Egypt, the Cairo bloodletting also highlights the uneven
> progress of the wider Arab Spring … Initial euphoria about an unstop-
> pable domino effect that would topple one Arab autocracy after another
> has given way to a more nuanced view that looks at specific local factors
> over a longer period, including the capacity of the old regimes to fight
> back and hold on.

TUESDAY 11 OCTOBER

1.55pm: Egypt's deputy prime minster and finance minister, Hazem
al-Beblawy, has resigned, al-Jazeera television is reporting. Al-Jazeera correspondent Rawya Rageh says he has quit over the violence on Sunday. Beblawy
was appointed by the ruling military council after popular protests in July.

WEDNESDAY 12 OCTOBER

1.34pm: The battle for Sirte appears to be reaching its final stages with resistance from Gaddafi loyalists crumbling, according to troops loyal to the interim government and observers. Fighting has become focused on a fort-like high rise building in district two. One commander of the revolutionary forces claimed that they were in control of 80% of the ousted dictator's hometown.

1.50pm: In Egypt, military rulers have washed their hands of responsibility for the violence at Sunday's demonstration by Coptic Christians in Cairo. At a press conference they claimed their troops were attacked by Christians at the protest. Amnesty International has called for an independent investigation into Sunday's events to "urgently explain how a protest against religious discrimination turned into a bloodbath".

Hazem al-Beblawy, who yesterday submitted his resignation over the violence at the march, says it has been refused by the military rulers. Al-Masry al-Youm reports that Beblawy "said he will continue to consider the issue and has not yet made a final decision regarding the military council's refusal".

2.44pm: Syria's state news agency Sana is claiming one million people have rallied in the capital Damascus in support of the Assad regime.

MONDAY 17 OCTOBER

10.52am: Troops loyal to the Yemeni president have been engaged in heavy fighting against forces opposed to Saleh across much of the capital, Sana'a, this morning, with AP reporting rockets, mortars and heavy machine guns being used. Six people were shot dead last night when plain-clothes government loyalists launched a sniper attack on a rally in Sana'a calling for Saleh's resignation.

TUESDAY 18 OCTOBER

1.08pm: Israeli soldier Gilad Shalit has been freed five years after being seized by Hamas gunmen, in a deal that involves the release of 1,027 Palestinians. A gaunt Shalit told Egyptian TV that he missed his family and hoped the deal would promote peace between Israel and the Palestinians.

WEDNESDAY 19 OCTOBER

8.45am: During a visit to Tripoli yesterday, Hillary Clinton admitted that the US would like to see Muammar Gaddafi killed. "We hope he can be captured or killed soon so that you don't have to fear him any longer," Clinton told students and others at a town hall-style gathering in the capital city.

2.38pm: The opposition Syrian National Council has been invited to take over the Syrian embassy in Tripoli, according to Council member and head of foreign relations Radwan Ziadeh.

Speaking to the Turkish website Zaman, he said:

The Libyan Transitional Council recognised the SNC, and they closed the embassy of the Assad regime in Libya. They are willing to give us responsibility for the embassy ... We have gotten recognition from different political parties in Egypt and Tunisia. In addition, we have high-level channels with some of the Arab countries, [for example] Saudi Arabia and Qatar.

3.32pm: "Your revolution has been stolen," a defiant Yemeni president has said in a TV address as he again refused to step down.

Reporting from Sana'a, Tom Finn said Saleh was trying to portray the uprising as hijacked by his rival and former general Ali Mohsen.

[Saleh] looked pretty much at ease. He said that people calling on him to step down were not just calling for one man to leave power, but also his four million supporters who voted for him in the elections in 2006. It doesn't look like he is anywhere near to stepping down or signing anything.

After four days of violence left more 35 people dead in Sana'a, the streets have been calmer today, Tom reports.

THURSDAY 20 OCTOBER

10.16am: Sirte has fallen, according to wire reports. From AP:

Libyan fighters have overrun the last positions of Gaddafi loyalists holding out in the city of Sirte and the revolutionaries now have all of the ousted leader's hometown within their hands.

Reporters on the scene say the final push to capture the remaining pro-Gadhafi positions began around 8am on Thursday and was over after about 90 minutes.

Reuters has quotes from commanders:

"Sirte has been liberated. There are no Gaddafi forces any more," said Colonel Yunus Al Abdali, head of operations in the eastern half of the city. "We are now chasing his fighters who are trying to run away."

Another front line commander confirmed the capture of the Mediterranean coastal city, which was the last remaining significant bastion of pro-Gaddafi fighters almost three months after the ex-leader was overthrown by rebels.

12.07pm: The Misrata Military Council is reporting that Gaddafi himself has been arrested. In an email, it said:

Now in contact with our correspondent at the front of the Sirte. The tyrant Muammar Gaddafi was arrested. God is great and thank God.

12.15pm: Mahmoud Shammam, the NTC's information minister, has just been on al-Jazeera, and alluded to the capture of Gaddafi but refused to confirm it. He said:

I think we can say that Sirte is liberated … I think the celebrations are going on right now. Also there's big talk about some big fish on their way to Misrata. I cannot confirm anything but people over there are talking they caught a big fish.

Asked what would happen if Gaddafi had been captured, Shammam said, "We are going to put him in front of the court, we're not going to hang him in the street … I think every Libyan wants to see Gaddafi stand trial."

12.53pm: Al-Jazeera is now reporting that Gaddafi was killed in Sirte. Reuters is saying that Gaddafi died of his wounds.

1.20pm: Guma el-Gamaty, the former NTC coordinator in the UK, is telling Sky News Gaddafi and his close aides tried to escape and freedom fighters tried to capture them. There was an exchange of fire and reports claim he was killed or injured, Gamaty says.

2.57pm: Sky News is showing video of Gaddafi's body being dragged through the streets of Sirte. It is very graphic.

3.22pm: AP is saying that the Libyan prime minister, Mahmoud Jibril, has confirmed Gaddafi is dead.

4.43pm: Nato commanders are recommending the Libya air campaign should now be brought to an end, according to the Guardian's Julian Borger. The formal decision will be taken tomorrow, but he has just received this comment from a Nato official.

> A military assessment of the current situation in Libya and a recommendation for the wrapping up of the Nato operation is on its way to Nato HQ. This will most likely prompt a special meeting of the North Atlantic Council tomorrow to consider the recommendation and decide on the future of the current mission.

6.02pm: The National Transitional Council says the former leader died on the way to hospital in Sirte; AP reports that a doctor who was part of the medical team accompanying Gaddafi to hospital has said he died from two bullet wounds to the head and chest.

The AP story also has more detail about Gaddafi's final moments.

> Footage aired on Al-Jazeera television showed Gaddafi was captured wounded but alive in Sirte. The goateed, balding Gaddafi, in a blood-soaked shirt and his face bloodied, is seen standing upright being pushed along by fighters, and he appears to struggle against them, stumbling and shouting. The fighters push him on to the hood of a pickup truck, before dragging him away, apparently toward an ambulance.
>
> Later footage showed fighters rolling Gadhafi's body over on the pavement, stripped to the waist and his head bloody.

7.08pm: President Obama has been speaking in Washington. He said:

> Today we can definitively say that the Gaddafi regime has come to an end. One of the world's longest serving dictators is no more ... The

Libyan people now have a great responsibility to build an inclusive, tolerant and democratic Libya.

9.26pm: Here are some voices from the streets of Tripoli, filed by Andrei Netto for the Guardian. Hussan Imbess, 28, chemical engineer:

Even the fact that he was in his hometown fighting doesn't make him a hero or a martyr. He was not fighting, he was in a hole. He could be a hero for some Libyans, but he's certainly not mine.

Mohamed Shawsh, 26, accountant:

We have never had this feeling before. That's freedom. You don't feel the freedom until the day you can say what you think and not be afraid of the consequences ... But this is just the end of the phase one. Our goal is not to kill Muammar Gaddafi. Our goal is to build a free country. Hopefully we are all united today. We have the same blood, the same languages and the same country to build in the future.

FRIDAY 21 OCTOBER

12.06pm: Anti-government protesters in Syria have been celebrating the death of Gaddafi and warning Assad that he will be next. In the town of Taftanaz in northern Syria protesters waved flags of the Libyan interim government.

12.39pm: Officials in Tripoli accept that the confusing circumstances of Gaddafi's death will have be investigated, Ian Black reports from the Libyan capital.

There is an awareness that this issue will have to be looked into. The circumstances of his death are, at the very least, confusing and ambiguous. I think we will see the rebel government sounding co-operative about this. But there are very few people who will be shedding a tear about the circumstances of his demise. We will have to be aware of that difference between international expectations and the mood here ...

What's going to happen now is that Mustafa Abdul Jalil is going to make that declaration [of liberation] tomorrow in Benghazi. That is causing some annoyance. There is political unease around the issue of the declaration coming from Libya's second city rather than Tripoli, the formal capital. There's a sense that it is time for the revolution to move to the capital.

1.42pm: It remains unclear exactly how Gaddafi died. Nato says it bombed a convoy near Sirte yesterday, unaware that Gaddafi was a part of it. This seems to have led to Gaddafi and others escaping into a drainage pipe. After this, the picture becomes unclear. Mahmoud Jibril, Libya's prime minister, said Gaddafi was taken out of the pipe, shot in his right arm "when we started moving him", and put in a truck, which moved away, at which point he was "caught in crossfire between the revolutionaries and Gaddafi forces" and shot in the head. He died before reaching hospital, Jibril said.

If Jibril's version is true, it is unclear at what point Gaddafi, still alive, was manhandled on to the bonnet of a car, and paraded around by a crowd of fighters, apparently in Sirte, before his body was rolled around in the street, and then paraded on a car through Misrata, as mobile phone video footage shows. A doctor who examined Gaddafi's body said he was killed by a bullet to his intestines, and was also shot in the head.

Gaddafi's burial has been delayed while the circumstances of his death are examined.

5.15pm: Al-Jazeera is leading its news bulletin with a claim that Gaddafi was captured unharmed. Reporter Tony Birtley said that according to sources and human rights groups the ousted dictator was then placed on a car and driven through the streets but fell off and was injured. He said Gaddafi was then kicked and punched.

SUNDAY 23 OCTOBER

7.32am: Nine months after they took to the streets en masse and forced their president on to a plane to Saudi Arabia, Tunisians vote today in the first free election in their history and the first to have come from the tumult of the Arab Spring.

Across the country of the Jasmine revolution, millions are expected to cast their vote to elect an assembly which will then have the powers to draw up a constitution and appoint a new transitional government. It is, as the electoral commission this morning declared, *le jour-J* – D-Day.

12.22pm: The Guardian's Angelique Chrisafis has been out and about in Ettadhamen, a poor suburb of Tunis where hundreds were queuing to vote along "dusty, litter-strewn streets". A selection of her latest Tweets:

\# Teacher in ettadhamen: "9 months ago you cdn't even talk about politics in the street for fear of secret police. So proud to vote"

\# Cleaning lady in ettadhamen: "before, every election here was fixed. Let's hope we can trust the politicians of tomorrow"

\# Student in ettadhamen: "i'm so excited to be voting to change tunisia's future. I'm nearly 20, I'd like at least some hope of a job"

MONDAY 24 OCTOBER

12.10pm: The US state department says America has withdrawn Robert Ford, its ambassador to Syria, because of "credible threats against his personal safety". According to AP, spokesman Mark Toner could not say when Ford would return, saying it depended on a US "assessment of Syrian regime-led incitement and the security situation on the ground".

1.42pm: Libya's transitional leader has ordered an investigation into the death of Gaddafi after the US and other international powers pressed for the probe.

Mustafa Abdul Jalil has said that the NTC formed a committee to investigate the killing on Thursday, amid conflicting reports of how the dictator who ruled Libya for four decades died.

TUESDAY 25 OCTOBER

9.06am: Some details are emerging about the burial of Gaddafi, his son Mutassim and a senior official. AP has this:

A Misrata military council official says Muammar Gaddafi, his son Mutassim and a top aide have been buried in a secret location, with a few relatives and officials in attendance.

In a text message spokesman Ibrahim Beitalmal is quoted as saying the burial took place at 5am today, and that Islamic prayers were read over the bodies.

4.01pm: The Yemeni government has signed a ceasefire with a dissident general to try to end weeks of violence, Reuters is reporting. Explosions and gunfire could still be heard in the north of the capital, Sana'a, however.

The deal between the governemnt of Ali Abdullah Saleh and General Ali Mohsen was due to come into effect today at 3pm local time.

THURSDAY 27 OCTOBER

12.21pm: Amid reports of an increase in violence in the country, the Syrian opposition is naming tomorrow's protest "the Friday of the no-fly zone". They are calling for the same protection that was offered to Gaddafi's opponents in Libya.

3.37pm: The 15-nation UN security council has unanimously approved a resolution terminating the UN mandate, which set the no-fly zone over Libya and permitted foreign military forces, including Nato, to use "all necessary measures" to protect Libyan civilians.

The resolution said the UN authorisation for foreign military operations in Libya will lapse at 11.59pm local Libyan time on 31 October.

FRIDAY 28 OCTOBER

10.21am: The moderate Islamist party An-Nahda, has been declared as the victor in Tunisia's first free elections, taking 90 of 217 seats in an assembly that will write a new constitution.

1.00pm: The chief prosecutor of the international criminal court has told the Associated Press he is in indirect contact with Muammar Gaddafi's son Saif al-Islam about the possibility of surrendering for trial.

Luis Moreno-Ocampo said talks are being held through intermediaries whom he did not identify. He also said he did not know exactly where Islam is.

2.59pm: The death toll in Syria today seems to be rapidly escalating. Reuters says at least 20 have been killed, probably more, citing activists and residents, as people demonstrate for a no-fly zone.

"God, Syria, We want a no-fly zone," shouted protesters in the Bab Tadmur neighbourhood of Homs.

In Hama, activists and one resident said Assad loyalists fired at a demonstration demanding his overthrow as soon at it broke out from Abdelrahman Bin Aouf mosque.

"They attacked the protest immediately because the mosque is near the old Hamiuidya neighborhood and they did not want the two protests to meet," said one activist, who did not want to give his name for fear of persecution.

MONDAY 31 OCTOBER

11.13am: The "No to military trials" movement in Egypt is calling on all Egyptians to stop co-operating with any military tribunals, in the wake of the detention of blogger Abd El Fattah for such a refusal. It said:

At least 12,000 Egyptian civilians have been subjected to summary, covert military trials. The accused are often denied counsel, the opportunity to review evidence or examine witnesses; there are limited avenues of appeal. Eighteen death sentences have been handed down so far.

Abd El Fattah's targeting is only the latest example of the systematic targeting of journalists, media figures, bloggers and activists by Scaf.

4.57pm: The Nato secretary general, Anders Fogh Rasmussen, has ruled out the possibility of a no-fly zone for Syria. Asked at a press conference in Tripoli if there was a possibility Nato would now spearhead a no-fly zone in Syria he responded: "It's totally ruled out. We have no intention whatsoever to intervene in Syria."

TUESDAY 1 NOVEMBER

8.32am: Libya's interim leadership has chosen an electronics engineer from Tripoli as the country's new prime minister. Abdurrahim el-Keib was chosen yesterday by 51 members of the NTC and will appoint a cabinet in the coming days. Keeb's appointment helps correct the Benghazi bias of the interim government, according to the New York Times. He has spent most of his career abroad, it notes, but "for the purposes of Libyan politics Keeb is considered a resident of the western city of Tripoli, the capital, offering regional balance to the interim president, Mustafa Abdul Jalil, who is from the east."

9.50am: How many civilians lost their lives in the Nato airstrikes, asks the BBC's Jonathan Beale.

Estimates of those killed – including pro-Gaddafi forces, "rebel" forces and civilians – currently vary between 2,000 and 30,000, Beale writes.

As the Guardian's Data blog has noted, the UN's new body in Libya, Unsmil, has not been able to find any verifiable figures for the number of civilian dead.

12.47pm: The Assad regime has ignored an Arab League proposal for ending the violent crackdown in Syria. As many as 13 people were killed yesterday as security forces fired at protesters across the country, according to Syrian Observatory for Human Rights.

4.46pm: Syrian state television is reporting that a final agreement has been reached between the authorities and an Arab League committee charged with finding a solution to the unrest, according to Reuters. It says an official announcement will be made tomorrow at the Arab League headquarters in Cairo. The chief of the League, Nabil al-Arabi, has told AFP that a road map revealed on Monday urged Assad's regime to remove tanks from the streets and for talks to take place between the regime and its opponents.

WEDNESDAY 2 NOVEMBER

10.31am: Details about the Arab League's Syria plan continue to dribble out, ahead of a meeting in Cairo. But there is confusion about whether Damascus has agreed to the plan as the regime's news agency claims.

From an AP report filed in Cairo:

Arab League diplomats say the organisation is about to unveil a plan to ease violence in Syria that calls for the withdrawal of tanks and armored vehicles from the streets and free elections.

Syria's state-run media said late Tuesday that Damascus has agreed to an Arab League plan, but a senior Arab League official said they had not yet received any response from Syria.

Arab diplomats involved in the process said the proposal also calls for release of all political prisoners and a new constitution as well as free presidential and parliamentary elections. They spoke on condition of anonymity because the proposal is not yet public.

1.40pm: Activists in Syria say the security forces have killed 13 people in Homs. The Local Co-ordination Committees are describing the killings as the Hawleh massacre, after the district in Homs where the killings took place. Bound and gagged victims of this apparent execution, whose bodies were filmed today near Homs, were killed by plain-clothed security forces in an revenge attack, local sources have told Amnesty International.

6.24pm: Syria has reportedly accepted an Arab League road map aimed at ending the bloody crackdown. The proposal calls for the regime to withdraw armoured vehicles from the streets, stop violence against protesters, release all political prisoners and begin a dialogue with the opposition within two weeks. Syria also agreed to allow journalists, rights groups and Arab League representatives to monitor the situation in the country.

THURSDAY 3 NOVEMBER

9.56am: So much for tanks being withdrawn from Syria's streets. Video footage has already emerged showing tanks shelling residential areas in Homs, the centre of the Syrian uprising. Activists who circulated the footage said it was filmed today.

10.43am: Lebanon's Daily Star has a useful summary of the main points of the Arab League road map.

1. Complete halt to the violence, whatever its origin, to protect Syrian civilians.
2. Release of people detained as a result of the recent events.
3. Withdrawal of every type of military presence from towns and residential districts.
4. Allow concerned organisations from the Arab League, Arab and international media to move freely throughout Syria and find out the reality of the situation.

2.52pm: As many as 72 people were reported to have been killed in the central city of Homs within the last 24 hours according to the semi-official Syria News website.

It quotes a doctor giving the figure. One source said 27 bodies were found in a food truck near a cemetery in the city.

FRIDAY 4 NOVEMBER

8.34am: Syrian opposition groups have called on protesters to take to the streets in large numbers to test the sincerity of the regime's commitment to an Arab League agreement to end its violent crackdown on dissent.

"We were hoping the violence might stop after the authorities agreed to the initiative, but the scene is still unbearable," Mohammed Saleh, a resident of Homs, told the New York Times. "The bloodshed hasn't stopped, and the army and security forces haven't left the streets."

Meanwhile, the head of the Free Syrian Army, Colonel Riad Assad, said he wants his force to be recognised as the military wing of the opposition Syrian National Council. "We are waiting for them to appoint a high delegation and send a representative to speak to us about how we can support their aims militarily," he told the Daily Telegraph.

11.08am: A Syrian activist claims to be live tweeting directly from a demonstration in the central city of Hama.

Here's a selection of his updates within the last hour.

\#   This is the first time security forces use nail bombs.

\#   My mother says I should not go to protest today, I said to her: how many times can one person die?

\#   She said: we just want to celebrate victory like Egyptians, I said: then we must sacrifice.

\#   intensive gunfire directly at us

\#   My house is one street away but I can't get there.

4.21pm: The Syrian Observatory for Human Rights says there have been 19 civilian deaths reported across the country today. Homs again emerges the worst hit with at least six people reported to have been killed.

TUESDAY 8 NOVEMBER

10.49am: Another grim milestone for Syria: nearly eight months into the uprising against Assad's regime, at least 3,500 people have been killed, according to the UN.

In mid-October, a senior UN official said the Syrian death toll had risen above 3,000. That would mean around 500 people have been killed in the country in the past three-and-a-half weeks.

THURSDAY 10 NOVEMBER

4.29pm: Syrian security forces have today killed at least 21 people across the country, according to an AP report citing activists and the Syrian Observatory for Human Rights.

> In some of the attacks, security forces opened fire as they conducted raids in search of dissidents in areas including the suburbs of the capital, Damascus, Deir Ezour, Hama and Homs, which has emerged as the epicenter of the uprising.
>
> An eight-year-old girl was among the victims in Homs, said Rami Abdul-Rahman, head of the British-based Syrian Observatory for Human Rights.

6.29pm: Pressure is mounting on the Arab League to take a much tougher line with Syria ahead of an emergency meeting on Saturday. The opposition Syrian National Council said the League should expel Syria. Amnesty said it should refer Syria to the international criminal court after reports that more than 100 people have been killed within a week of the government agreeing to an Arab League deal to end the violence.

FRIDAY 11 NOVEMBER

3.56pm: Protesters in over 20 major cities worldwide are preparing to take action against Egypt's military junta tomorrow, as part of a global day of solidarity to "defend the Egyptian revolution", writes Jack Shenker.

> Rallies and marches have been scheduled across four continents following an appeal from Cairo-based activists who accuse army generals of launching a systematic crackdown on human rights in a bid to crush

meaningful political change in the aftermath of this year's anti-regime uprising, which toppled Mubarak and left a Supreme Council of the Armed Forces in his place.

Saturday's protests come as a new video is released purporting to show further evidence of military involvement in the violence which erupted at a Coptic rally in October, leaving at least 27 people dead. The clashes took place against a backdrop of multiple human rights abuses by the authorities which have driven a wedge between army generals and revolutionaries.

5.15pm: In Yemen, at least 11 people have been killed in heavy fighting in the central city of Taiz, a day after a UN envoy began a new mission to push President Saleh to quit under a Gulf peace plan.

SUNDAY 13 NOVEMBER

9.32am: The Assad regime has reacted with fury to the Arab League's surprise decision to suspend Syria over its refusal to end the violent assaults against dissent. Pro-Assad supporters in Damascus stormed the embassies of Saudi Arabia and Qatar in protest at the Arab League's decision. Saudi Arabia strongly condemned the attack on its embassy and said it held Syria responsible.

The Syrian government has accused the Arab League of acting under orders of the United States and said that the suspension violates the League's charter. In a defiant press conference Syria's representative to the League, Yousef Ahmad, claimed that the army had left the streets, that pro-regime protests outnumbered anti-government protests and that there had been no more than around 300 deserters from the army.

Writing on his blog al-Bab, Brian Whitaker considers the likely consequences of the League's action.

First, it makes a mockery of Assad's claims that the uprising is some kind of American/Zionist plot against his regime. He may well try to make out that the Arab League has been nobbled by Americans and Zionists too but, even for the Assad loyalists, that would surely be stretching credulity too far …

Perhaps most important of all, the League's decision implies that Arab states no longer expect Assad to survive. Theoretically, he could be rehabilitated in the unlikely event that he complies with the "peace plan" but, for all practical purposes, 18 of the league's 22 members have now burnt their boats and are beginning to prepare for the post-Assad era.

4.22pm: Activists claim 23 people have been killed by the security forces in Syria today. More than half of the deaths occurred in the central city of Hama where crowds were seen fleeing gunfire and snipers were filmed from a rooftop in the city.

MONDAY 14 NOVEMBER

10.57am: Syria has accused Arab states of plotting against it after the Arab League's decision to suspend Damascus. Speaking this morning, foreign minister Walid al-Moallem said the move was an "illegal" decision prompted by US "incitement". The suspension – due to take place on Wednesday – was "an extremely dangerous step", added al-Moallem, as he expressed trust in Russia and China to stick by their supportive stance at the UN, thus ruling out a UN-mandated military intervention.

2.53pm: Three weeks after it held its first free elections, Tunisia finally has confirmed results. The final figures confirm a victory for the moderate Islamist An-Nahda party, whose leader returned to the country of the Jasmine revolution after years in exile and which won 89 of the 217 seats available in the new constituent assembly.

3.12pm: An Egyptian judge has overturned a decision which barred members of Mubarak's former ruling party from standing in the upcoming elections.

TUESDAY 15 NOVEMBER

8.37am: Jordan's King Abdullah has become the first Arab leader to call for Syria's president to step down. In carefully crafted remarks to the BBC he said:

> If I were in his shoes, I'd step down. If Bashar considers the interest of his country, he would step down, but he would also create an ability to reach out and start a new phase of Syrian political life.

Estimates of the death toll in Syria yesterday have dramatically increased, with more than 70 people, mostly soldiers, now thought to have been killed, AFP reports. The Britain-based Syrian Observatory for Human Rights said 27 civilians were shot dead by security forces while 34 soldiers and 12 suspected army deserters were killed in clashes.

1.10pm: Syria is trying to head off suspension from the Arab League which is due to begin tomorrow. It is scrabbling to find the mandatory 15 of the 22 states onside to convene a meeting of League ambassadors in an attempt to stall, or overturn, the suspension.

WEDNESDAY 16 NOVEMBER

8.26am: Syrian army defectors say they have launched several attacks on President Assad's military bases near Damascus, including one on an intelligence facility. Meanwhile, Syria has announced the release of 1,180 political prisoners as part of its commitments to the initial Arab League deal agreed almost two weeks ago.

11.03am: Syria has promised that there will be no more attacks on foreign embassies after a spate of incidents involving pro-regime supporters at missions of countries perceived as hostile to the Assad government, including Jordan, Qatar, Saudi Arabia and Turkey, according to the Jordanian foreign ministry.

1.05pm: The Free Syrian army has launched several attacks on President Assad's military and intelligence bases near the capital. An eyewitness described seeing "huge explosions". The Free Syrian Army said in a statement the target was a compound run by the air force intelligence in the Damascus suburb of Harasta.

2.03pm: Today's attacks by the Free Syrian Army have targeted a feared symbol of the Assad regime's repression, writes Guardian Middle East editor Ian Black.

> Syria's air force intelligence directorate is a central part of the Assad regime's repressive apparatus – less concerned with aviation matters than keeping tabs on the opposition. The rocket and machine gun attack on

one of its facilities at Harasta on the Damascus-Aleppo highway looks like the most audacious and precisely-targeted attack yet by Assad's enemies.

It symbolic significance will not be lost on ordinary Syrian citizens. This feared directorate owes its ostensibly anomalous role to the fact that the president's father and predecessor, Hafez, was commander of the air force before coming to power in 1968 …

AFI personnel have often been seen in action against protesters and are reported to have fired live ammunition to disperse demonstrators in Damascus in April, killing 43.

3.40pm: The French foreign minister, Alain Juppe, says he is recalling the ambassador to Syria because of the violence in the country. He told parliament:

There has been renewed violence in Syria, which has led me to close our consular offices in Aleppo and in Latakia as well as our cultural institutes and to recall our ambassador to Paris.

THURSDAY 17 NOVEMBER

8.35am: Interpretations vary on exactly what the Arab League has agreed about Syria. The New York Times reports this morning that the League has given Syria three more days to end the crackdown in a surprise reprieve during its meeting in the Moroccan capital Rabat.

The League's turnabout raised questions about whether an organisation long derided in the region as ineffectual, even a joke, could take on a more vigorous role in a tumultuous time. Expelling Syria would have offered the most vivid illustration of the country's growing isolation, as European and American sanctions accumulate, countries withdraw ambassadors from Damascus and its former interlocutors become sharp critics.

But AP says Syria's suspension from the League has been confirmed. The protocol did not specifically say if Syria's suspension from the organisation has remained in force, but an official from the Moroccan foreign ministry confirmed that is the case, it said.

5.52pm: A march of Coptic Christians to mark the end of 40 days of mourning after a demonstration ended with 27 dead – mainly Copts – has come under attack in Cairo. Some reports blamed the assault, in which stones and Molotov cocktails were hurled, on Islamists. The ministry of health reported 29 injured protesters. One is reportedly in intensive care.

FRIDAY 18 NOVEMBER

8.31am: The family of jailed Egyptian activist and blogger Alaa Abd El Fattah have called for his supporters to gather in Tahrir Square today to mark his birthday and call for an end to military trials. Abdel Fattah, one of almost 12,000 people detained by the military since the start of the revolution, is in high spirits, according to his mother. "All this solidarity goes to your head," she says. "The only thing he feels really bad about is missing the birth of his son."

The protest is being dubbed the "Friday of the One Demand" in reference to opposition to a draft constitution granting unfettered power to the army.

8.50am: Germany, France, the UK and four Arab countries have tabled a new UN resolution calling for an end to human rights violations in Syria, the BBC reports. With the UN Security Council divided on Syria, the resolution has been tabled in a committee of the general assembly.

Syria has refused to respond to a warning by the Arab League to halt the bloodshed within three days or face economic sanctions. Activists claim 26 people died yesterday including four soldiers. Burhan Ghalioun, the exiled head of the opposition Syrian National Council, said the regime was responsible for sectarian killings but he also urged supporters to halt attacks, warning that they offered "a big service to the regime".

10.53am: Breaking news on AP: A Syrian official says Damascus has agreed "in principle" to allow an Arab League observer mission into the country. The official said that Syria was still studying the details and asked not to be named because the issue is so sensitive.

1.27pm: Tens of thousands of people have taken part in protests across Syria, according to video footage from activists. Today's demonstrations have been dubbed "the Friday of departing ambassadors" in reference to a call by activists for foreign countries to withdraw their representatives.

1.46pm: The Arab League has turned down last-minute amendments by Damascus on a deal to allow observers to enter Syria, unnamed diplomats have told Lebanon's Daily Star.

MONDAY 21 NOVEMBER

9.15am: Thousands of protesters have remained in Tahrir Square overnight and clashed with riot police. Violent exchanges were reported over the weekend as Cairo plunged into some of the worst violence seen since the anti-Mubarak revolution, with at least 11 people killed and hundreds injured. The protests spread beyond the capital, with large demonstrations against the Supreme Council of Armed Forces (Scaf) seen in several towns throughout the Nile Delta and southern Egypt.

The violence has thrown plans for upcoming parliamentary elections into doubt.

Resistance to the ruling junta has been building for many months, but exploded into the open after Scaf attempted to push through a piece of legislation that would have shielded the military from political scrutiny for decades, writes Jack Shenker:

> By yesterday morning, following 24 hours of fierce street fighting and the conquest of Tahrir by revolutionaries, the furniture of the anti-Mubarak uprising was once again wheeled into place in the capital.

9.28am: In Libya, Saif al-Islam and Abdullah al-Senussi have been arrested. It remains unclear whether or not the people who captured Gaddafi's son and his former intelligence chief will hand them over to the authorities in Tripoli. The prosecutor of the international criminal court, which has charged the men with war crimes, is expected to visit Tripoli today.

10.01am: Jack Shenker has filed from Cairo:

> Clashes are currently concentrated on the south-west corner of the square, where a heavily-fortified line of security forces has been holding steady for a full 48 hours now, pumping endless volleys of teargas and other ammunition from their stronghold in Mohamed Mahmoud street, which is a block away from the interior ministry.
>
> Earlier in the night an uneasy agreement was reached between some protesters and the authorities which would allow the anti-junta crowds to remain in the square in return for attacks on its fringes coming to an end. But that ceasefire collapsed within the last hour and violence has resumed. The health ministry has confirmed that the death toll from the

unrest has now reached at least 22, while more than 1,700 are believed to be injured.

5.23pm: Thirty-three people are reported to have been killed in Egyptian violence over the past three days according to morgue officials. The ministry of health said more than 1,500 have been injured in the latest clashes in and around Tahrir Square – the worst bout of violence in Egypt since the revolution that ousted Mubarak. Witnesses said protesters had been hit by rubber bullets and suffocated with aggressive teargas. Video has been circulating of police apparently beating protesters.

7.00pm: The Egyptian cabinet has tendered its resignation to the ruling military council. There is some confusion as to whether the resignation has been accepted by Scaf.

The cabinet said they will run the nation's day-to-day affairs until elections are held at the end of November. Plans for the elections have been thrown into chaos, however, with several political parties and individual candidates saying they will suspend their campaigns. Protesters are demanding that the military quickly announce a date for the handover of power to a civilian government.

9.42pm: From Reuters:

> As midnight approached, about 20,000 people packed Tahrir Square, the epicentre of the anti-Mubarak revolt early this year, and thousands more milled around in surrounding streets.
>
> "The people want the fall of the marshal," they chanted, referring to Field Marshal Mohamed Hussein Tantawi, Mubarak's defence minister for two decades and head of the army council.

TUESDAY 22 NOVEMBER

9.02am: In Egypt, activists have called for protesters to descend on the streets en masse today for a "million man" march aimed at easing the grip of military rule. An estimated 20,000 people flocked to Tahrir Square last night after the government offered to resign despite bloody clashes with riot police that have left at least 33 dead. It is still unclear whether or not the Scaf authorities have accepted the resignation.

The interim military rulers are guilty of abuses which in some cases have been worse than those committed under Mubarak, according to a new report by Amnesty International. Criticising the Scaf authorities for failing "to live up to their promises" on human rights, the organisation denounced the use of military courts for civilians and crackdowns on peaceful protest. The report was written before the latest violence.

11.12am: Turkey's prime minister has called on Assad to step down as Syria's president. In a strongly worded warning, Recep Tayyip Erdogan compared the Syrian leader's position to that of Adolf Hitler in the dying days of Nazi Germany. "For the welfare of your own people and the region, just leave that seat," he said. The appeal comes after Abdullah Gul, the Turkish president, told the Guardian that Ankara no longer trusted the Damascus regime.

2.18pm: The trickle of developments that collectively suggest Scaf's days could be numbered is rapidly becoming a torrent, says the Guardian's Cairo correspondent Jack Shenker.

> The latest is a statement made by 245 leading Egyptian diplomats, calling on the ruling generals to "stop systematic assaults by security on protesters" and demanding civilian power be restored by mid-2012 at the latest (under the military council's current plan, it would remain in control well into 2013).

7.06pm: Field Marshal Hussein Tantawi has said the armed forces are prepared to hold a referendum on immediately transferring power to a civilian authority if people demand it. AP reports:

> Tantawi also told the nation in a televised address that presidential elections will be held before 30 June, but did not specifically mention a date for the transfer of power.
>
> In his brief address, Tantawi sought to cast the military as the nation's foremost patriots and angrily denounced what he called attempts to taint its reputation.

7.41pm: Martin Chulov writes from Tahrir Square:

> People are settling in for what seems to be a long haul. Tantawi's speech was poorly received. Vague pledges, opaque timelines for change and

general torpor are the very reasons that Egyptians now find themselves back where it all began.

Teargas is still being fired with abandon in parts of the square. It's hard to imagine anywhere else on earth has been gassed more this year than this over-run roundabout in the centre of Cairo.

WEDNESDAY 23 NOVEMBER

8.28am: Yemen's President Saleh has flown to Saudi Arabia to finally sign a deal to transfer power in return for immunity from prosecution. Opposition politicians are expected to join him there later today. Saleh has backed down from signing the Gulf Co-operation Council initiative on three occasions.

9.43am: Thousands of anti-government demonstrators have marched in the Yemeni capital to express disgust at the immunity deal for Saleh, Tom Finn reports from Sana'a.

> Hundreds of people have been killed and thousands wounded [so] the idea that Saleh and his sons can get off the hook is impossible for [protesters] to accept. One man said to me, "if you cut off the head of a plant, it doesn't take long for the plant to grow back," suggesting there hasn't been the widespread changes that people have been calling for.

10.24am: Egyptian police have clashed with anti-government protesters for a fifth night, AP reports.

> Elnadeem Center, an Egyptian rights group known for its careful research of victims of police violence, said late Tuesday that the number of protesters killed in clashes nationwide since Saturday is 38, nine more than the health ministry's death toll. The clashes also have left at least 2,000 protesters wounded, mostly from gas inhalation or injuries caused by rubber bullets fired by the army and the police. The police deny using live ammunition.

1.22pm: Several political parties are reportedly discussing the possibility of calling for next week's elections to be postponed due to the violence. Ahram Online said they were keen for voters in Cairo and Alexandria – and other protest hotspots – to not go to the polls until next year. The Muslim

Brotherhood is opposed to such a move, insisting the first round of the parliamentary elections must go ahead later this month.

1.53pm: A report by the Bahrain Independent Commission of Inquiry into human rights abuses during the Pearl revolution has just been published. From Reuters:

> Bahrain's security forces used excessive force to suppress protests earlier this year, an inquiry commission said, and urged a review of sentences handed down by authorities against those it held responsible for the turmoil.
>
> The panel, led by Egyptian-American international law expert Cherif Bassiouni, was formed and funded by Bahrain's government five months ago to investigate any crimes committed during the worst unrest seen in the island kingdom since sectarian-tinged political violence shook Bahrain in the mid-1990s.
>
> Confessions were extracted under duress and detainees were tortured, Bassiouni said in a speech delivered at the palace of Bahrain's King Hamad, adding that 35 were killed, including five security personnel.

4.11pm: With King Abdullah of Saudi Arabia sitting alongside him, Saleh has signed on the dotted line of the GCC-backed deal to usher him from office. The president is currently speaking, blaming "Zionists" for some of the violence that has beset the country in recent months and saying it will take years for Yemen to recover from the crisis. He is acknowledging the lives lost during the uprising.

4.22pm: The deal that Saleh has signed means he will immediately transfer his powers to the vice president and that he will be given immunity from prosecution, writes Tom Finn in Sana'a.

> The deal, first drawn up by the gulf monarchies back in April, sees Saleh retain the honorary title of president while his deputy, Abd-Rabbu Mansour Hadi, forms and presides over a government of national unity until early presidential elections in February. In return for signing, Saleh and his family are guaranteed immunity from prosecution.
>
> But the deal, which will see many of Saleh's relatives retaining government and military positions, is unlikely to appease the thousands

of youthful protesters who remain camped out in city squares across the country demanding Saleh's prosecution. As news of Saleh's departure for Riyadh spread, a spontaneous march broke out in Sana'a.

5.34pm: There is no sign of clashes in Cairo dying down. Martin Chulov reports on Twitter:

\# More injured in Tahrir now than at any other time today. Teargas hanging like heavy mist. Triage centres over-run

\# Saw 2 girls violently convulsing for 20 min after gassed near Tahrir. Drs said reaction psychic. Looked much more than that

THURSDAY 24 NOVEMBER

8.41am: Egyptian security forces are believed to be using a powerful incapacitating gas against civilian protesters in Tahrir Square following multiple cases of unconsciousness and epileptic-like convulsions among those exposed. The Guardian has collected video footage as well as witness accounts from doctors and victims who have offered strong evidence that at least two other crowd control gases have been used on demonstrators in addition to CS gas.

11.23am: The writer Mona Eltahwy, who has been released after being detained for 12 hours at the interior ministry, has claimed, in a series of tweets, that she was beaten and sexually assaulted by the central security forces (CSF).

\# 5 or 6 surrounded me, groped and prodded my breasts, grabbed my genital area and I lost count how many hands tried to get into my trousers.

\# Besides beating me, the dogs of CSF subjected me to the worst sexual assault ever

\# Another hour later I was free with apology from military intelligence for what CSF did. Took pics of my bruises and recorded statement

Eltahwy also said she was blindfolded for two hours and posted a picture of her swollen hand.

12.51pm: Scaf leaders have said in a press conference that elections will start as scheduled on Monday despite the widespread protests and calls for a postponement. Earlier the interior ministry said it could no longer secure the elections but the Supreme Council said the army would help with the security. It said the elections were the best way to help the country at present and they would go ahead no matter what. The military rulers said they hoped to appoint a new government before the elections.

3.15pm: Syria has been given until tomorrow to sign a protocol allowing in observers. It has been invited to sign the protocol in Cairo. If it does not sign, it could face sanctions.

9.33pm: Sky are reporting that former prime minister Kamal al-Ganzouri has been asked to form a new cabinet by the military junta.

> Previously prime minister from 1996 to 1999 under ousted former president Hosni Mubarak, Ganzouri agreed to lead a so-called national salvation government after meeting the head of the ruling army council, Field Marshal Mohamed Hussein Tantawi.
>
> His administration will replace the military-appointed cabinet of Essam Sharaf, which resigned en masse on Sunday amid widespread criticism over its perceived subservience to the ruling generals.

9.58pm: Egypt's Social Democratic party have withdrawn from Monday's planned election, according to Ahram Online.

A statement from the party criticised the behaviour of the military council for monopolising power and called for a national salvation government to supervise elections, naming Mohamed ElBaradei as somebody they would like to see involved.

FRIDAY 25 NOVEMBER

8.33am: Crowds are gathering in Cairo's Tahrir Square, for what is expected to be a massive protest against the military government. The protest, which has been dubbed the "Friday of the last chance" comes after the Supreme Council of the Armed Forces refused to postpone elections scheduled for Monday. "There is a general feeling to call off the elections completely," said Nasser Abdul Mohsena, an opponent of the junta who has been demonstrating in the capital.

The White House has called on the military council to transfer power to a civilian government as soon as possible.

11.40am: Presidential hopeful Mohamed ElBaradei was surrounded by supporters when he turned up in Tahrir Square to take part in Friday prayers, John Dokomos reports from Cairo.

> ElBaradei was totally surrounded by supporters going crazy for him. He was mobbed, he had handlers trying to protect him. People were telling us that he's the "symbol of the revolution" ... People were very ecstatic to see him.

1.36pm: Syria has missed a deadline set by the Arab League for it to allow in international observers or face a vote on sanctions. Syria did not respond to the Arab League but Reuters reported that the deadline had been extended until the end of the day. Meanwhile, the Local Co-ordination committees say 18 people have been killed so far in Syria today, including two children.

1.44pm: Two uniformed army officers have appeared on a balcony over-looking Tahrir Square and joined the crowds in chants of "The people want the downfall of the field marshall", Jack Shenker reports from Cairo.

> It adds to a sense that, although we are yet to hear from senior officers, the mid-ranking officers do seem to be getting more and more scepti-cal of the rule of the military council. There is huge excitement in the crowd. They [the officers] are actually conducting some of the anti-Scaf chanting.

5.05pm: Mohammed Bassendoua has been nominated to form the new government in Yemen, according to al-Arabiya citing opposition sources. He will be the country's new prime minister.

There has been heavy fighting today in Sana'a between security forces and an army unit that joined the popular uprising against Saleh, according to Yemeni officials. The troops fired machine guns and mortars, some of which landed on civilian homes and scarred the facades of buildings.

SATURDAY 26 NOVEMBER

3.45pm: A moderate Islamist party has claimed victory in Morocco's parliamentary elections. The interior ministry confirmed that the Justice and Development party is on track to form the next government. Turnout was low amid calls by pro-democracy campaigners for a boycott.

4.36pm: Reuters is reporting that 10 people have been killed in clashes between rival Muslim factions in north Yemen today. Shia Muslim rebels shelled positions held by Sunni Islamist Salafi fighters after the collapse of a week-old ceasefire, a Salafi spokesman said.

SUNDAY 27 NOVEMBER

11.11am: The head of Egypt's Supreme Council of the Armed Forces has said that elections will go ahead tomorrow, notwithstanding violently repressed protests this week in which 42 people have died. Hussein Tantawi called on voters to turn out at the polls tomorrow and said that there would be "extremely grave consequences" if the current crisis were not overcome.

MONDAY 28 NOVEMBER

8.43am: Early turnout is reported to be high as Egypt goes to the polls despite continuing protests.

Martin Chulov tweets from Cairo:

> It's chaotic & confused. But under way. Flyers near polling booths (a no-no). Crowds & optimism growing @ Egypt's 1st free vote

The Muslim Brotherhood is poised to make sweeping gains solidifying the conservative Islamic movement as a powerhouse in post-revolution Egypt and an emerging force in a volatile region.

It's too late to boycott the elections as some activists have urged, writes the prominent blogger Zeinobia on Egyptian Chronicles.

> Activist are calling the people to boycott the elections in order not to give Scaf a legitimacy, the problem is that even if we boycott the elections, it will claim to have legitimacy in one way or another … Boycotting elections need a campaign, a long one, not just [a] week.

9.09am: Egyptians have flocked to the polling stations in their millions amid a string of logistical problems, Jack Shenker reports from Cairo.

> We are already getting a lot of reports of [voting] violations. In Alexandria there have been a number of cases of people spying pre-marked ballot papers before the polls had even opened …
>
> Logistically the system is creaking and it's struggling to cope with the numbers. People know that, which is why they are turning up early to vote and it is why they are having to queue for so long. But it doesn't seem to have put people off … they seem incredibly optimistic and excited.

4.05pm: A report for the UN's Human Rights Council has accused Syria of committing "gross violations of human rights" during its crackdown against protests. It found that 256 children had been killed by government forces.

4.19pm: Egyptian polling stations have been ordered to open for two more hours to cope with a higher than expected turnout. Despite the chaotic scenes at some polling stations, the first day of voting has passed off better than many expected after concerns about a lack of preparation and widespread calls to postpone the ballot.

TUESDAY 29 NOVEMBER

8.43am: On the opening day of the election Egyptians came out to vote in record numbers, defying widespread predictions of violence and chaos. Arabist blogger Issandr El Amrani says Egypt has a come a long way since last year's disastrous elections under Mubarak when there was widespread vote buying and police collusion. "So far what we have seen, despite being an election that was tremendously badly prepared, is going OK," he says.

2.05pm: Egypt's military rulers are reportedly importing a shipment of 21 tonnes of teargas from the US, following eight days of street clashes in which countless gas cannisters were launched at civilians.

WEDNESDAY 30 NOVEMBER

8.23am: The Muslim Brotherhood's Freedom and Justice party candidates are in the lead in most of the counts in the election so far, according to local press reports. The Brotherhood said the high turnout in the election indicated that Egyptian's wanted a parliamentary system of government.

11.37am: Turkey has imposed sanctions on Syria. Outlining the measures foreign minister Ahmet Davutoglu said Syria "has squandered the last chance that it was given". A summary, from Reuters:

> Strategic cooperation between the Turkish and Syrian governments has been suspended until a "legitimate government which is at peace with its people is in charge in Syria". All relations with Syria's central bank to be frozen. All bank assets of the Syrian government in Turkey to be frozen. Delivery of weapons and military supplies to Syria will be blocked. All financial credit dealings with Syria to be stopped.

Mahir Zeynalov, news editor of Turkey's Zaman news site, tweets:

It took nine months and 4,000 lives for Turkey to finally announce mild sanctions on Syria.

1.32pm: The Egyptian election results are to be delayed until Thursday, a day later than planned, state TV has reported. An official at the electoral commission told Reuters votes were still being counted.

THURSDAY 1 DECEMBER

8.20am: Amnesty International has accused Saudi Arabia of launching a wave of repression and attempts to criminalise dissent to prevent Arab uprisings spreading to the kingdom. Interim Middle East and North Africa director Philip Luther said:

> Peaceful protesters and supporters of political reform in the country have been targeted for arrest in an attempt to stamp out the kinds of call for reform that have echoed across the region.

8.41am: Egyptian activist and blogger Nelly Ali confesses her sense of betraying the revolution after voting in the elections. She writes:

> I ended up standing in this queue for five hours and 45 minutes. I ended up voting for a party I knew not much about and a candidate to represent

me only because he had gone through as many ideological changes in his political life as I have religions. In total there were three ticks. I walked out knowing I had ticked for a party, a member of parliament and a representative of the workers. In my dreams that night I had a tick beside betrayal, a tick beside allowing the villains to get away and a tick beside handing over part of the revolution to the enemy …

I do not know if by voting I was celebrating democracy or dancing on the graves of those whose blood and tears fell on the ground nourishing freedom on the land on which they fell.

11.06am: The renegade Free Syrian Army has agreed to change tactics by ending its attacks on the regular army following a meeting with the opposition Syrian National Council, the Turkish daily Hurriyet reports.

Both parties have decided that the Free Syrian Army will "not organise any assault" against the Syrian regime any more, and will resort to "armed resistance" only for "defensive reasons".

"The leader of the Free Syrian Army, Col Riad al-Asaad, has agreed that the movement in Syria will stay as civilian. [The army] will be responsible for protecting civilians during protests," SNC Executive Committee member Ahmed Ramadan, one of the attendees at the secret meeting, said.

5.51pm: The announcement of Egypt's election results, already 24 hours late, has been delayed further. The Egyptian electoral commission blamed the delay on the high number of votes cast. State TV said they would be released on Friday. Scaf said they would now be revealed on Friday or Saturday.

FRIDAY 2 DECEMBER

9.21am: The big surprise in the first round of the Egyptian election is the success of the Salifist party al-Nour, according to Shadi Hamid, Islamist expert from the Brookings Institute. Speaking to Bloggingheads TV he said some predictions indicated al-Nour could get as much as 20% of the vote. "Elections are not about popularity, they are about organisation, strategy and manpower and on those three counts no one does it better than the Islamists," he said.

Al-Nour is expected to come second in the poll behind the Muslim Brotherhood.

10.07am: Navi Pillay, the UN's high commissioner for human rights, has called for Syria to be referred to the international criminal court over its brutal crackdown. Speaking in Geneva at today's emergency meeting on the Syria crisis, Pillay said:

> In light of the manifest failure of the Syrian authorities to protect their citizens, the international community needs to take urgent and effective measures to protect the Syrian people.

AP adds:

> A draft resolution backed by African, European, Asian, Arab and American members of the 47-nation rights council calls for the establishment of a special investigator on Syria, but leaves open the issue of whether the more powerful security council should refer the country to the ICC.

4.12pm: The Muslim Brotherhood has spent a lot of time this week trying to reassure people that its Freedom and Justice party is not going to impose orthodox Islam on the citizens of Egypt, assuming that it is going to be the biggest winner in the elections.

Part of its case has been its insistence that it is not interested in forming a coalition with the Salafist al-Nour party. But now the ultra-conservative al-Nour party is attempting some reassurance of its own.

Spokesman Mohamed Nour told AFP that Christians have nothing to fear:

> We are talking about a state that was under Islamic law for 1,300 years. Touching one hair on a Copt's [Coptic Christian's] head violates our programme. The results in these elections are the best response [to such fears], despite a campaign of fear-mongering and slander in the past 10 months. A large part of the public trusts us.

6.38pm: We still await any conclusive results from voting in Egypt, but AP has this:

Egypt's election commission announced few results, but said turnout was 62%, the highest in the country's modern history.

Leaked preliminary counts indicated that the Muslim Brotherhood's political arm took the largest share of votes. Following closely behind was the ultra-conservative Islamist Nour party and a liberal coalition, according to unofficial counts.

As votes were being counted in nine provinces, accounting for about 30% of the 498 seats in parliament's lower house, anti-military protests continued in Cairo. Two more rounds, ending in January, will cover Egypt's other 18 provinces.

MONDAY 5 DECEMBER

8.50am: Syria says it is still negotiating with the Arab League over the bloc's request to send observers into the country, despite missing the latest deadline to respond. On Saturday, the League gave the Assad regime until Sunday to sign up to the League's proposal in order to prevent the sanctions taking effect.

9.16am: Hamas is preparing to abandon its political headquarters in Damascus in a bid to distance itself from the current Syrian regime, according to Haaretz. But Iran, one of the few remaining supporters of Assad, is threatening to cut the Palestinian group's funds if it does so, reports the Israeli daily.

> The Iranian pressure also included an unprecedented ultimatum – namely, an explicit threat to stop supplying Hamas with arms and suspend the training of its military activists ...
>
> Haaretz has learned that Hamas has made a decision to abandon Damascus without letting the Syrian authorities know. The decision was made by the organisation's senior leadership in the wake of the harsh criticism voiced against top Hamas officials in Gaza and abroad because of their ties with the Syrian regime.

10.22am: An online campaign has been launched to free Razan Ghazzawi, the US-born Syria blogger who was arrested on Sunday on her way to attend a workshop for advocates of press freedoms in the Arab world. If that seems ironic, in her last post – on Thursday – before being detained,

Ghazzawi celebrated the release of another Syrian blogger, Hussein Ghrer, who had been held for 37 days, Global Voices (for whom she sometimes writes) points out.

1.25pm: The Assad regime has said that it is willing to sign an Arab League protocol to send international observers into Syria but only on certain conditions. The foreign minister, Walid al-Moallem, said all resolutions passed by the league, in the absence of Syria, namely those suspending it from the bloc, and imposing sanctions, must be annulled. He also said that the plan must be signed in Damascus and that the movement of the observers must be co-ordinated with the Syrian authorities.

2.36pm: Twitter has revealed the "hottest topics" wordwide in 2011 and the Middle East uprisings figure prominently. The most popular hashtag was #egypt. At number 10 was #jan25.

4.04pm: Doctors say the death toll from the past four days of fighting in Yemen, between government troops and tribal fighters, has reached 30. Activist Nouh al-Wafi told AP more than 200,000 protesters took to the streets of Taiz on Monday demanding a halt to the army's random shelling of residential areas. Both sides had pulled out at least partially of parts of the city on the orders of a committee of MPs, set up by acting head of state Abd-Rabbu Mansour Hadi over the weekend.

TUESDAY 6 DECEMBER

8.33am: The Arab League said it will maintain sanctions imposed on Syria, after Assad's government demanded the removal of the measures as a condition for admitting observers, Bloomberg reports. The League secretary general Nabil al-Arabi suggested he was not prepared to bargain on the issue. The League "will not lead to suspending Arab sanctions on Syria", he said.

9.22am: Yesterday saw one of the bloodiest days in Syria since the start of the uprising in March, according to the Syrian Observatory for Human Rights, who say 50 civilians were killed, with as many as 34 deaths reported in Homs.

12.06pm: The Assad regime has lost control of about a tenth of Syria, according to the Syrian Observatory for Human Rights. Rami Abdulrahman, head of the UK-based group, told the Guardian a "civilian war" is now a reality in the country.

1.36pm: Voting is continuing in the run-offs in the Egyptian elections but turnout has been low according to media reports. Radio Masr put the turnout at 20% compared to 52% in last week's first round. The run-offs are taking place for seats in which no individual won 50% or more of the vote in the first round.

2.08pm: Hezbollah's leader Hassan Nasrallah has backed the Assad regime in a TV address after a rare public appearance in Lebanon. He accused the United States of seeking to destroy Syria "to make up for its defeat in Iraq," AP quotes him saying.

> He accused some in the Syrian opposition of catering to US agendas in Syria and the region, and called on protesters to realise that they were being "used" for the wider aim of striking at Assad's regime for its support for Hezbollah and other anti-Israel groups in the region.

3.09pm: Robert Ford, the outspoken US ambassador to Syria is to be sent back to Damascus, according to AP. It cites a senior administration official. Ford was withdrawn from Syria in October for his own safety after a number of attacks against him by pro-Assad supporters. Ford infuriated the government by visiting an anti-government protests in Hama at the height of the demonstrations during the summer.

3.18pm: Alaa Abd El Fattah, the prominent Egyptian activist who has been in jail since being arrested on October 30, has become a father. His wife has given birth to their first child, according to the Egyptian blogger Zeinobia. Fattah was arrested on charges of inciting violence against the military relating to the bloodshed at a march of Coptic Christians on 9 October after he spoke out against the army's involvement in the violence.

He, and his wife, Manal Hassan, have called their son Khaled, after Khaled Said, whose death at the hands of two police officers helped inspire the revolution that ousted Mubarak.

4.23pm: Hillary Clinton has arrived in Geneva for a meeting with Syrian opposition members and has said they will be discussing how to ensure minorities are protected.

Sitting across a table from six members of the opposition Syrian National Council, she said:

> Obviously, a democratic transition is more than removing the Assad regime. It means setting Syria on the path of the rule of law ... The Syrian opposition that is represented here recognises that Syria's minorities have legitimate questions and concerns about their future and that they need to be assured that Syria will be better off under a regime of tolerance and freedom.

5.57pm:. Violence appears to be increasing in the central city of Homs, with 31 people killed so far in Syria today, all but one in Homs, according to activists. The violence in Homs has become increasingly sectarian, with tit-for-tat attacks pitting majority Sunnis against members of Assad's minority Alawite sect, according to AP.

WEDNESDAY 7 DECEMBER

8.34am: President Assad has tried to claim he is not responsible for the country's violence by suggesting that the army is outside his control. In a preview of an interview with ABC News due to be broadcast later today Assad said of the army: "I don't own them. I'm president. I don't own the country, so they're not my forces." At a state department press conference a reporter for ABC also quoted Assad saying: "There's a difference between having a policy to crack down and between having some mistakes committed by some officials. There is a big difference."

US state department spokesman Mark Toner has dismissed the remarks. He said: "There's just no indication that he's doing anything other than cracking down in the most brutal fashion on a peaceful opposition movement."

1.28pm: Assad's denial that killings had been ordered in Syria have no logic, according to Amnesty. Neil Sammonds, Amnesty's Syria researcher says:

> It has been clear for eight and half months that the security forces, including the army, have been shooting all over the place at peaceful protesters and people at funerals. There is no logic to what he [Assad] has being saying. He is the supreme commander of the Syrian armed forces. That is his title. Article 103 of the Syrian constitution makes that clear.

3.35pm: The Bahrain Youth Society for Human Rights says Bahraini security forces are attacking protesters who have headed back to Pearl Square, which was the heart of protests against the regime before the square was raided and destroyed by security forces earlier this year.

The society says:

> Hundreds of protesters decided to return to the Pearl Square and sit there. Security forces used stun grenades and rubber bullets and teargas. Members of the BYSHR confirm that there are many injuries.

3.57pm: Is the Arab League softening its stance on Syria? Algeria's foreign minister Mourad Medelci has today said a League deal to end the crisis should be given a "maximum chance" to succeed. Last month the League imposed sanctions on Syria and suspended its membership after Damascus ignored a ceasefire agreement.

4.41pm: Yemen's official news agency says a national unity government has been created, says AP.

Vice President Abd-Rabbu Mansour Hadi has reportedly issued a decree approving the formation of the new 35-member Cabinet headed by the veteran independent politician Mohammed Basindwa. The Cabinet posts are equally divided between Saleh's Congress party and the opposition.

5.58pm: Scores of Libyan judges and lawyers have been protesting in Tripoli against lawless behaviour in the capital by former rebel groups, whom they said should now leave the city and return to their home towns. Judges and lawyers said they decided to protest after an armed militia raided the offices of the prosecutor general on Tuesday.

The crowd of about 250, carrying placards reading "No to weapons; Yes to justice!" gathered outside Tripoli's courthouse before marching to the central Martyrs' Square. The head of Tripoli's city council has given the rebels until the end of the year to hand in their weapons to authorities.

THURSDAY 8 DECEMBER

12.16pm: The new Egyptian parliament may not have a single woman in it, Daily News Egypt reports. No female won a seat in parliament in the first round and there were no women contesting the run-offs, it says. It quotes women's groups as voicing further concern about what the success of Islamist parties means for women's rights.

4.41pm: The Local Co-ordination Committees of Syria, which until now have played down the increasingly sectarian nature of the uprising, have acknowledged that tensions between ethnic groups are spiraling out of control in the city of Homs.

But in a report on the problem the LCC blames the government for stirring up ethnic tensions and urges the opposition, activists, defected soldiers, religious leaders and the media to intervene to help stop it.

It says activist websites should stop showing videos and images of a sectarian nature that might fuel tensions.

FRIDAY 9 DECEMBER

8.36am: The Syrian army has surrounded Homs and is preparing to launch a "massacre" according to a warning from the opposition Syrian National Council. In a press statement it said:

> Evidence received from reports, videos and information obtained by activists on the ground in Homs indicates that the regime [is] paving the way to commit a massacre in order to extinguish the revolution in Homs and to discipline, by example, other Syrian cities that have joined the revolution.

9.40am: The most cited source on events in Syria lives in a terraced house in Coventry where he combines monitoring the Assad regime's brutal crackdown with running a clothing business, Reuters reports in a fascinating piece:

> With only a few hours sleep, a phone glued to his ear and another two ringing, the fast-talking director of arguably Syria's most high-profile human rights group is a very busy man.
>
> "Are there clashes? How did he die? Ah, he was shot," said Rami Abdulrahman into a phone, the talk of gunfire and death incongruous with his two bedroom terraced home in Coventry, from where he runs the Syrian Observatory for Human Rights.
>
> When he isn't fielding calls from international media, Abdulrahman is a few minutes down the road at his clothes shop, which he runs with his wife.

MONDAY 12 DECEMBER

8.46am: Local elections are being held across Syria today despite the ongoing crackdown by Assad's regime and the opposition's call for a boycott. Authorities have insisted the vote will be freer than in previous years, but with tensions as high as they are, few Syrians are likely to go out to cast their vote.

12.45pm: David Cameron has held talks with the King of Bahrain, who is under pressure in his country to adopt reforms and ease an oppressive crackdown. The meeting, which Downing Street said was an opportunity for the British prime minister to press upon Hamad bin Isa Al Khalifa the need for reform, was seen by many as a chance for Britain to patch up relations. Protesters greeted the news with fury, calling for a demonstration to be held outside the prime minister's residence.

4.18pm: Around 200 people have gathered for a protest in the Libyan city of Benghazi to protest against the National Transitional Council. The protesters say they were particularly enraged by comments made by NTC head Mustafa Abdul Jalil at the weekend, when he said the Libyan people were prepared to forgive those who fought for Gaddafi during the war.

TUESDAY 13 DECEMBER

8.47am: More than 5,000 people have died in the nine-month-long Syrian uprising, according to UN human rights chief Navi Pillay. The UN high commissioner for human rights has recommended that the security council refer Syria to the international criminal court for investigation of possible crimes against humanity.

WEDNESDAY 14 DECEMBER

1.31pm: A renewable energy specialist and long-suffering former dissident who spent 15 years in Ben Ali's jails has been appointed Tunisia's new prime minister.

Hamadi Jebali, 62, secretary general of the moderate Islamist party An-Nahda, now has three weeks to form the next interim government but he is expected to present it as soon as the end of the week because of the pressing problems the country faces, according to AP.

2.30pm: Time magazine has named "the protester" as its person of the year.

5.25pm: Rival militia groups are becoming increasingly entrenched in the post-Gaddafi era in Libya and won't hand in their weapons until they trust the government, according to a new report by the International Crisis Group. The report found that around 125,000 Libyans are armed and are loyal to one of up to 300 rival militia. The groups have been given until the end of the year to hand in their weapons, but they are unlikely to do so because they don't trust the NTC, the report found. It said:

> In the meantime, violence between militias is increasing, despite government attempts to curb it. One military commander, Abdul Hakim Belhaj, leader of the Tripoli Military Council, emerges as a particularly divisive figure whose sudden rise to power is viewed by some as "tantamount to a coup". Belhaj has become a "lightning rod for anxieties about Islamism and symbol over the country's future identity", the report says.

THURSDAY 15 DECEMBER

4.45pm: Egyptians mostly in rural areas have been continuing to vote in the second round of the country's first post-Mubarak parliamentary elections, with accusations from both Islamists and liberals that election officials have been filling out ballot forms for "elderly or confused" voters, according to AP.

FRIDAY 16 DECEMBER

8.45am: Russia has circulated a surprise draft resolution aimed at resolving the crisis in Syria. The BBC's UN correspondent Barbara Plett writes:

> Western diplomats say they are willing to negotiate the draft, but they want changes – such as much stronger language on human rights abuses, and endorsement of Arab League sanctions. Crucially they say the resolution should spell out that Damascus is primarily responsible for the violence, and not assign equal blame to the government and the opposition.

Vitaly Churkin, Russia's ambassador to the UN, said the resolution was aimed at reviving an Arab League plan which has stalled over Syria's refusal to allow in monitors.

9.05am: The killing of Muammar Gaddafi could have been a war crime and will be investigated, according to the chief prosecutor of the international criminal court. Luis Moreno-Ocampo told reporters: "I think the way in which Mr Gaddafi was killed creates suspicions of ... war crimes. We are raising this concern to the national authorities and they are preparing a plan to have a comprehensive strategy to investigate all these crimes."

4.40pm: Up to 17 people have been killed by Syrian security forces, according to reports, after another Friday of large protests across the country. Up to 200,000 people took to the streets in various demonstrations in Homs, according to the Syrian Observatory for Human Rights. The slogan of today's demonstration in Syria is "the Arab League silence is killing us".

MONDAY 19 DECEMBER

9.34am: Clashes between Egypt's ruling military and protesters insisting that they cede power have continued in Cairo's Tahrir Square for a fourth day.

The health ministry said on Sunday that 10 people had been killed in the violence since Friday. Some activists have put the number of people killed at 13. There have also been reports that five people were killed overnight. In Sunday's clashes, protesters and troops battled on two main streets off Tahrir Square, trading volleys of stones and firebombs around barriers that the military set up to block the two central avenues.

2.00pm: The Syrian government has signed the Arab League initiative to end the violence in its country. Under the plan it must allow Arab monitors into the country, withdraw the army from towns, release political prisoners and start a dialogue with the opposition. The Syrian foreign minister, Walid al Muallem, said the observers will have a one-month mandate that can be extended by another month if both sides agree. The observers will be "free" in their movements and "under the protection of the Syrian government", he said, but will not be allowed to visit sensitive military sites.

An advance party, led by a top Arab League official, will head to Syria within two or three days to prepare for the arrival of the monitors, Reuters reports. Meanwhile the Local Co-ordination Committees say 13 people have been killed by security forces today.

PART TWO

Essays, analysis and commentary

We finally have revolution on our minds

SAMI BEN HASSINE • Guardian, 13 January

I am part of the new generation that has lived in Tunisia under the absolute rule of President Zine al-Abidine Ben Ali.

In high school and college, we are always afraid to talk politics: "There are reporters everywhere," we are told. Nobody dares discuss politics in public; everyone is suspicious. Your neighbour, your friend, your grocer might be Ben Ali's informer: do you or your father want to be forcibly taken to an undefined place one night at 4am?

We grow up with this fear of activism; we continue studying, going out and partying, regardless of politics.

During high school, we begin to find out the intricacies of the "royal" family and hear stories here and there – about a relative of Leila Trabelsi, the president's wife, who took control of an industry, who has appropriated the land of another person, who dealt with the Italian mafia. We talk and discuss it among ourselves – everybody is aware of what's going on, but there is no action. We quickly learn that Tunisian television is the worst television that exists. Everything is relayed to the glory of President Ben Ali, who's always shown at his best. We all know he dyes his hair black. Nobody likes his wife, who has a wooden smile: she never seemed sincere.

We do not live, but we think we do. We want to believe that all is well since we are part of the middle class, but we know that if the cafes are packed during the day, it is because the unemployed are there discussing football. The first nightclubs open their doors and we begin to go out, to drink and enjoy the nightlife around Sousse and Hammamet. Other stories are circulating – about a Trabelsi who gave someone a horrible kicking because he felt like it, or another who caused a car accident only to return home to sleep. We exchange stories, quietly, quickly. In our own way, it is a form of vengeance: by gossiping, we have the feeling we're plotting.

The police are afraid: if you tell them you're close to Ben Ali all doors open, hotels offer their best rooms, parking becomes free, traffic laws disappear.

The internet is blocked, and censored pages are referred to as pages "not found" – as if they had never existed. Schoolchildren exchange proxies and the word becomes cult: "You got a proxy that works?"

We all know that Leila has tried to sell a Tunisian island, that she wants to close the American school in Tunis to promote her own school – as I said, stories are circulating. We love our country and we want things to change, but there is no organised movement: the tribe is willing, but the leader is missing.

The corruption, the bribes – we simply want to leave. We begin to apply to study in France, or Canada. It is cowardice, and we know it. Leaving the country to "the rest of them". We go to France and forget, then come back for the holidays. Tunisia? It is the beaches of Sousse and Hammamet, the nightclubs and restaurants. A giant ClubMed.

And then, WikiLeaks reveals what everyone was whispering. And then, a young man immolates himself. And then, 20 Tunisians are killed in one day.

And for the first time, we see the opportunity to rebel, to take revenge on the "royal" family who has taken everything, to overturn the established order that has accompanied our youth. An educated youth, which is tired and ready to sacrifice all the symbols of the former autocratic Tunisia with a new revolution: the Jasmine revolution – the true one.

This article was first published in French on nawaat.org, where it originally appeared, as it did on the Guardian website, under the pen-name Sam. The byline was later updated at the author's request

TUNISIA/LIBYA

Our neighbours have shown us a way out

HISHAM MATAR · Guardian, 22 January

In the 1970s, the young Libyan leader, Colonel Muammar Gaddafi, was the most impatient exponent of Arab unity. In 1973, he flew to Tunisia in order to convince his next-door neighbour to form a union with Libya. What happened during that summit says a lot about why Tunisia is the first Arab nation to overthrow a dictator through peaceful mass protest.

The first president of Tunisia, Habib Bourguiba, 70 years old by then, sat at a simple table with a microphone in front of him and a small glass of water to one side. He wore a French suit, his grey hair was slicked back, and he had on a pair of square dark glasses. He looked like Jorge Luis Borges. But, unlike the Argentinian author, Bourguiba wasn't a gifted orator. As a public speaker, the Sorbonne graduate lacked tact and was given to excitement. "What is the point of uniting 1.5 million Libyans with 5 million Tunisians?" he asked, mockingly.

It became clear, as Bourguiba went on, that he had two objectives in mind: to deflate and mildly humiliate the young Nasserist Libyan, and to outline his vision of the Arab world. Bourguiba's thesis was as simple as it was poignant: for the Arab people to build secure states and societies, they ought to concern themselves not with Arab unity, but with education and development.

Sadly, his first motive reduced the credibility of his second. He stated his opinion, that Tunisia was socially and politically superior to its north African neighbour, with enthusiasm and, one couldn't help but detect, delight.

As the Tunisian crowd cheered, the Libyan leader sat to one side looking unimpressed. Gaddafi was only 31. He had all the confidence and swagger of a young man at the height of his powers. He sat in his military uniform, his shaven chin pointing up. Every now and then he would laugh or yawn theatrically.

There was little doubt as to what Gaddafi made of the older man's remarks. As there was little doubt, among Arab observers and commentators, that Bourguiba, the seasoned politician, knew perfectly well what he was doing – that this was the best way to offend his hot-blooded guest. This fact, as well as the Tunisian's lack of enthusiasm for Arab unity, served to distract many Arabs from the valuable and pertinent recommendations the Tunisian president was offering.

This was a heady time. The bitter taste of 1967 was still in the mouth. Every Arab state had a European ex-colonial power breathing down its neck. Yet winning independence was within living memory, and confidence was still high. In the middle of it all there were these two north African men, born more than 30 years apart, both dictatorial, both with prisons full of dissidents, both with egos the size of their two countries combined, and each pointing towards a different path. Bourguiba favoured institutions and a robust bureaucracy, while Gaddafi distrusted institutions and sought to dismantle every union and club.

One of the main reasons Tunisians were able to rid themselves of Ben Ali – who was bequeathed to them by Bourguiba – was less because of the claim, endlessly repeated in the western media, that Tunisia is more European in its thinking than its neighbours, and more because of the extent to which Tunisian civil society and state bureaucracy have been allowed to develop since independence.

We Libyans are just as hungry for a just and accountable government as our Tunisian brothers and sisters. The lack of resilient institutions will make our task more difficult. However, a worried Gaddafi was the first Arab leader to give an address on television about the events in Tunisia. He obviously disapproves, but also hopes to quell the protests that have started in some Libyan towns and cities.

I am, by instinct, wary of revolutions. The gathering of the masses fills me with trepidation. But seeing the Tunisian crowds in Habib Bourguiba Avenue, the familiar street throbbing like a hot vein, was one of the most glorious things I have seen in all of my 40 years. From before I was born, we Arabs have been caught between two forces that, seemingly, cannot be defeated: our ruthless dictators, who oppress and humiliate us, and the cynical western powers, who would rather see us ruled by criminals loyal to them than have democratically elected leaders accountable to us. We have been sliding towards the dark conclusion that we will forever remain trapped between these two beasts. The men and women of Tunisia took us back from the brink of that precipice.

Hisham Matar is a Libyan novelist

Challenges for the trailblazers

JONATHAN STEELE · Guardian, 26 October

Having launched what became known as the Arab Spring, Tunisia has now led the region by holding a clean election with an enthusiastic turnout and highly encouraging results. The three parties that have come out on top in the most democratic of north African states have no links with the capital city's upper middle class or those sections of the business community that benefited from the ousted Ben Ali dictatorship. They both have a tradition of struggling for democratic values.

As in post-Mubarak Egypt, there was reason to fear that the old regime would re-emerge in Tunisia with new faces, but this now seems unlikely. The party that has emerged from the poll most strongly is An-Nahda (Renaissance), which suffered massive repression under Ben Ali and has won great respect for its sacrifices. This party of modern democratic Islam campaigned hard on the two issues that concern most Tunisians: corruption and unemployment, particularly youth unemployment.

While several smaller secular parties tried to manipulate Islamophobia – a relatively easy card to play given the official state-controlled media's demonisation of the Islamists over several decades – their efforts have failed. Voters had their first chance to listen to An-Nahda's candidates and they were not put off by what they heard. An-Nahda made special efforts to show that it wanted an inclusive government of national unity and would respect all points of view. It also reached out to voters in the more impoverished interior, making it clear it would not be just a party of the Mediterranean coast as Ben Ali's regime had been.

The main runners-up, The Congress for the Republic and Ettakatol, the Democratic Forum for Labour and Liberties, both have a strong and principled record in the struggle against corruption and dictatorship. Ettakatol has a distinguished background in the trade union movement, which, again as in Egypt, was one of the main pillars of the struggle to oust Ben Ali.

While Egypt is inevitably linked with Tunisia in the world's headlines as the only other Arab country to have achieved regime change this year by nonviolent means, Turkey may provide a better paradigm for Tunisia's future political development. Under Kemal Ataturk, Turkey went through forced secularisation and modernisation just as Tunisia did under its first president,

Habib Bourguiba. Women were obliged to remove the veil in schools, universities and public jobs, and were also allowed to run for parliament. Abortion was made legal and polygamy banned. Marriage required the bride's consent.

But there was a severe downside to the regime in Turkey: a highly political army that enriched itself, mounted coups and imprisoned hundreds of opponents. In Tunisia similar repression occurred under the guise of curbing the Islamists.

Now, a new generation in Tunisia is keen to turn its back on such practices just as a similar generation did in Turkey a decade ago when the Justice and Development party, the moderate Islamists, were elected to power. North Africa has moved on from the time when the army in Algeria foolishly blocked an election victory by moderate Islamists in 1991, plunging the country into civil war and creating opportunities for supporters of a more extreme form of Islamism to take up guns. Tunisia always was an altogether more civil society and will not repeat such folly now that Islamists have won its first free election.

One issue is whether the secular fundamentalism that banned the hijab will give way. An-Nahda would find it easier to restore women's right to wear what they please in government buildings than it has been in Turkey, where the hijab ban is enshrined in the constitution and continues in force. In Tunisia, the ban was enacted by legislation, and a new parliament could change the law. As Rachid Ghannouchi, An-Nahda's founder, said during the campaign: "We are against the imposition of the headscarf in the name of Islam and we are against the banning of the headscarf in the name of secularism or modernity."

But dress code is not Tunisia's top priority. The country's big challenge is to draw up a constitution which safeguards the political freedoms that those who rose up against Ben Ali in January demanded. The assembly elected on Sunday is tasked to do that. It will also appoint a government that will have to start tackling unemployment. Europe's financial crisis will not make that easy. Tourism has collapsed and may not quickly revive even though the country has shown itself to be safe for foreign visitors.

So after the elections, Tunisia's road ahead remains tough. At least, the omens are clearer than in Egypt or its neighbour, Libya.

Jonathan Steele is a former Guardian foreign correspondent

EGYPT

'This brutality is why we are protesting'

JACK SHENKER · Guardian, 27 January

In the streets around Abdel Munim Riyad Square the atmosphere had changed. The air which had held a carnival-like vibe was now thick with teargas. Thousands of people were running out of nearby Tahrir Square and towards me. Several hundred regrouped; a few dozen protesters set about attacking an abandoned police truck, eventually tipping it over and setting it ablaze. Through the smoke, lines of riot police could be seen charging towards us from the south.

Along with nearby protesters I fled down the street before stopping at what appeared to be a safe distance. A few ordinarily dressed young men were running in my direction. Two came towards me and threw out punches, sending me to the ground. I was hauled back up by the scruff of the neck and dragged towards the advancing police lines.

My captors were burly and wore leather jackets – up close I could see they were *amin dowla*, plainclothes officers from Egypt's notorious state security service. All attempts I made to tell them in Arabic and English that I was an international journalist were met with more punches and slaps; around me I could make out other isolated protesters receiving the same brutal treatment and choking from the teargas.

We were hustled towards a security office on the edge of the square. As I approached the doorway of the building other plainclothes security officers milling around took flying kicks and punches at me, pushing me to the floor on several occasions only to drag me back up and hit me again. I spotted a high-ranking uniformed officer, and shouted at him that I was a British journalist. He responded by walking over and punching me twice. "Fuck you and fuck Britain," he yelled in Arabic.

One by one we were thrown through the doorway, where a gauntlet of officers with sticks and clubs awaited us. We queued up to run through the blows and into a dank, narrow corridor where we were pushed up against the wall. Our mobiles and wallets were removed. Officers stalked up and down, barking at us to keep staring at the wall. Terrified of incurring more beatings, most of my fellow detainees – almost exclusively young men in their 20s and 30s, some still clutching dishevelled Egyptian flags from the protest – remained silent, though some muttered Qur'anic verses and others were shaking with sobs.

We were ordered to sit down. Later a senior officer began dragging people to their feet again, sending them back out through the gauntlet and into the night, where we were immediately jumped on by more police officers – this time with riot shields – and shepherded into a waiting green truck belonging to Egypt's central security forces. A policeman pushed my head against the doorframe as I entered.

Inside dozens were already crammed in and crouching in the darkness. Some had heard the officers count us as we boarded; our number stood at 44, all packed into a space barely any bigger than the back of a Transit van. A heavy metal door swung shut behind us.

As the truck began to move, brief flashes of orange streetlight streamed through the thick metal grates on each side. With no windows, it was our only source of illumination. Each glimmer revealed bruised and bloodied faces; sandwiched in so tightly the temperature soared, and people fainted. Fragments of conversation drifted through the truck.

"The police attacked us to get us out of the square; they didn't care who you were, they just attacked everybody," a lawyer standing next to me, Ahmed Mamdouh, said breathlessly. "They … hit our heads and hurt some people. There are some people bleeding, we don't know where they're taking us. I want to send a message to my wife; I'm not afraid but she will be so scared, this is my first protest and she told me not to come here today."

Despite the conditions the protesters held together; those who collapsed were helped to their feet, messages of support were whispered and then yelled from one end of our metallic jail to another, and the few mobiles that had been hidden from police were passed around so that loved ones could be called.

"As I was being dragged in, a police general said to me: 'Do you think you can change the world? You can't! Do you think you are a hero? You are not'," confided Mamdouh.

"What you see here – this brutality and torture – this is why we were protesting today," added another voice close by in the gloom.

Speculation was rife about where we were heading. The truck veered wildly round corners, sending us flying to one side, and regularly came to an emergency stop, throwing everyone forwards. "They treat us like we're not Egyptians, like we are their enemy, just because we are fighting for jobs," said Mamdouh. I asked him what it felt like to be considered an enemy by your own government. "I feel like they are my enemies too," he replied.

At several points the truck roared to a stop and the single door opened, revealing armed policemen on the other side. They called out the name of

one of the protesters, "Nour", the son of Ayman Nour, a prominent political dissident who challenged Hosni Mubarak for the presidency in 2005 and
was thrown in jail for his troubles.

Nour became a cause celebre among international politicians and pressure
groups; since his release from prison security forces have tried to avoid attacking him or his family directly, conscious of the negative publicity that would
inevitably follow.

His son, a respected political activist in his own right, had been caught in
the police sweep and was in the back of the truck with us – now the policemen were demanding he come forward, as they had orders for his release.

"No, I'm staying," said Nour simply, over and over again and to applause
from the rest of the inmates. I made my way through the throng and asked
him why he wasn't taking the chance to get out. "Because either I leave with
everyone else or I stay with everyone else; it would be cowardice to do
anything else," he responded. "That's just the way I was raised."

After several meandering circles which seemed to take us out further and
further into the desert fringes of the city, the truck finally came to a halt. We
had been trapped inside for so long that the heat was unbearable; more people
had fainted, and one man had collapsed on the floor, struggling for breath.

By the light of the few mobile phones, protesters tore his shirt open and
tried to steady his breathing; one demonstrator had medical experience and
warned that the man was entering a diabetic coma. A huge cry went up in the
truck as protesters thumped the sides and bellowed through the grates:
"Help, a man is dying." There was no response.

After some time a commotion could be heard outside; fighting appeared
to be breaking out between police and others, whom we couldn't make out.

At one point the truck began to rock alarmingly from side to side while
someone began banging the metal exterior, sending out huge metallic clangs.
We could make out that a struggle was taking place over the opening of the
door; none of the protesters had any idea what lay on the other side, but all
resolved to charge at it when the door swung open. Eventually it did, to
reveal a police officer who began to grab inmates and haul them out, beating them as they went. A cry went up and we surged forward, sending the
policeman flying; the diabetic man was then carried out carefully before the
rest of us spilled on to the streets.

Later it emerged that we had won our freedom through the efforts of
Nour's parents, Ayman and his former wife Gamila Ismail. The father, who
was also on the demonstration, had got wind of his son's arrest and apparently

followed his captors and fought with officers for our release. Shorn of money and phones and stranded several miles into the desert, the protesters began a long trudge back towards Cairo, hailing down cars on the way.

The diabetic patient was swiftly put in a vehicle and taken to hospital; I have been unable to find out his condition.

Jack Shenker is the Guardian's Cairo correspondent

EGYPT

United by an injustice and anger that won't be tamed

ALAA AL ASWANY · Guardian, 28 January

It was an unforgettable day for me. I joined the demonstrators in Cairo, along with the hundreds of thousands across Egypt who went on to the streets on Tuesday demanding freedom and bravely facing off the fearsome violence of the police. The regime has a million and a half soldiers in its security apparatus, upon which its spends millions in order to train them for one task: to keep the Egyptian people down.

I found myself in the midst of thousands of young Egyptians, whose only point of similarity was their dazzling bravery and their determination to do one thing – change the regime. Most of them are university students who find themselves with no hope for the future. They are unable to find work, and hence unable to marry. And they are motivated by an untameable anger and a profound sense of injustice.

I will always be in awe of these revolutionaries. Everything they have said shows a sharp political awareness and a death-defying desire for freedom. They asked me to say a few words. Even though I've spoken hundreds of times in public, this time it was different: I was speaking to 30,000 demonstrators who were in no mood to hear of compromise and who kept interrupting with shouts of "Down with Hosni Mubarak!" and "The people say, out with the regime!"

I said I was proud of what they had achieved, and that they had brought about the end of the period of repression, adding that even if we get beaten up or arrested we have proved we are not afraid and are stronger than they are. They have the fiercest tools of repression in the world at their disposal, but we have something stronger: our courage and our belief in freedom. The crowd responded by shouting en masse: "We'll finish what we've begun!"

I was in the company of a friend, a Spanish journalist who spent many years in eastern Europe and lived through the liberation movements there. He said: "It has been my experience that when so many people come out on to the streets, and with such determination, regime change is just a matter of time."

So why have Egyptians risen up? The answer lies in the nature of the regime. A tyrannical regime might deprive the people of their freedom, but in return they are offered an easy life. A democratic regime might fail to beat poverty, but the people enjoy freedom and dignity. The Egyptian regime has deprived the people of everything, including freedom and dignity, and has failed to supply them with their daily needs. The hundreds of thousands of demonstrators are no more than representatives of the millions of Egyptians whose rights have been invalidated.

While public calls for reform in Egypt long predated the dissent in Tunisia, events there were of course inspiring. Now people could clearly see the security apparatus could not protect the dictator for ever. And we had greater cause than our Tunisian counterparts, with more people living in poverty, and under a ruler who has held the reins of power even longer. At some point, fear made Ben Ali flee Tunisia. We could emulate the success of that protest; some people on Cairo's streets copied the same French slogan, *Dégage, Mubarak*.

Already the authorities are finding their tactics cannot stop the protests. Demonstrations have been organised through Facebook as a reliable, independent source of information; when the state tried to block it, the people proved cleverer, and bloggers passed on ways to bypass the controls. And the violence of the security services is a risk for both sides: in Suez people have risen up against police who shot demonstrators. History shows that at some point ordinary policemen will refuse to carry out orders to kill fellow citizens.

More ordinary citizens are now defying the police. A young demonstrator told me that, when running from the police on Tuesday, he entered a building and rang an apartment bell at random. It was 4am. A 60-year-old man opened the door, fear obvious on his face. The demonstrator asked the man to hide him from the police. The man asked to see his identity card and invited him in, waking one of his three daughters to prepare some food for the young man. They ate and drank tea together and chatted like lifelong friends.

In the morning, when the danger of arrest had receded, the man accompanied the young protester into the street, stopped a taxi for him and offered him some money. The young man refused and thanked them. As they embraced the older man said: "It is I who should be thanking you for defending me, my daughters and all Egyptians."

That is how the Egyptian spring began. Tomorrow, we will see a real battle.

Alaa Al Aswany is an Egyptian writer, and a founding member of the political movement Kefaya

EGYPT

The tyrant has gone.
Now the real struggle begins

PANKAJ MISHRA · Guardian, 12 February

For the last two weeks I have, like innumerable others, careened from the television news to internet updates and back, longing for the moment that came last night, when the tyrant finally yielded to a brave and spirited people. History has been made; celebrations are in order. But it is not too early to ask: what next?

The so-called Higher Military Council inspires no confidence. Does another military strongman lurk in the regime's entrails? I wonder if western leaders, shamed into moral bluster after being caught in flagrante with Mubarak, will, when we relax our vigils, tip the balance towards "stability" and against real change.

I grow a bit apprehensive, too, recalling the words of an extraordinarily perceptive observer of Egypt's struggles in the past: "The edifice of despotic government totters to its fall. Strive so far as you can to destroy the foundations of this despotism, not to pluck up and cast out its individual agents."

This was the deathbed exhortation-cum-warning of the itinerant Muslim Jamal al-Din al-Afghani (1838–97) who pursued a long career in political activism and trenchant journalism. Travelling through Afghanistan, Iran, Egypt and Turkey in the last half of the 19th century, al-Afghani saw at first hand how unshakeable the "foundations of despotism" in Muslim countries had become.

That they were reinforced in the next century, even though many of the "individual agents" of despotism were plucked up and cast out, would not have surprised him.

He spent eight years in Egypt at a crucial time (1871–79), when the country, though nominally sovereign, was stumbling into a long and abject relationship with western powers. Invaded by Napoleon in 1798, Egypt had become the first non-western country to try to catch up with western economic and military power. Building a modern army and bureaucracy required capital, and Egypt's rulers began large-scale plantations of a cash crop highly valued in Europe: cotton.

This led, in the short term, to great private fortunes. But, having bound its formerly self-sufficient economy to a single crop and the vagaries of the international capitalist system, Egypt was badly in debt to European bankers by the late 1870s. Unable to generate sufficient capital on its own, Egypt became heavily dependent on huge high-interest loans from European banks.

For British and French bankers, the state's treasury was, as the economic historian David S Landes wrote, "simply a grab-bag". Egypt's nascent manufacturing industry stood no chance in an international economic regime whose rules were rigged in favour of free-trading Britain. At the same time, early modernisation in Egypt had unleashed new classes with social and political aspirations that could not be fulfilled by a despotic regime beholden to foreigners.

In the late 1870s and early 80s, Egyptian resentment finally erupted in what were the first nationalist upsurges against colonial rule anywhere in Asia and Africa. Predictably, the British invaded and occupied Egypt in 1882 in order to protect their interests, most important of which was the sea route to India through the Suez canal.

In Ottoman Turkey, al-Afghani observed a similar advance of western economic and strategic interests backed by gunboats. In his native Persia, he participated in mass protests against the then shah's sale of national land and resources to European businessmen.

Al-Afghani came to realise that the threat posed to the traditionally agrarian countries of the east by Europe's modern and industrialised nation-states was much more insidious than territorial expansion. Imposing, for instance, the urgencies of internal modernisation and the conditionalities of "free trade" on Asian societies, European businessmen and diplomats got native elites to do their bidding. In turn, local rulers were only too happy to use western techniques to modernise their armies, set up efficient police and spy networks and reinforce their own autocratic power.

This was why, al-Afghani explained presciently in the 1890s, Muslims moved from despising despots coddled and propped up by the west to despising the west itself. Al-Afghani saw, too, the proliferation of the now-ubiquitous binaries (western liberalism versus religious fanaticism, stability versus Islamism), which ideologically justified to Europeans at home their complicity with brutal tyranny abroad. In 1891 he attacked the British press for presenting Iranian protesters against the Shah as Islamic fanatics when, in fact, they articulated a profound longing for reform.

Al-Afghani wouldn't have been surprised to see that even national sovereignty and electoral democracy were no defence against such materially and intellectually resourceful western power. The secular nationalist Wafd party won Egypt's first elections in 1924; and they kept up their winning streak over the next decade. But, acting in concert with the Egyptian monarch, the British made it impossible for the Wafd party to exercise any real sovereignty. (This was when, feeding on widespread frustration with conventional democratic politics, Egyptian Islamists first came to the fore – the Muslim Brotherhood was founded in 1928.)

As the Indian anti-imperialist leader Jawaharlal Nehru, who followed the slow strangling of Egyptian democracy from a British prison, caustically commented in 1935, "democracy for an Eastern country seems to mean only one thing: to carry out the behests of the imperialist ruling power."

This dismal truth was to be more widely felt among Arabs as the United States replaced Britain and France as the paramount power in the Middle East; and securing Israel and the supply of oil joined the expanding list of western strategic interests in the region.

The rest of this story would have been as familiar to al-Afghani as it is to us. Gamal Abdel Nasser presided over a relatively brief and ecstatic interlude of Egyptian freedom. But his socialistic reforms did not rescue Egypt from the perennially losing side in the international economy; and Nasser's successors, all military strongmen, worked on reinforcing the foundations of their despotism: they struck military alliances with western governments, opened the national economy to foreign investors, creating a small but powerful local elite committed to the status quo, while a fully modernised police state bullied the steadily pauperised majority into passivity.

The edifice of this despotism was always bound to totter in the age of instant communications. Cursing the Muslim despots of his time, al-Afghani lamented on his deathbed: "Would that I had sown all the seed of my ideas in the receptive ground of the people's thoughts." Al-Jazeera and the internet have now helped accomplish what al-Afghani only dreamed of doing: rousing and emboldening the politicised masses, shattering the cosy consensus of transnational elites.

The protests grow bigger every day, swelled by new social classes, beneficiaries as well as victims of the ancien régime. Even the stalwart propagandists on state TV have found their inner voices. Assisted by YouTube, the demonstrators praying unflinchingly on Kasr al-Nil as they are assaulted by water cannons have swiftly accumulated even more moral-spiritual power than the resolute satyagrahis of Mahatma Gandhi did in their own media-deprived time. Amazingly, in less than two weeks, the protesters in Midan Tahrir have stripped the local despot and his foreign enablers of their moral authority and intellectual certainties.

The essential revolution in the mind has already been accomplished. A radical transformation of political and economic structures would be an even more extraordinary event. But achieving it won't be easy, as Tunisia's example already reveals; and Egypt's own history warns us that the foundations of despotism are deep and wide. It is now clear that our virtual vigils will have to continue long after the western media's very recent fascination with Egypt trails off, and assorted neocons and "liberal" hawks emerge from the woodwork to relaunch their bogey of "Islamism". We may also have to steel ourselves, as victory appears in sight, for some more bitter setbacks in the long Egyptian battle for self-determination.

Pankaj Mishra is a writer based in the UK and India

EGYPT

The unknown woman shows the struggle is not over

AHDAF SOUEIF • Guardian, 19 December

The woman is young, and slim, and fair. She lies on her back surrounded by four soldiers, two of whom are dragging her by the arms raised above her head. She's unresisting – maybe she's fainted; we can't tell because we can't see her face. She's wearing blue jeans and trainers. But her top half is bare: we can see her torso, her tummy, her blue bra, her bare delicate arms. Surrounding this top half, forming a kind of black halo around it, is the abaya, the robe she was wearing that has been ripped off and that tells us that she was wearing a hijab.

Six years ago, when popular protests started to hit the streets of Egypt as Hosni Mubarak's gang worked at rigging the 2005 parliamentary elections, the regime hit back – not just with the traditional Central Security conscripts – but with an innovation: militias of strong, trained, thugs. They beat up men, but they grabbed women, tore their clothes off and beat them, groping them at the same time. The idea was to insinuate that females who took part in street protests wanted to be groped.

Women developed deterrent techniques: layers of light clothing, no buttons, drawstring pants double-knotted – and carried right on protesting. Many of the smaller civil initiatives that grew into the protest movement: "We See You", "Against Corruption", "The Streets are Ours" were women-led.

But, a symbiotic relationship springs up between behaviours. Mubarak and Omar Suleiman turn Egypt into the US's favourite location for the torture of "terror suspects" and torture becomes endemic in police stations. The regime's thugs molest women as a form of political bullying – and harassment of women in the streets rises to epidemic levels.

Until 25 January. The revolution happened and with it came the Age of Chivalry. One of the most noted aspects of behaviour in the streets and squares of the 18 days of the Egyptian revolution was the total absence of harassment. Women were suddenly free; free to walk alone, to talk to strangers, to cover or uncover, to smoke to laugh to cry to sleep. And the job of every single male present was to facilitate, to protect, to help. The Ethics of the Square, we called it.

Now our revolution is in an endgame struggle with the old regime and the military.

The young woman is part of this.

Since Friday the military has openly engaged with civilian protesters in the heart of the capital. The protesters have been peacefully conducting a sit-in in Ministries' Street to signal their rejection of the military's appointment of Kamal al-Ganzouri as prime minister.

Ganzouri announced that no violence would be used to break up the Cabinet Office sit-in. Moments later the military took on the protesters. For a week military police and paratroopers had kidnapped activists from the streets, driven them off in unmarked vehicles, interrogated them and beaten them. On Friday they kidnapped Aboudi – one of the "Ultras" of the Ahli Football Club. They gave him back with his face so beaten and burned that you couldn't see features – and started the street war that's been raging round Ministries' Street for the last three days.

The protesters have thrown rocks at the military. The military has shot protesters, and thrown rocks, Molotov cocktails, china embossed with official parliament insignia, chairs, cupboards, filing-cabinets, glass panes and fire-works. They've dragged people into parliament and into the Cabinet Office and beaten and electrocuted them – my two nieces were beaten like this.

They beat up a newly elected young member of parliament, jeering: "Let parliament protect you, you son of …" They took a distinguished older lady who's become known for giving food to the protesters and slapped her repeatedly about the face till she had to beg and apologise. They killed 10 people, injured more than 200, and they dragged the unconscious young woman in the blue jeans – with her upper half stripped – through the streets.

The message is: everything you rose up against is here, is worse. Don't put your hopes in the revolution or parliament. We are the regime and we're back.

What they are not taking into account is that everybody's grown up – the weapon of shame can no longer be used against women. When they subjected young women to virginity tests one of them got up and sued them. Every young woman they've brutalised recently has given video testimony and is totally committed to continuing the struggle against them.

The young woman in the blue jeans has chosen so far to retain her privacy. But her image has already become icon. As the tortured face of Khaled Said broke any credibility the ministry of the interior might have had, so the young woman in the blue jeans has destroyed the military's reputation.

Ahdaf Soueif is a novelist and commentator based in London and Cairo

LIBYA

Please don't intervene in our people's uprising

MUHAMMAD MIN LIBYA · Guardian, 1 March

"Kiss my mum goodbye for me, and tell her that her son died a hero," said my friend Ahmed, 26, to the first person who rushed to his side after he was shot in a Tripoli street.

Two days later, my friend Ahmed died in the hospital. Just like that.

That tall, handsome, funny, witty, intellectual young man is no more. No longer will he answer my phone calls. Time will stand still on his Facebook account for ever.

An hour before he was shot, I called Ahmed. He sounded at his best. He told me that he was in Green Square in the heart of Tripoli, and that we were free. Then bad telephone connections meant I couldn't reach him again for two whole days.

That was when I called Ahmed's best friend, who broke the devastating news to me. They were about to bury him, he told me. I rushed to the cemetery, and arrived there right after the burial. I found some of our friends. They pointed at a spot on the ground telling me it was where Ahmed's body lay. We all hugged each other and just cried our hearts out.

This is the kind of story you get out of Tripoli these days. Hundreds of them, perhaps even thousands. The kind of stories that you could never imagine on your doorstep.

Like when you hear a six-month-old baby has been murdered, you just hope with all your heart that Saif al-Islam Gaddafi's claims turn out to be true that there's precious little violence here, that al-Jazeera fabricated the story. You hope that infant is right now sleeping peacefully in his mother's arms. Like when you hear of someone from Tajura who had a bullet in his head for two days before dying, leaving behind a bereaved wife and child. You have been praying to God that the father be there playing with his child. But the photos, the video show you the cold truth. The wails that need no translation: loved ones being snatched away by death. All humans understand that scream.

This has been the life of Tripoli for quite some time. This is why the city is now called the "City of Ghosts" by its inhabitants, who have despaired at seeing protesters flee the teargas. The city has ground to a halt, with the vast majority of shops closed and schools and universities shut down. Only a few shops selling basic supplies remain open, and even that only for a few hours each day.

But despite this bleak picture of Tripoli, people have high hopes and faith that we are now witnessing the last moments of Gaddafi's regime. This man no longer rules Libya; he is merely a man with a gun turned to the people.

His two speeches, and his son's before that, were nothing but threats – they all backfired in favour of the Libyan revolution. Libyan tribes from the east to the west went out to assert national unity.

Abroad his record is no better. Gaddafi wanted to scare the western world off with the alleged threat of an Islamic emirate. The international community answered him by barring him from exile abroad, freezing his assets and referring his regime's crimes to the international court of justice with almost unprecedented international unanimity.

All Libyans, even the pro-Gaddafi minority, believe that it's only a matter of time before Libya regains its freedom. But the frightening question remains: how many martyrs will fall before Gaddafi does? How many souls will he take before the curse is broken?

This happy ending, however, is marred by a fear shared by all Libyans; that of a possible western military intervention to end the crisis.

Don't get me wrong. I, like most Libyans, believe that imposing a no-fly zone would be a good way to deal the regime a hard blow on many levels; it would cut the route of the mercenary convoys summoned from Africa, it would prevent Gaddafi from smuggling money and other assets, and most importantly it would stop the regime from bombing weapons arsenals that many eyewitnesses have maintained contain chemical weapons; something that would unleash an unimaginable catastrophe, not to mention that his planes might actually carry such weapons.

Nevertheless, one thing seems to have united Libyans of all stripes; any military intervention on the ground by any foreign force would be met – as Mustafa Abud Al Jeleil, the former justice minister and head of the opposition-formed interim government, said – with fighting much harsher than what the mercenaries themselves have unleashed.

Nor do I favour the possibility of a limited air strike for specific targets. This is a wholly popular revolution, the fuel to which has been the blood of the Libyan people. Libyans fought alone when western countries were busy ignoring their revolution at the beginning, fearful of their interests in Libya. This is why I'd like the revolution to be ended by those who first started it: the people of Libya.

So as the calls for foreign intervention grow, I'd like to send a message to western leaders: Obama, Cameron, Sarkozy. This is a priceless opportunity that has fallen into your laps, it's a chance for you to improve your image in the eyes of Arabs and Muslims. Don't mess it up. All your previous programmes to bring the east and the west closer have failed, and some of them have made things even worse. Don't start something you cannot finish, don't turn a people's pure revolution into some curse that will befall everyone. Don't waste the blood that my friend Ahmed spilt for me.

Let us just live as neighbours on the same planet. Who knows, maybe I as your neighbour might one day show up at your doorstep to happily shake your hand.

Muhammad min Libya is a pseudonym. The author is a Tripoli-based blogger. This article was commissioned and translated in cooperation with Meedan

LIBYA

A chance to repair the reputation of intervention

ALAA AL-AMERI · Guardian, 18 March

How are the numbers for UN resolutions chosen? I sincerely hope it's just a poetic coincidence that the resolution authorising international assistance for the democratic movement in Libya bears the number "1973".

This was the year that Muammar Gaddafi began his purge against the "politically sick" which saw students, professors, writers, judges, lawyers, military officers and anyone who questioned his authority hanged in public or murdered in private. How fitting then that the world should finally come to the assistance of the long-suffering Libyan population under this of all banners.

Not everyone is happy to help, though. The Germans were joined by the usual suspects against resolutions aimed at protecting populations from their governments – Russia and China. It was, however, disappointing to see India and Brazil among the abstainers. Still, I suppose it's not fun when your business dealings with unhinged mass murderers are rudely interrupted by people asking for basic freedoms.

We can't celebrate too soon, however. By definition, all UN resolutions are toothless. They simply provide international approval for intervention in national matters. Pressure must therefore be maintained for a swift and effective intervention. Personally, I am sceptical about the regime's "ceasefire" announcement: my sources on the ground are saying that it is just a ploy and that the shelling of Misrata continues unabated.

There's no lack of countries, including Turkey, wishing to slow the process of intervention. There are still many who insist that military intervention must only go ahead with the involvement of members of the Arab

League and African Union. This outdated ethnic filter puts people into different jurisdictions based on race and cultural identity. The deference to Arab and African opinion is not a matter of geographical location – Libya is closer to Italy, Spain and France than it is to Saudi Arabia, Zimbabwe and South Africa. It's frustrating as a Libyan to be told as you scream for help that your case is being referred to Syria and the Democratic Republic of Congo.

This is a genuine opportunity to cleanse the reputation of humanitarian military intervention. There is a clear mandate, credible counterparts, a well-defined mission with an obvious exit strategy. The Libyan interim National Transitional Council has made it clear there is no need or desire for troops on the ground, which must make the job of convincing domestic constituencies in the US and Europe that much easier. Libya even has the means to pay for the cost of the intervention upon victory.

Those who don't want to be involved should stay out of the way. Disruption of the process will cost lives. Turkey and others should be aware of their shortsightedness and remember that Libya will soon have a new government, freely elected and representative of people who fought tooth and nail for their freedom, no thanks to them.

Just as we will not forget those who stand against us, we will owe a great debt to those who have chosen to stand with us. The UK and France, regardless of previous dealings with the Gaddafi regime, have made an honourable stand. France is still the only country to formally recognise the Libyan Interim National Transitional Council as the sole legitimate representative of the Libyan people. The friendship and support of Lebanon, Qatar, the UAE and other allies across the world must not and will not be forgotten. Even though the US came late to the party, it was its involvement that helped to swing the security council resolution, and US forces will almost certainly be involved in the implementation of any no-fly zone. It is now the job of Libyans to live up to the confidence of those who have come to their aid, and to the aspirations of those who have died fighting for a future that many of us believed we wouldn't see in our lifetimes.

Alaa al-Ameri is a pseudonym. The author is a British-Libyan economist and writer

LIBYA

How Gaddafi became a plonker

MARINA HYDE · Guardian, 27 August

Did you see that gold mermaid sofa which belonged to Colonel Gaddafi's daughter? To adapt George Orwell's famous observations on the goosestep, a gold mermaid sofa is only possible in countries where the common people dare not laugh at the army. "Its ugliness is part of its essence," Orwell went on of the preposterous high kick, in words which might just as easily be applied to that gilded monster of an arse-rest. "For what it is saying is 'Yes, I am ugly, and you daren't laugh at me.'"

Well, they dare now, even as Tripoli's death-toll mounts, and it's hard not to smile at every photo of a rebel posing with a goofy two-finger salute on the sea-beast, like some malarial parody of a DFS advert. See also pictures of rebels posing in canoes in Gaddafi's swimming pool; laughing at his fairground; or tinkling on his white baby-grand pianos with sarcastically raised eyebrows.

It's such a fine line between stupid and clever, as Spinal Tap's Nigel Tufnel once had cause to remark, and it's a similarly gossamer boundary between murderous and feared tyrant, and that plonker who bought some of the most tasteless nafferies in the wider north-African area.

Gaddafi may not be in rebel clutches (at least at time of writing), but he is now, unquestionably, a joke. And it's hard not to be swept along in the exhilaration of the great dictator becoming a joke. Ridicule is powerful, which is why the likes of Gaddafi threaten everything to suppress it, and in the free exchange of irreverence is the seed of Libyan democracy. This week, one of the country's most prominent comedians spoke of the challenges of a newly empowered audience. "Now it's very difficult to make them laugh about politics because they're joking themselves," explained Milood Amroni. "Now the people are making the jokes and we're laughing."

It's infectious. Spotting a cockroach in the sunken bath at the ransacked compound of Gaddafi's brutal intelligence chief Abdullah Senussi, a rebel saluted it. "Hello, Mr Abdullah," he is reported to have deadpanned. "We thought we'd find you here." For some, Gaddafi is even beyond a joke. "If I make jokes about Gaddafi they wouldn't be good jokes," Amroni continued, "because he's too weak now and it's not good to make jokes about a weak guy."

Ouch. And yes, I'm afraid I found the discovery of Gaddafi's Condoleezza Rice scrapbook almost too pathetic, and have filed it alongside the revelation from a former Bin Laden concubine that the late al-Qaida CEO had a massive crush on Whitney Houston, and was forever banging on about how "truly Islamic" she would be if only she hadn't been brainwashed by her then husband Bobby Brown.

Bin Laden understood the terrible threat of people laughing at him, which he deemed a fate worse than death. Death he was ready for, he would often say, but in 2006 he admitted in a taped address: "I fear to be humiliated." As well he might. It is incredibly difficult to fight ridicule. The only way is to be a self-deprecatingly good sport, or to be funnier back, both of which are rather tricky if your entire shtick is built on fear. And these days you can't keep a good joke down, which is presumably why Pakistan's president Asif Ali Zardari has made any quips about him sent via text, email or Twitter punishable by 14 years' imprisonment.

In his wise little book Fighting the War of Ideas Like a Real War, J Michael Waller insists dictators' desperate fear of being giggled at is justified. "The more autocratic or extreme the leader," he adds, "the more vulnerable he is to ridicule." He reminds readers that Augustus Caesar outlawed rib-ticklers about himself, while jokes about the Nazi regime carried a death sentence and Soviet comedians had to appear before cultural censors nicknamed the Department of Jokes. On seizing power, Fidel Castro ordered official buildings to display signs reading "Counter-revolutionary jokes forbidden here", while in the 1980s Iran assassinated even exiled humorists, bumping off a comedian in Germany and a seller of satirical CDs in London.

It's easy to think of other examples. Brazil's hangover from its dictatorial era is manifested in a law which bans ridiculing candidates in the three months prior to an election. Then there's everybody's favourite cuddly authoritarian socialist Hugo Chávez, who seeks to imprison satirists, and who last year banned any unauthorised use of even his name or image. In North Korea, only Kim Jong-il is permitted to make jokes, though he is, according to officials, "a priceless master of witty remarks". Sample gag? "Those who love the future have nothing impossible to do."

Mm. I don't want to stick my neck out on this one, but I can't help feeling that somewhere in North Korea, someone is telling a rather better joke than that, and the lesson of history is that eventually, some day, enough North Koreans will even dare to laugh at their goosestepping army. For now, though, the joke is on Colonel Gaddafi – his madness and mermaid sofas – and given that the Libyans will need a laugh in the difficult times to come, it seems churlish not to join in.

Marina Hyde is a Guardian columnist

LIBYA

Nato's intervention was a catastrophic failure

SEUMAS MILNE • Guardian, 27 October

As the most hopeful offshoot of the "Arab Spring" so far flowered this week in successful elections in Tunisia, its ugliest underside has been laid bare in Libya. That's not only, or even mainly, about the YouTube lynching of Gaddafi, courtesy of a Nato attack on his convoy.

The grisly killing of the Libyan despot after his captors had sodomised him with a knife, was certainly a war crime. But many inside and outside Libya doubtless also felt it was an understandable act of revenge after years of regime violence. Perhaps that was Hillary Clinton's reaction, when she joked about it on camera, until global revulsion pushed the US to call for an investigation.

As the reality of what western media have hailed as Libya's "liberation" becomes clearer, however, the butchering of Gaddafi has been revealed as only a reflection of a much bigger picture. On Tuesday, Human Rights Watch reported the discovery of 53 bodies, military and civilian, in Gaddafi's last stronghold of Sirte, apparently executed – with their hands tied – by former rebel militia.

Its investigator in Libya, Peter Bouckaert, told me yesterday that more bodies are continuing to be discovered in Sirte, where evidence suggests about 500 people, civilians and fighters, have been killed in the last 10 days alone by shooting, shelling and Nato bombing.

That has followed a two month-long siege and indiscriminate bombardment of a city of 100,000 which has been reduced to a Grozny-like state of destruction by newly triumphant rebel troops with Nato air and special-forces support.

And these massacre sites are only the latest of many such discoveries. Amnesty International has now produced compendious evidence of mass abduction and detention, beating and routine torture, killings and atrocities by the rebel militias Britain, France and the US have backed for the last eight months – supposedly to stop exactly those kind of crimes being committed by the Gaddafi regime.

Throughout that time African migrants and black Libyans have been subject to a relentless racist campaign of mass detention, lynchings and atrocities on the usually unfounded basis that they have been loyalist mercenaries. Such attacks continue, says Bouckaert, who witnessed militias from Misrata this week burning homes in Tawerga so that the town's predominantly black population – accused of backing Gaddafi – will be unable to return.

All the while, Nato leaders and cheerleading media have turned a blind eye to such horrors as they boast of a triumph of freedom and murmur about the need for restraint. But it is now absolutely clear that, if the purpose of western intervention in Libya's civil war was to "protect civilians" and save lives, it has been a catastrophic failure.

David Cameron and Nicolas Sarkozy won the authorisation to use "all necessary means" from the UN security council in March on the basis that Gaddafi's forces were about to commit a Srebrenica-style massacre in Benghazi. Naturally we can never know what would have happened without Nato's intervention. But there is in fact no evidence – including from other rebel-held towns Gaddafi re-captured – to suggest he had either the capability or even the intention to carry out such an atrocity against an armed city of 700,000.

What is now known, however, is that while the death toll in Libya when Nato intervened was perhaps around 1,000–2,000 (judging by UN estimates), eight months later it is probably more than ten times that figure. Estimates of the numbers of dead over the last eight months – as Nato leaders vetoed ceasefires and negotiations – range from 10,000 up to 50,000. The National Transitional Council puts the losses at 30,000 dead and 50,000 wounded.

Of those, uncounted thousands will be civilians, including those killed by Nato bombing and Nato-backed forces on the ground. These figures dwarf the death tolls in this year's other most bloody Arab uprisings, in Syria and Yemen. Nato has not protected civilians in Libya – it has multiplied the number of their deaths, while losing not a single soldier of its own.

For the western powers, of course, the Libyan war has allowed them to regain ground lost in Tunisia and Egypt, put themselves at the heart of the upheaval sweeping the most strategically sensitive region in the world, and secure valuable new commercial advantages in an oil-rich state whose previous leadership was at best unreliable. No wonder the new British defence secretary is telling businessmen to "pack their bags" for Libya, and the US ambassador in Tripoli insists American companies are needed on a "big scale".

But for Libyans, it has meant a loss of ownership of their own future and the effective imposition of a western-picked administration of Gaddafi defectors and US and British intelligence assets. Probably the greatest challenge to that takeover will now come from Islamist military leaders on the ground, such as the Tripoli commander Abdul Hakim Belhaj – kidnapped by MI6 to be tortured in Libya in 2004 – who have already made clear they will not be taking orders from the NTC.

No wonder the council's leaders are now asking Nato to stay on, and Nato officials have let it be known they will "take action" if Libyan factions end up fighting among themselves.

The Libyan precedent is a threat to hopes of genuine change and independence across the Arab world – and beyond. In Syria, where months of bloody repression risk tipping into fullscale civil war, elements of the opposition have started to call for a "no-fly zone" to protect civilians. And in Africa, where Barack Obama has just sent troops to Uganda and France is giving military support to Kenyan intervention in Somalia, the opportunities for dressing up a new scramble for resources as humanitarian intervention are limitless.

The once savagely repressed progressive Islamist party An-Nahda won the Tunisian elections this week on a platform of pluralist democracy, social justice and national independence. Tunisia has faced nothing like the backlash the uprisings in other Arab countries have received, but that spirit is the driving force of the movement for change across a region long manipulated and dominated by foreign powers.

What the Libyan tragedy has brutally hammered home is that foreign intervention doesn't only strangle national freedom and self-determination – it doesn't protect lives either.

Seumas Milne is a Guardian columnist

LIBYA

Reunion with my jailer

GHAITH ABDUL-AHAD · Guardian, 31 October

I remembered that Hatem was tall and wore spectacles and had a pudgy, smiling face that didn't seem to fit his profession. But I was not prepared for the warmth he showed. Meeting him again was like encountering an old friend. The questions came tumbling out. "How are you? How did you find me? What happened after you left?"

In the early days of the Libyan revolution, Hatem had been the officer in charge of my custody during two weeks of solitary confinement inside one of Gaddafi's notorious Tripoli prisons. The last time I saw him we had been separated by an iron door. Only his face and his hands had been visible as he passed food through the tiny hatch.

Outside, the revolution was fermenting in the mountains and the streets of the coastal cities, but inside the prison the officers had been confident. Hatem was angry, frustrated, and sometimes deluded, ranting against the rebels – "the rats", as Gaddafi had dubbed them – the agents of Nato, and the crusaders plotting against his country. He accused journalists of being spies and enemies of Libya.

"What do you want from us?" he would ask every night as he stood outside my cell, drinking coffee. Sometimes, in a sudden burst of generosity, he would pass a small cup through the hatch for me. But he never came inside. "We love Gaddafi. We love him. What's happening is all because of you journalists. It's a plot by Nato and Arab reactionary countries."

Months after I had been released, and after Tripoli had fallen to the rebels, I went to look for Hatem. I wanted to ask him if he believed in what he was telling me or if it was all part of an act. Through him I wanted to tell the story of the security apparatus of the regime in its final days and what's happening to them now.

The mood in Tripoli was jubilant. In Martyrs' Square car horns were honking, children waved flags, women ululated and celebratory bursts of gunfire peppered the sky.

But the signs of the difficult relationship between the old and the new were surfacing. In front of ministries and public buildings there were small demonstrations against old regime officials. In my hotel room I spread my clues out on the bed. I knew what Hatem looked like. I knew he worked in a prison of one of the many security services, but that was it. How do you look for the defeated in the city of victors?

For a city with a single main hospital and one university, Tripoli was well-equipped when it came to prisons. There was the infamous Abu Salim prison, where 1,200 inmates were killed in 1996; the military police prison; the criminal investigation prison. In the last days of the revolution, farms and company offices were converted into prisons and every military or security unit ran its own detention centre.

We drove to the prison of the external security service, where other journalists had been held. The main building was like a dead animal, its spine broken in half by a massive bomb. Around it were manicured lawns and a basketball court and pleasant gardens, smaller white buildings scattered among the shrubs and trees.

With a government guard I went into one of the smaller buildings. Inside, it was efficiently divided into small cells. But they were bigger and lighter than my cell. We walked into another building. During my incarceration I was blindfolded all the time while outside my cell. But I had drawn a map of the place in my mind. I thought I'd recognise it when I saw it. I didn't. Instead, recognition came in flashbacks. I am crouching blindfolded facing a wall, three men in military uniform sifting through our belongings. The room smells of hospital detergent. I can see a man in a surgical mask and rubber gloves. The Brazilian journalist I was captured with is led away. A big door slams.

Now the realisation hits me. I'm in that room again. A few bits of furniture lie overturned on the dark grey, mottled carpet. I can taste the feeling of terror that came over me in this place a few short months ago.

Flashback: three faceless officers interrogating me for hours. "You can tell us what we need to know or we can make you talk."

We walked further, into a long neon-lit corridor, huge black doors lining one side. Behind them lay dark cells with grimy mattresses, filthy, broken toilets. The ghosts of guards and their captives lingered in the air. Here, then. It was here.

I walked into different cells and wondered what had happened to the other inmates: the man who screamed all night, the Egyptian, the Tunisian, the American. "That building was called the Market," a former intelligence officer told me later. "There were food and clothing shops for the members of the service, officers who had to spend weeks without leaving would shop there. Then they converted it into a prison for high-value people, VIPs."

What about torture, I asked him. "Sometimes they would put the detainees in dog cages, just to scare them. It depended on the officer. Some would go out of their way to harm prisoners."

I was not beaten or tortured but I could hear the sounds of people getting beaten through the walls. The doctor had told me that the foreigners were treated differently. "Where they kept you the treatment was considered luxury compared to the guys who were kept in the back prison or with the dogs. The foreigners were not beaten but they beat and tortured the locals. They wouldn't beat the prisoners in front of me, but I did see officers walking with sticks made of palm tree reeds. But even without beating life was horrible, the dark, small dungeons, the fear, the sounds of the dogs. They terrorised the people in these dark cells. You lose your humanity, you lose your respect."

I asked Saleh, a former intelligence officer who spent some time in jail for aiding the rebels in the first days of the uprising, to help me track some of the former officers who worked in the "Market" prison. Two days later we managed to locate one of the guards that I knew. Abdul Razaq was lean and medium height, handsome with grey hair. I remembered him to be always in a good mood but now he looked years older. Dark, sagging rings had formed under his twitching eyes.

We sat outside his house in a small, dusty lane of low, brick houses in Tajoura. The metal shutters of shops were down but neighbours stood outside the high gates of their houses talking. He was scared and anxious. He didn't know why I had come to see him, and he was worried that I might be seeking some form of revenge. His daughters were playing around him like three little kittens. He sent one inside to bring tea. She came back carrying a white plastic tray that had a silver teapot and three very small cups. He held the teapot high while pouring.

"Look, I am still in charge of feeding you," he said, attempting to break the awkwardness of sharing tea with his prisoner. "When you were there things were good, after you left [mid-March) the prisons started filling. In the small cells we started putting five or six. The big ones held up to 60. The corridors were filled with detainees. It became horrible."

"For you or the prisoners?" I asked, half-jokingly. "For us," he said seriously, handing me the small cup. "Imagine the smell, of all those people squeezed together, we went there with masks on.

"When Nato started bombing us, I knew it was over. We can detain people and put them in jail but we can't resist Nato. We all started to defect."

"I couldn't handle the pressure after that," said Razaq. "I asked for a medical leave and I stayed in my house from June. "I didn't sign up for this, I didn't join the service to be under Nato bombing. Now in the middle of the night I jump. My wife says, what's happening? I say, bombs, bombs. She says, go back to sleep, these are your dreams."

I asked him if he knew the officer I was looking for. He said yes. He asked one of his daughters to bring him his phone and made a call and 10 minutes later the officer came. Tall and striding confidently, it was Hatem.

He was smiling. Abdul Razaq offered him a glass of tea. He drank it and kept asking how I found him.

It was a strange moment. We were meeting like old friends. There was some kind of shared camaraderie between us. Yet can I draw a line between the man and his job? Can you befriend your jailer? He told me about what happened to the jail after I left. He spoke about it fondly, as if it was a place filled with happy memories.

"We knew Nato was going to bomb us, we sent most of the prisoners to another place, a company compound. But we stayed in the headquarters. Most of the nights you can hear the sound of missiles and then you hear the explosion. That night we just heard a huge explosion, the floor underneath my feet went and then there was another explosion, everything was covered with smoke and dust, all the doors burst open from the explosion. The building that was hit was our communication centre. The monitoring equipment was there and we could listen to any phone number we wanted. How do you think we found you?" he smiled.

"We could have [survived] if it was Nato alone, but Libya was infested with spies," Hatem added bitterly. "So many people here defecting in the end – not because they didn't agree or benefit from the regime, but because they knew it was game over."

I asked the two officers about another jailer. He was short, stocky and rude and used to burst into the cell in the middle of the night asking random questions. A couple of times he blindfolded me and handcuffed me and marched me around the corridors, just to then bring me back to the cell.

"This guy had a psychological problem," said Hatem. "Sometimes he was nice, and then sometimes something in him clicks and he becomes very aggressive, making life for prisoners hell. In the last days there was paranoia. They were throwing anyone and everyone in prison. The [Gaddafi] militias would grab people in the street, take their money and phones, and hand them to us. We started refusing to receive detainees."

Hatem stood up: "What are you up to now? Let's drive around town."

Tripoli has the most beautiful sunsets in the world. A burning orange disc was sinking slowly into the sea. I watched his face change every time we passed a checkpoint. He would force a meek, uneasy smile, the smile of someone not used to relinquishing power.

People like Hatem are being detained all over Tripoli. They are stopped at checkpoints and pulled out of their cars when they show their ID cards.

"This is a very dangerous time," Hatem said. "No one has credibility. [The rebels] call you, they say we need to talk to you, you go, and you find yourself detained. The Gaddafi regime used to detain people and no one would know where they are and who detained them. Now it's the same thing."

There comes a point when people know that the days of the regime are over. This point comes at different times to different people. Saleh switched sides in March. Abdul Razaq lost his nerve in June. I asked Hatem, when did he reach that point?

"I never defected. I worked until 20 August (the day rebels entered Tripoli). Only then I couldn't go to work because of the fighting. But I didn't pick up a gun and fight the rebels. Those are Libyans. I think they are mistaken, but it's not my job to fight in the streets."

The perfect disc was half-submerged now in the water. Families were filling the small playground on the edge of the sea. A traffic jam built up in front of Martyrs' Square, honking and selling flags.

"The same people who were carrying the green flag in Gaddafi's one million people march are the same people carrying the flag of the revolution," Hatem says.

"Gaddafi didn't import people to cheer for him. They were Libyans. It's fine. People can change their mind." But, he adds, it is wrong for those same people now to claim they had nothing to do with the regime, and to say that everyone who did should be locked up. Two days later, I met Hatem again. We sat in an old cafe in the centre of old Tripoli, in the courtyard of a beautiful old Italian palazzo.

Men smoked and discussed the politics of post-Gaddafi Libya. Hatem ordered two machiatos. I asked Hatem if he or others tortured people in the prison.

"Look, what do you expect from us? We are an intelligence service. We needed to get confessions from people, but it all depends on the officer. Some officers enjoy the pressure on people. Some just do it to get information. Most of the times you don't need to torture people to get information – you just buy it off them."

The more I talked to Hatem, the more resentfully he spoke of the rebel movement.

"Muammar [Gaddafi] is to be blamed for all that happened," he said. "He should have left from the beginning. He was great in his foreign policy. I knew as a Libyan nothing can happen to me overseas because the regime will defend us. But at home, he was a disaster. His sons looted all the foreign investment and they left the country hungry, and when the war happened the poor people became the victims."

In words almost identical to that of Iraqi army officers who found themselves shunned or hunted after the fall of Baghdad, he said: "Five of my friends have been killed in the last month. We were almost 10,000 members of the intelligence service.

"We haven't been paid for two months now. In another month or two, 5,000 will start to rebel against the transitional council if they continue with the assassinations of the former officers. Then we are heading to civil war."

Ghaith Abdul-Ahad is a Guardian correspondent

SYRIA

The boldness of Bashar al-Assad

BRIAN WHITAKER • Guardian, 31 March

Bashar al-Assad doesn't really look like an Arab president. Or a dictator, come to that. He doesn't have the arrogant grandeur of a Ben Ali or the self-centred pomposity of a Mubarak. Seeing him reminds me of some gangly scoutmaster: the sort who gets very dogmatic about granny knots and clove hitches but still has trouble keeping tents up in a strong wind.

Considering the public mood in the Middle East this may even give Assad an advantage. The less any leader resembles Ben Ali or Mubarak at the moment, the better, and his pep talk on Wednesday to the Damascus scout troop – sorry, parliament – seemed to be much appreciated. "Dib dib dib dob dob dob," they chanted at every opportunity. Well, not exactly, but they might just as well have done. They clapped a lot, interrupted him with loyal declarations of support and even lauded him with poems.

Assad, for his part, looked comfortable and relaxed (he was, after all, among friends) and seldom referred to his notes. He smiled from time to time and chuckled at his own jokes. It's easy to see why many Syrians prefer him to his dad – though, to be honest, it's very hard not to be more likeable than Hafez al-Assad.

It was when Assad came to the now-obligatory section of his speech where embattled presidents blame foreign conspiracies for the demonstrations that I started to feel confused. Surely he had got it the wrong way round. Others have been saying that the aim of the "foreign conspiracy", if such it is, is to keep Assad in power, not to remove him. What about that article in Haaretz the other day describing Assad as "Israel's favourite Arab dictator"? Or Hillary Clinton praising him as a "reformer"?

Contrary to the impression given in some of the news reports, Assad did talk about reform, and talked about it rather a lot. Syria is already reforming, he said, and will continue to do so. But just when it seemed that he might be on the point of announcing some specific new reforms, he stopped speaking and the parliament gave him a final round of applause.

To understand why, we have to look at an interview Assad gave to the Wall Street Journal at the end of January – which he also mentioned in his speech on Wednesday. Interviewed shortly after Ben Ali had been ousted from Tunisia and when the Egyptian uprising was just a few days old, he said: "If you did not see the need for reform before what happened in Egypt and in Tunisia, it is too late to do any reform. This is first. Second, if you do it just because of what happened in Tunisia and Egypt, then it is going to be a reaction, not an action; and as long as what you are doing is a reaction you are going to fail."

So Assad is trying a different tack. Reform, yes, but all in good time. There will be no hasty concessions to protesters as happened in Tunisia and Egypt; that would be a sign of weakness and would only encourage further demands. Instead, the relevant ministries will announce their plans in due course, after full and careful consideration, etc, etc.

That is certainly a bold strategy, but in the midst of growing turmoil it's either a sign of supreme confidence or extreme recklessness.

So how will it play out in Syria? For hardcore regime supporters, it's an attitude they can understand and admire. One of them, quoted in Joshuah Landis's Syria Comment blog, said:

Finally, I respect Bashar. He has showed that he is a real man. He has spared the country bloodshed. Any sign of weakness, it would have been the start of the end … All the modern and reform-minded people are dreamers. They live abroad and think that Syria can become a London/Paris/NY if we just reform. It is either civil war or the status quo ...

Kentucky Fried Chicken? We can do without it. Those that don't like it can leave to their fancy foreign capitals or Beirut. They are welcome [to visit Syria] in the summer to enjoy the food and arghile and go back to their democracy.

But what of the others, almost certainly the majority, who are not hard core? What faith can they place in the assurances of steady reform? Since Assad came to power 11 years ago, a few reforms – very modest ones in comparison with what needs to be done – have been accomplished, perhaps not at a snail's pace but certainly at a speed that could be overtaken by a tortoise. Even Assad conceded in his speech: "The state has made promises of reform and they have not been carried out."

There is no guarantee, though, that reforms promised for the future will be any more radical than those of the past. In the words of another Syrian quoted by Landis: "Somebody has decided that either all Syrians are dumb and [the regime] can continue to trick them for ever or that civil war is much better than giving the people more power."

One of the most telling parts of Wednesday's performance was not Assad's speech itself but what it revealed about the sycophancy of Syria's parliament. This is clearly not a place for hammering out laws and policies through the cut and thrust of debate. It is a temple for the Assad cult and changing that will take more than reform. It will take a revolution.

Brian Whitaker is a Guardian Middle East specialist

SYRIA

Sanctions: damned if we do, damned if we don't

GEORGE MONBIOT • Guardian, Tuesday 20 September

I would rather not be writing this column. To argue against the course of action I'm discussing is to tolerate collusion with a murderous regime. To argue in favour is to risk promoting wider human suffering. The moral lines are tangled and the progressive response is confused: perhaps it is unsurprising that this issue has attracted little public discussion. Should we or should we not support wider economic sanctions on Syria?

I felt obliged to tackle this question when I discovered last week that Shell, the most valuable firm listed on the London Stock Exchange, is directly connected to the economic interests of Bashar al-Assad's government. It has a 21% share in the Al Furat Petroleum Company, 50% of which is owned by the state. Ghassan Ibrahim, CEO of the Global Arab Network and a prominent opponent of the regime, tells me that the government permits foreign companies a share of its booty only if they can offer expertise it does not otherwise possess. As much of the wealth produced by Syrian state companies goes into the pockets of the elite, it seems clear that if Shell were not useful to the regime, it would no longer be there.

Shell says: "We condemn any violence and the human rights abuse it represents and we have deep concern over the loss of life … we comply with all applicable international sanctions." But, though complying with current sanctions, it is enriching a government that is violently repressing peaceful protest. The regime has killed some 2,600 Syrian people since March. Its interrogators have tortured and mutilated its prisoners, cutting off genitals and gouging out eyes.

The likely outcome of Shell's investment is that Assad has more money to spend on soldiers, weapons and prison cells. The argument for forcing Shell and other investors to leave and for finding further means of starving the government of money is a strong one.

But no one with an interest in human rights can be unaware of what happened when western nations applied sanctions to Syria's neighbour, Iraq. No one who has seen it can forget the CBS interview in 1996 with Madeleine Albright, Bill Clinton's secretary of state. The interviewer pointed out that half a million children had died in Iraq as a result of sanctions. "We think the price is worth it," Albright replied. The sanctions on Iraq could scarcely have been better designed to cause mass mortality. But even measures that are narrower in scope and applied more humanely will add economic distress to the suffering of Syria's people. Sanctions broad enough to hurt the government's ability to deploy troops will also be broad enough to hurt the people they are meant to protect.

And if not sanctions, then what? So far the only alternatives on offer are vacuous condemnation and demands from the likes of Nick Clegg that "it's time for Assad to go", which, in terms of efficacy, is like being mauled by a giant sock.

So far the European Union has imposed travel bans on members of the regime and frozen some of their assets. The impact is likely to be limited, not least because Assad and his close associates are said to have stashed far greater sums beyond the reach of the EU (and beyond the reach of any kind of scrutiny or accountability) in Swiss banks. It wasn't until May that European governments decided to impose an arms embargo on Syria, which tells us more than is comfortable about their priorities. But better late than never.

More recently, Europe banned the import of Syrian oil. Because the EU imported over 90% of Syria's oil, because oil provides 25% of state revenue and because the state has a monopoly on its sale, this would have stung – had Italy not insisted that the ban be delayed until mid-November. This gives the government time to find new customers. An investment ban, which would reduce the value of assets that enrich the political elite, could hit the government much harder.

The obvious means of resolving this question is to ask the Syrian people what they want. But there is no clear consensus. Of the three opponents of the Assad regime I've consulted, two are in favour of wide-ranging sanctions, one is against. Chris Doyle, director of the Council for Arab-British Under-standing, who has spoken to a much larger number of dissidents, tells me that "Syrians are hugely divided on this issue". Almost everyone in the protest movement supports sanctions aimed specifically at members of the regime and their businesses, but they are split over wider measures, such as the EU's oil embargo.

Ghassan Ibrahim told me that opponents of the government recognise that "freedom is very expensive and you have to pay the price. Let's pay it once and for good." He argues that sanctions are likely to be more effective than they were in Iraq, as the regime's resources are smaller. Even today it can scarcely afford to sustain its army. The government's oil revenues provide few benefits for the people.

Samir Seifan, a prominent economist who sought to reform the regime, argues in favour of a wider embargo, including sanctions on investments in the oil and gas sector. This would, he concedes, hurt people because of its impact on industry, farming, transport and electricity, but it also restricts "army movements which are using a huge amount of oil products". Others have argued, Doyle says, that as well as hurting the people more than the regime, sanctions would give Assad an excuse to blame the Americans and Europeans for the economic crisis he has caused.

So I posted the question on Comment is Free, in the hope that Guardian readers would help to resolve it. There was a big response. It provided no clear answers, but it helped to clarify some of the issues.

The most widespread objection to the sanctions was that the governments imposing them are selective in their concerns and lacking in moral credentials. This is true on both counts. This column is discussing sanctions on Syria only because they are being imposed there, rather than on Saudi Arabia or Bahrain, which are also run by violently repressive regimes. Far from restraining them, the UK and other European nations continue to supply them with a hideous array of weapons. Though both the UK and the US committed the crime of aggression in Iraq, there is no prospect of sanctions against them. This is the justice of the powerful.

But these concerns, while valid, do nothing to resolve the question. You could just as well argue that because the grisly Russian and Chinese governments oppose further sanctions, they must be a good idea. The brutality of Assad's government is not altered by the nature of the states that oppose him, or by the incoherence and self-interest of their foreign policy. We must make our own moral judgments.

The division on this question among Syrians, the difficulty in predicting the outcome of measures that might help and will harm, a repulsion from collaboration pitched against a fear of aggravation, lead me to an unusual place for a polemicist. There is no right answer.

George Monbiot is a Guardian columnist

SYRIA

Why Russia is sticking by Damascus

DAVID HEARST · Guardian, 2 December

While an international noose is tightening around the neck of Bashar-al Assad's regime in Syria, with Turkey this week doing most of the pulling, one country, other than Iran, is intent on bucking the trend – Russia.

A day after the UN human rights council said that Syrian forces were committing crimes against humanity, and Turkey was considering imposing a buffer zone along its border to protect Syrians, Sergei Lavrov, the Russian foreign minister, said further attempts should be made to engage with Damascus.

Lavrov opposed the idea of an arms embargo, saying it was unfair to expect the Syrian government not to respond to unrest. He thought that for the most part armed opposition groups were provoking the Syrian authorities. These were not empty words.

On Monday the state-run English-language channel, Russia Today, reported that Moscow would be sending the aircraft-carrying missile cruiser, Admiral Kuznetsov, and two escort ships on a two-month tour of the Mediterranean and would be dropping in on the Syrian port of Tartus. Six hundred Russian technicians are currently working there to renovate it as a base for Russian ships. Russia Today said the deployment had been long planned, but no one lost sight of the fact that the USS George HW Bush had just appeared off the coast of Syria. On Thursday, a consignment of Russian Yankhont anti-ship cruise missiles arrived in Syria.

Why is Russia engaging so heavily with Syria, where it did not with Libya or Iran? After all, the Russian president Dmitry Medvedev banned the sale of R-300 anti-aircraft missiles to Tehran.

The first answer is money. Apart from active arms contracts worth $4bn, the Moscow Times reported recently that Russia's investment in Syrian infrastructure, energy and tourism amounts to $19.4bn in 2009. A Russian company, Stroitransgaz, is building a natural gas processing plant 200km east of Homs and is providing the technical support for the Arab gas pipeline. The Tatarstan-based Tatneft began pumping Syrian oil last year and in January vowed to spend $12.8m drilling wells near the Iraqi border.

But that is by no means all of the story. The shadow of Libya weighs heavily on Russia's policy with Syria. Throughout the Nato intervention, Lavrov said Russia would not recognise the rebels (although that is what they ended up doing), that there was no UN mandate for a ground forces operation, that the Nato intervention caused more casualties than would otherwise have occurred. Back in August Lavrov said: "Russia will do everything it can to prevent a Libyan scenario happening in Syria."

Even though such a scenario has for now been ruled out by Nato, Admiral Viktor Kravchenko, former chief of naval staff, said Moscow was sending a message to the US and Europe. "Having any military force other than Nato's is very useful for the region because it will prevent the outbreak of armed conflict," he said.

This is not as daft as it first seems, although Russia's naval deployment is no match for Nato, and indeed will be eagerly awaited by them. Naval watchers will be agog to know whether Russia can keep three large ships on the seas without one of them breaking down.

Russia's fears about a civil war developing in Syria are geostrategic and may not be too dissimilar to some of the more cautious western foreign policy analysts, war-gaming the effects it would have on the region. Russian middle eastern experts compare Syria to Russia's own province of Dagestan in the North Caucasus.

Unlike its neighbouring Chechnya, Dagestan is a patchwork of competing tribes, religions, ethnicities and loyalties, more than 150 of them. If a breakaway Muslim insurgency took hold there, Dagestan would explode like a grenade, sending hot shards of metal and people across southern Russia.

Russian fears of a Lebanese-style civil war breaking out in Syria, with the country fissuring on sectarian lines, may not be as far fetched in three months' time as they currently seem. Keeping Syria together while getting rid of a vile dictatorship may conversely be a harder task than western leaders pressing for more sanctions realise. Turkey for one is talking big, but acting on the ground more cautiously.

David Hearst is a Guardian leader writer

SYRIA

Why we must stay out of Syrians' struggle

MEHDI HASAN · Guardian, 12 December

Given the events of the Arab Spring, some might say that the tell-tale sign that a dictator's days are numbered is when his defiance turns to delusion. Last Wednesday, in an interview with ABC's Barbara Walters, a chuckling and snorting Bashar al-Assad, the Syrian dictator, tried to deny any responsibility for the attacks on his own people: "They are not my forces. They are the forces belonging to the government. I don't own them, I'm president."

This, of course, is denial of the highest order. Syria is a police state in which Assad and his Ba'ath party cronies call all the shots – literally. According to the

United Nations, Syrian security forces have killed more than 4,000 since protests against the regime broke out in March. ("Some mistakes committed by some officials," shrugged Assad.)

His television interview has been interpreted by some as further evidence that the Syrian regime is on the back foot. But is Assad really close to quitting? Or being toppled? Of the three dictators who have fallen since the start of the Arab Spring, one (Gaddafi) is dead, one (Mubarak) is on trial, and one (Ben Ali) is in exile. Assad is reported to have turned down offers of safe haven in the Gulf and continues to show no mercy to the protesters. His Shabiha militias roam Syria's streets, shooting, maiming and torturing. On Sunday at least nine people were killed in clashes as opposition activists tried to call a general strike.

So it would be a mistake to write off the ruthless Syrian president, no matter how deluded he might seem on television. His regime has been remarkably resilient, despite having endured US-imposed sanctions for the past seven years. In 2005, following the assassination of the former Lebanese prime minister Rafiq al-Hariri – allegedly on the orders of Syrian intelligence – many western analysts assumed that Assad, the young, pampered, UK-educated eye doctor, was finished. Yet he not only survived but emerged stronger, more determined and more outspoken on issues of Middle East diplomacy (from the civil war in Iraq to the calcified politics of the Arab-Israeli conflict).

Syria, of course, is a key player in the region: the Americans and Israelis want Assad gone in order to try and pull Syria out of Iran's orbit and thereby further isolate the mullahs in Tehran (as well as Syrian-sponsored militant groups like Hamas and Hezbollah); the Russians are defending Assad in order to protect their business interests in Damascus and to prevent any knock-on effects from a Syrian civil war on Russia's own restive province of Dagestan; the Turks have turned on Assad, their former ally, in order to bolster their new position as a regional power and diplomatic linchpin; and the Gulf Arabs just want to back a Sunni majority against a minority Shia/Alawite regime.

Yet, as Flynt Leverett, a former Middle East analyst for the US National Security Council and the CIA, has observed: "It is far from clear that the Assad government is actually imploding ... Moreover, no one has identified a plausible scenario by which the 'opposition', however defined, can actually seize power."

Leverett is right to put the word "opposition" in quotation marks. There is no singular, unified or cohesive movement against Assad. In a reflection perhaps of the country's array of religions, sects and ethnicities, Syria's dissident groups are diverse and divided. They cannot agree on tactics or goals, with credibility and legitimacy varying from group to group.

The biggest point of tension is between exiled opposition activists and protesters on Syria's streets. "There have been a dozen conferences and statements in several cities but nothing to show for it," a protester told the Economist back in September. "Meanwhile we continue to go out and take the bullets."

Another major tension is between the Syrian National Council (SNC) – formed in August from a multiplicity of opposition groups, including the Muslim Brotherhood and the Kurdish Future Movement party, and led by the Paris-based Syrian academic Burhan Ghalioun – and the Free Syrian Army (FSA), composed of around 15,000 defectors from the armed forces.

Ghalioun is a popular figure in Washington, having told the Wall Street Journal earlier this month that a post-Assad Syria would cut off military ties with Iran and reduce its support for Hamas and Hezbollah. Yet his SNC insists that the Syrian opposition must not resort to violence or turn to armed resistance. The FSA, however, has launched attacks on Syrian soldiers and Ba'ath party offices. "We don't like [the SNC] strategy," the FSA coordinator Abdulsatar Maksur told the New York Times last week. "We favour more aggressive military action."

Then there are the sectarian and ethnic tensions. The opposition has been desperate to downplay the fact that it is largely drawn from Syria's Sunni Arab majority and rejects claims that it is directing its protests and anger towards the privileged Shia Alawite minority that rules the country. Yet in July the International Crisis Group, an independent, Brussels-based thinktank, published a report that claimed the opposition had "edit[ed] out sectarian (ie anti-Alawite) slogans that at times are voiced on the streets" from the videos of protests that it regularly posts on the internet. In August, at a meeting of opposition figures in Turkey, the Kurdish delegation is reported to have staged a walkout when the other opposition groups declared their wish to keep the word "Arab" in the name of the Syrian republic.

Since Friday, however, the SNC has been focused on one particular task: warning western governments and journalists that Syrian forces are planning a massacre in the western city of Homs.

There are reports that western intelligence agencies have been training the FSA. More worryingly, if one looks at precedents from Kosovo in 1999 to Libya this year, this could mark the beginning of a descent down the slippery slope to war.

But a western-led military intervention in Syria would be a disaster. Unlike with Libya, there is no prospect of a UN security council resolution, and nor has there been a call for military action from the Arab League – or from Syria's internal opposition groups. "We reject foreign intervention – we think it is as dangerous as tyranny. We reject both," says Hassan Abdul-Azim, a leading member of the National Co-ordination Committee, a grassroots (and anti-SNC) umbrella group of nonviolent opposition activists inside Syria.

Logistically, a no-fly zone would be of little value in Syria, where Assad's security forces and militias are carrying out small-scale, street-by-street operations against unarmed civilians, rather than launching massed army assaults or air strikes.

So the west's approach in Syria should be Hippocratic: first, do no harm. Further sanctions might succeed in squeezing Assad's mafia-like regime, but sending British or American planes to carpet-bomb the suburbs of Damascus or Aleppo will do little to protect civilian lives or bolster the opposition.

The youth of Syria – brave, unarmed, idealistic – are being cut down by Assad's troops and yet the grim reality is that there is little the west can do to help them: we cannot control events in Syria or bring about a speedy end to the crisis. If the popular uprising against the Ba'athists is to succeed, Syrians – of all parties, sects and ethnicities – will have to make it happen on their own. The sad truth is, it is not our job to topple Assad.

Mehdi Hassan is senior editor (politics) at the New Statesman

BAHRAIN

Political art blossoms at Pearl roundabout

OMAR AL-SHEHABI • Guardian, 6 March

It is 5am, the sun is yet to rise, and it is a perfect time to visit "Lulu", Pearl roundabout, which is the centre of Bahrain's opposition movement. The hard core of people are just arising from their slumber, but our aim is to check out the street art on display.

The country's political street slogans have been dominated over the past 20 years either by huge banners congratulating the royal family on being good leaders, or hastily scribbled graffiti of "Down with Al Khalifa", which are then quickly washed over by the security forces. The settlement established at Lulu has provided a fertile ground for new forms of political street art – though how long it will remain is unclear.

A busy traffic junction with a large flyover overlooking it, Pearl roundabout contains thousands of messages. Many deliver the usual motifs that have become the opposition's staple diet: martyrs, sacrifice, glory. Graphic pictures of the recently killed and imprisoned fill the roundabout. "We will write our victory with our martyrs' blood," says a popular slogan.

The less formal ones signal new signs of creativity. "We won't move even if summer comes. The air conditioners are ready," says a placard with the front of a real air conditioner plastered on it, referring to the searing temperatures that can reach 50C in July.

One of the more striking artworks is a chair, crooked, with a toy machine gun strapped on it. Through the chair are two arrows, one labelled "martyrs" and the other "political naturalisation". Underneath the chair is a picture of superglue. The label reads: "Tested on the Bahrain PM's chair for 40 years" – in reference to the longevity of the current prime minister in his position.

Others follow the same theme. One shows a picture of the eight British prime ministers since 1970, starting with Edward Heath all the way to David Cameron. Below are pictures of all the prime ministers in Bahrain over the same period – one.

A big banner hangs from the side of the flyover: "We have heard of people changing their regimes. Have you ever heard of a regime changing its people?" This refers to the widespread accusation regarding the government bringing in thousands of carefully selected foreigners and fast-tracking their citizenship to re-engineer the country's demographic makeup.

On the neatly designed centre-stage of the roundabout, the Arabic arches are topped with "We are here until the regime falls". A few days earlier, members of an officially recognised Islamist party erased the slogan. It does not chime with their declared stance on a constitutional monarchy. Not much later other youths were repainting it.

"By the end of this week these banners calling for the fall of the regime must be gone," said one leader of an officially recognised opposition party. Two weeks later, "The people want the downfall of the regime" is by far the most popular chant in the square.

"For me, the fall of the regime could be a proper constitutional monarchy," explains one protester. "However, 'The people want a constitutional monarchy with full separation of powers and an elected assembly and an accountable prime minister' does not make for a catchy chant."

Although so far leaderless, no movement can be complete without icons. One is the "popcorn guy". He was present selling popcorn from the first day of the occupation of Lulu. Two nights later the security apparatus forcibly scattered the campers, killing five protesters. When protesters retook the roundabout two days later, the guy was back but his popcorn machine was gone.

"Popcorn guy" now wanders the square carrying a placard saying: "The people demand the army returns the popcorn machine" (it rhymes in Arabic). In this video, he sarcastically tells the government that you have stolen the sea and he can no longer fish (in reference to vast areas of reclaimed land that went to private hands), and now they have also stolen his popcorn machine. His livelihood has been cut off. He promises to share the popcorn returns 50–50 (in reference to a long-held accusation that the head of the government takes half of the profits from any largescale projects on the island).

Nick Kristoff, the Pulitzer prize-winning American journalist, is another recent household name. While the opposition has been appreciative of his reporting, with one promising to rename a street after him should the movement succeed, he is now the main subject of the government sympathisers' ire, with petitions against him circulating widely. This follows a series of tweets and articles in which he lambasted the Bahraini authorities for their bloody treatment of the protesters.

There is a battle for hearts and minds on the streets of Bahrain, to use a phrase often abused by American officials. The most widespread symbol has become the Bahraini flag. Tailors are the busiest traders on the island, hardly able to keep up with demand. This red-and-white zig-zagged flag, designed under British orders after the signing of the protectorate treaty more than 150 years ago, is being reclaimed by all sides.

Flags of Hezbollah and pictures of its charismatic leader, Hassan Nasrallah, have disappeared from opposition rallies. Pro-government rallies have also witnessed a noticeable decline in the pictures of the Bahraini leadership. They have all been replaced by the national flag, a significant change for some of the opposition, who used to see the flag as a symbol of the ruling dynasty.

"National" and "unity" have become the catchphrases of the times. "No Sunni, no Shia, national unity," is a very popular chant, implicitly underscoring the sectarian tensions. The new pro-government movement is called the National Unity Gathering, while a group of independents of largely oppositional leanings took up the name the National Coalition. Although yet to be fully implemented in practice, if these words do get cemented into political reality, the government could be in for an even bigger headache.

Omar al-Shehabi is a Bahraini citizen and director of the Gulf Centre for Policy Studies

BAHRAIN

A nation of deepening divisions

IAN BLACK · Guardian, 8 August

Midsummer nights are steamy in Manama, and sweat glistened on thousands of faces as Sheikh Abdel-Latif Al Mahmoud boomed out a warning to Bahrain's citizens to stand guard against criminals and conspiracies.

Cries of *Allahu akbar* went up from a sea of red and white national flags and pictures of King Hamad bin Isa al-Khalifa – teenage girls in jeans alongside veiled women and heavily bearded men in dishdashas. "This land will not be sold," they chanted. "In spirit and blood we will redeem you, O Bahrain."

Sheikh Mahmoud, a Sunni religious leader, heads the Tajammu' al-Wahda al-Wataniya (national unity gathering), formed in February when the revolutions in Egypt and Tunisia inspired peaceful anti-government protests in the Arab world's smallest country, triggering a violent backlash whose consequences still reverberate.

Pro-reform demonstrations at Pearl roundabout were followed by marches that paralysed Manama's financial district and one that headed for the royal palaces in al-Rifa'a.

The drama peaked in mid-March when Saudi forces moved across the King Fahd causeway in a show of force that underlined Bahrain's particular fragility in a tough and intolerant neighbourhood. Five months on, international interest in Bahrain has faded, but emotions here are still running high.

"My country was almost destroyed by political extremists," rages one Sunni businessman. Isa Darwish, a Christian from the city of Muharraq, complained of harassment by Shias from an adjacent village. "For the foreign media the Sunnis simply don't exist – so please tell our side of the story," a banker says.

Bahrain's status quo has been shaken. "Whoever invented the term Arab Spring deserves a prize," quipped Sheikh Mahmoud, displaying gory pictures of wounds inflicted on Sunnis as the unrest escalated. "And they called them peaceful protests!"

Shias demanding equal rights are portrayed by Sunnis as fanatics who are cheered on by Iran. The communities' narratives, like in Northern Ireland and Israel/Palestine, are hard to reconcile. Both see themselves as victims – though the suffering has been one-sided: most of the 33 dead, and the hundreds injured and imprisoned, are Shias and 30 Shia mosques, built without licences, have been demolished.

Ten days ago, on the eve of Ramadan, King Hamad – "a wise and democratic monarch", the media gushed loyally – was pondering the results of a "national dialogue" tasked to make recommendations for political and constitutional reforms, with slick western PR advisers on hand to spin the message.

Al-Wifaq, the main Shia opposition group, did not wait for the end. Its representatives walked out, protesting that their demands were being ignored.

"We met, we quarrelled, we drank tea and coffee and it provided some psychological relief," says, with a laugh, Munira Fakhro of the secular Wa'ad party (the National Democratic Action Society). "But it was a forum not a dialogue. The barrier is still there." The question, says a worried foreign diplomat, "is what does the king do with it all?"

Expectations are higher for an inquiry into the "events" of February and March. Set up by the king under the American-Egyptian international lawyer Cherif Bassiouni, its English title is the Bahrain Independent Investigation Commission – though tellingly, the local Arabic papers refer to it as the "royal" commission.

Its report, due in October, is likely to name those responsible for unlawful killings and other abuses. Bassiouni, a highly regarded veteran of UN and other inquiries, describes King Hamad as an "enlightened monarch who deserves support" and believes he will act on the recommendations.

Opposition supporters are not so sure – but hope he is right. "Terrible things were happening in Bahrain just a few months ago," says Mansoor al-Jamri, who has just been reinstated as editor of al-Wasat, the country's only independent newspaper, after being forced by the government to step down. "They've said, 'We've killed who we've killed and now let's move on.' Issuing press releases isn't going to be enough. There has to be substance."

Government officials in Manama are anxious to project a new sense of stability: the next Formula One Grand Prix is to be held in November

2012 and banking confidence is holding up – but restoring calm at home looks hard.

The national dialogue did express support for a "fairer" electoral system but there are no plans to change constituency boundaries or other mechanisms that preserve Sunni control: one Shia constituency has 15 times as many voters as a small Sunni one – classic gerrymandering.

No wonder critics were quick to dismiss the dialogue as a sham. "An exercise in make-believe," is the blunt conclusion of a new report by the International Crisis Group.

The king, it seems likely, will continue to appoint the prime minister and rely on an unelected upper chamber of parliament to keep MPs in check and his own power untrammelled.

And there is no sign that the government will halt its controversial policy of "political naturalisation" of non-Bahraini Sunnis – imported from Syria, Jordan, Yemen and even Pakistan – to fill the ranks of the security forces (from which Shias are largely excluded) to tip the demographic balance.

Census figures are not available but independent observers assume that Shias still make up at least 60% of Bahrain's native population. Sunnis dislike discussing this sensitive subject – and are not always consistent when they do.

"The Shia are not the majority," insists Anwar Abdulrahman, outspoken editor of the pro-regime daily Akhbar al-Khaleej. "Or if they are it is only 51% to 48%."

It was Abdulrahman's newspaper that famously called the US president "Mullah Obama" because of Washington's pressure for reforms that many Sunnis fear will empower the Shia and serve Iran's strategic interests.

In this highly charged atmosphere it is easy to forget that before this year's crisis, Bahrain, for all its shortcomings and sectarian divide, was the most liberal country in the Gulf.

Yet prospects for change now look bleak. Salman, the reformist crown prince, has been marginalised. Encouraged by the US and Britain to maintain dialogue with the opposition, he was outmanoeuvred by Sheikh Khalifa, the king's uncle, who holds the record as the world's longest serving prime minister – since 1971.

"An obvious move would have been for the king to sack Khalifa," says an intellectual, who defines himself as a member of the Sunni silent majority. "But that is harder now because it would be interpreted as sympathetic to Shia demands and would alienate the Sunnis, which he can't afford to do.

"You can use the police and the army to control the Shias but the Sunnis are the police and the army. Personally, I would rather live under a family than a sect."

The curiosity is that Bahrain might not have had its place in the Arab Spring at all. "If some people had kept their heads it could all have been avoided," suggests a foreign observer, who was in Manama as the government panicked and hardliners on both sides called the shots.

It will not be easy to repair the damage. Sheikh Mahmoud, talking long after the Tajammu rally ended and the shouts of patriotic support had died away, admits the government cannot embrace the reforms sought by the Shias at the same time as maintaining the Sunnis' traditional dominance.

"Our society has been broken in two," he says. "We are still guided by sectarian and tribal principles. Democracy is only a way for people to share in the running of the country when there is civil peace. "We want the rule of law, but if electoral reform leads to sectarian war in Bahrain should we go through that door? Any regime has to provide services and security for everyone."

Ian Black is the Guardian's Middle East editor

YEMEN

A better country awaits us all

TAWAKKUL KARMAN · Guardian, 9 April

The revolution in Yemen began immediately after the fall of Ben Ali in Tunisia on 14 January. As I always do when arranging a demonstration I posted a message on Facebook, calling on people to celebrate the Tunisian uprising on 16 January.

The following day a group of students from Sana'a University asked me to attend a vigil in front of the Tunisian embassy. The crowd was shouting: "Heroes! We are with you in the line of fire against the evil rulers!" We were treated roughly by the security forces, and we chanted: "If, one day, a people desires to live, then destiny will answer their call," and "The night must come to an end" – the mantra of the revolutionaries in Tunisia.

The demonstration was astonishing; thousands turned up, and Sana'a witnessed its first peaceful demonstration for the overthrow of the regime. "Go before you are driven out!" we cried.

That night student and youth leaders visited me, along with the human rights activist Ahmed Saif Hashid and the writer Abdul Bari Tahir. We agreed that we could not let this historic moment pass us by, and that we too could spark a peaceful revolution to demand an end to a despotic regime. We decided there was to be no backing down, despite the repression we knew would come. The rallies grew daily, even though the government deployed thugs against us.

After a week of protests I was detained by the security forces in the middle of the night. This was to become a defining moment in the Yemeni revolution: media outlets reported my detention and demonstrations erupted in most provinces of the country; they were organised by students, civil society activists and politicians. The pressure on the government was intense, and I was released after 36 hours in a women's prison, where I was kept in chains.

After my release I continued to demonstrate. Invitations were sent to all parties – including the people of the south, the Houthis in the north, the tribes, trade unions, civil society organisations and the army – to join the peaceful student revolution and demand an end to the regime. We encouraged them to overlook their differences and assured them that Yemen would be better off without Ali Abdullah Saleh; that the Yemeni people could resolve their own problems, including the war in Sa'ada, the issue of south Yemen and the question of terrorism. We believe we can establish a civil state with the rule of law. This was the message in the first weeks of the revolution.

Around the country, in places like Ta'az, Aden and Al-Hadidah, tents sprang up for vigils, copying Cairo's Tahrir Square. Hundreds of thousands poured into these "squares of liberation and change". With the inclusion of all sections of society, the revolution had outgrown the student movement.

So what happens when the regime falls, as it must? We are in the first stage of change in our country, and the feeling among the revolutionaries is that the people of Yemen will find solutions for our problems once the regime has gone, because the regime itself is the cause of most of them. A new Yemen awaits us, with a better future for all. We are not blind to reality, but the fact is that the revolution has created social tranquillity across the country as the people put their differences to one side and tackle the main issue together – no mean feat, given that there are an estimated 70 million weapons in Yemen.

In five years my country has witnessed six wars, but now the people's guns are silent; they have chosen peaceful change. Despite the fact that hundreds of protesters have been killed by the regime, not one police officer or security agent has been killed by the masses. Even Ma'arab, the most unruly and turbulent province, has witnessed its first peaceful demonstrations.

Violent tribesmen who have fought each other for decades have come together in "liberation squares"; blood feuds have been forgotten. When snipers killed more than 50 protesters and wounded 1,000 on the Friday of Dignity, it was the young who arrested the culprits; not one was attacked or injured, despite the anger and the blood that had flowed in the streets. This was the peaceful nature of the revolution in practice.

For the first time people in the south stopped calling for separation, raised the national flag and demanded an end to the regime. It's been truly historic. The country is united in its aim to rid itself of the regime through public vigils and rallies, civil disobedience and slogans instead of teargas and bullets.

This is a regime that carried out 33 years of rule through blood and corruption. We have brought it to its knees through our determination to remain in the squares for months if necessary, and through the steadfastness of our young people who have confronted the bullets of the regime with bared chests. With politicians and members of the army standing beside us, our success will go even further.

We cannot let the bogeyman of al-Qaida and extremism be used to stall historic change in our country; Saleh invokes this threat in an attempt to cling to power, as if he is the only one capable of bringing stability and tackling terrorism. It would be foolish to believe his lies.

Let us be clear: the Yemeni revolution has already brought internal stability to a state riddled with war and conflict. I call on the global community to support the peaceful revolution as it did in Tunisia and Egypt. I call on the United States and the European Union to tell Saleh that he must leave now, in response to the demands of his people. They should end all support for his regime, especially that which is used to crush peaceful opposition – teargas canisters have "Made in America" on them. They should freeze the Saleh family's assets and those of Saleh's henchmen and return them to the people.

If the US and Europe genuinely support the people, as they say, they must not betray our peaceful revolution. It is the expression of the democratic will of the overwhelming majority of the people of Yemen.

Tawakkul Karman is a Yemeni journalist and activist. She was awarded the Nobel Peace Prize in October 2011

YEMEN

Saleh resigns at last – but it changes little

BRIAN WHITAKER · Guardian, 24 November

After 33 years in power, nine months of deadly street protests calling for his resignation and weeks in hospital recuperating from a bomb attack on his palace, Yemen's Ali Abdullah Saleh finally signed away his presidency on Wednesday. He had come close to signing several times before – only to back off at the last moment.

Exactly what induced him to do the deed on this occasion is still unclear but the grisly fate of Muammar Gaddafi in Libya may have helped to focus his mind, along with international pressure. Yemen expert Ginny Hill suggests that a UN resolution approved unanimously by the security council last month may also have paved the way. The resolution, in effect, called on Saleh to go (it urged him to accept a transition plan hammered out by the Gulf Co-operation Council) and called for progress reports at 30-day intervals.

Just as the first of these reports was due, Saleh showed an increasing willingness to sign. Had he not done so, it's likely that the security council would have begun moving towards sanctions – starting by freezing the assets of Saleh and some of his immediate entourage.

Faced with the choice between a possible asset freeze and a promise of immunity from prosecution in the GCC deal, Saleh has opted for the latter. But although he has signed, he hasn't quite gone yet. He will nominally remain as president until a successor is elected, while the vice president – in theory at least – assumes all his powers. There are also rumours that Saleh may be bundled off abroad again for more medical treatment, this time to the US rather than Saudi Arabia.

Will this be enough to calm the situation on the ground in Yemen? Many are doubtful. Vice president Abd-Rabbu Mansour Hadi is a fairly weak figure who lacks a significant support base, either in politics or the military. At the same time, Saleh's numerous relatives continue to hold key positions from where they can manipulate the strings on his behalf.

If his relatives start causing trouble again – as they did during his absence after the bomb attack – Saleh will claim his country needs him again, because he is the only person who can rein them in. Even at this late stage, a further comeback attempt by Saleh cannot be ruled out.

According to the plan, though, Hadi will press ahead with forming a government of national unity ahead of an early presidential election – supposedly to be held 90 days from now. Rather than creating a breathing space, this could easily trigger a new power struggle as would-be presidents (conceivably including Saleh's son, Ahmed) jostle for position.

More generally, this emphasis on the presidency does not bode well because what Yemen really needs is a more effective parliament and a less powerful president. Ideally, there would have been a new constitution in place limiting presidential power before the installation of Saleh's successor but that seems unlikely to happen and curbing a new president after the election will be more difficult.

In the meantime, parliamentary elections are long overdue. They were supposed to have been held in April 2009 but parliament's term was extended for a further two years. The postponed elections failed to materialise again in April this year – ostensibly for technical reasons, though the turmoil in the country also made holding them impractical.

The upshot is that even without Saleh, Yemen still has a parliament in which Saleh's party, the General People's Congress, holds an overwhelming majority. It is a parliament with no real mandate and very little legitimacy, yet it is also the body charged by the constitution with the task of approving candidates for presidential elections.

Saleh may be on the way out but his regime – and everything it stands for – is still very much in place. That is basically what the GGC states were hoping for with their so-called transition plan: change at the top while preserving the status quo beneath.

There are parallels here with Egypt where the fall of Mubarak left key parts of his regime intact, as the protesters there are now discovering. For Yemenis who want real change, the struggle is far from over.

ALGERIA

Hopes of change remain alive

KARIMA BENNOUNE · Guardian, 24 March

A hundred stalwart demonstrators stand on the Place de 1er Mai (First of May Square) in Algiers, at what has become their weekly Saturday gathering. They include activists from opposition political parties, women's rights advocates, and people who are just plain fed up. This small but resolute troop is surrounded (and vastly outnumbered) by police who push them around and try to make them go away.

I was sorry to see fewer people demonstrating last weekend than in February, and asked Madjid Makedhi, who has reported many of the protests for El Watan newspaper, to explain. He told me the diminished numbers are entirely understandable in light of the massive security presence (there is even a helicopter overhead).

"Algerians have been separated from politics by these security policies of the government," Makedhi said. "Today ordinary Algerians can only think about their daily lives, about taking care of their children, and trying to have enough money to satisfy the needs of their families."

Still, the activists refuse to give up. Cherifa Kheddar, the women's rights advocate who I saw arrested last month, was in the square again last Saturday with her sign calling for the abolition of the gender-discriminatory family code, and carrying a bag full of similar placards for others to use.

The authorities ripped them all up, so she then raised her hand in the victory sign, and asked: "Are you going to try to take my fingers away from me now?"

On Sunday in Algiers, I interviewed protesting teachers and members of the new National Committee for the Defence of the Rights of the Unemployed. About 600 lined both sides of the street near the presidency building for hours, singing, chanting slogans – *hukuma dégage!* ("government out"), *al-hukuma dar al-ajaza* ("the government is an old folks' home") and many others.

Everyone has demands. The demonstrating teachers want better working conditions. The protesting unemployed want decent jobs. On the other side of the street, waving their Algerian passports, stood a group of now jobless workers who fled Libya during the current conflict and want to be assisted by the state. More than anything, they all want to be heard.

I wonder what the young policemen must be thinking as they stand in the street all day with their youthful counterparts. Fadia Babou, a serious 24-year-old unemployed woman who used to work for a radio station, tells me: "Really, the young policemen are living in the same situation we are."

In recent weeks, there have been multiplying manifestations of discord – communal guards marching, wounded veterans sitting in, doctors on strike, community meetings demanding change. Many more are planned. One of the young teachers tells me the problem is that each sector is demonstrating separately and there is currently no structure available to bring them all together. He is not hopeful about this as he says all the political parties are discredited and no single forum appeals to everyone.

Algeria's road ahead may be different from that of Tunisia or Egypt. The lingering nightmares of the 1990s, when some 200,000 died in a terrible war with fundamentalist armed groups, are partly responsible for this. According to this week's Jeune Afrique magazine, the distinction is also partially due to the fact that much more freedom of expression is possible here than in Ben Ali's Tunisia and this provides something of a pressure valve.

However, one of the biggest obstacles may be a lack of popular belief in the possibility of change.

Women's rights activist Fadila Chitour explains to me that many Algerians suffer from what she calls wounded memories, from the sense that so many deaths in the country since independence – in the protests of October 1988 and in the terrible 1990s – have been in vain. Hence, there is a pervasive feeling that making sacrifices now will not change anything.

This profound disillusionment with politics, which echoes Makedhi's assessment, makes rallying the population to protest much more difficult than elsewhere. Chitour is, however, confident that change will come to Algeria. "It is ineluctable," she asserts.

However, the big question for Chitour is not whether change will come or when, but how. "Will it be by peaceful means or not?" She says Algerians are terrorised by the idea that blood could flow in the streets again. And so she and the other members of the National Co-ordination for Change and Democracy will keep organising their peaceful protests every Saturday trying to make sure that grievances are channelled nonviolently.

Meanwhile, the Committee of the Unemployed will meet soon to assess its next move as well. My fervent hope is that the leaders of Algeria will heed the calls of the peaceful protesters, while that is possible. Among other things, change will require responsiveness to the youth, unity in the opposition and a seizing by all of this "moment of grace" as Tunisian human rights activist Alya Chamari described this spring across north Africa.

Is there a road that leads from Sidi Bouzid, the birthplace of the Tunisian revolution, to Algiers? That remains to be seen. Still, I cannot forget what Chamari says when I ask her if there is a message for Algerians, and others, from the Tunisian revolution: "You must never lose hope. And you must count on your youth."

Karima Bennoune is a US-based law professor

SAUDI ARABIA

A summer to follow the Arab Spring seems far off

JASON BURKE · Guardian, 30 June

The Bridges bookshop and cafe, on Arafat Street in an upmarket residential area of the southern Saudi port city of Jeddah, is quiet this weekend afternoon. Three young women sit on the floor working on a 13,000-piece jigsaw. Among the well-thumbed books for browsing on the artfully slanted shelves, next to works on Islamic calligraphy and architecture, are biographies of Mahatma Gandhi, Che Guevara and Nelson Mandela.

Yet Asma, Amna and Dina, all 23, are no revolutionaries. As educated, English-speaking, iPod and iPad-carrying young Arabs, they are very much in the same demographic as those who organised the mass demonstrations that ended the rule of President Hosni Mubarak in Egypt this year, but the three women are separated from their counterparts in Cairo by more than the Red Sea.

Images of the Arab Spring streaming into Saudi Arabia on the ubiquitous satellite TV channels may have meant that "people are realising the importance of being politically aware", Amna, a human resources management student, says. But, in the kingdom, "we don't actually do anything".

Such feelings explain, at least in part, why, while the rest of the Arab world is in ferment, Saudis, of whom 70% are under 30 and 35% are under 16, have remained largely quiet. Despite overseas attention focused on a few incidents of protest, scores of interviews over two weeks in deeply conservative areas, the capital, Riyadh, and relatively liberal Jeddah have revealed a country in which a growing desire for reform is a very long way from anything approaching mass dissent.

There is activism. The women working on the jigsaw are all involved in campaign groups, arguing for the right for women to vote in forthcoming municipal elections. Dina, who recently returned to Saudi Arabia after four years at a US college, says "nobody was doing much campaigning" when she left but now "lots is going on". Last month, several dozen women openly drove cars in defiance of custom, if not law.

"We cannot be a global leader and a medieval backwater at the same time," declared one headline in the Arab News newspaper.

There is also an increasingly vocal community of human rights activists, bloggers and tweeters. "Something is happening every week. Activism was not really in the social fabric here but, compared to five years ago, things are really picking up," says Mohammed al'Qahtani, a prominent human rights campaigner. Long-term observers of the kingdom – diplomats and analysts – agree.

Yet anyone hoping for major upheaval soon is likely to be disappointed. The word that recurs in Saudi Arabia is "gradual". The increase in activism is relative and demands remain modest. "We are asking to be allowed to drive," says Eman al-Nafjan, a female PhD student and blogger in Riyadh.

Any activism remains within very tightly constrained bounds in this still fiercely conservative country. The present ruler, King Abdullah, is known as more moderate on many issues than many predecessors and many other senior royals. He has tacitly encouraged campaigns for women's rights. His own decision to moderate the strict policy of gender segregation at the huge new research university he has had built on the outskirts of Riyadh enraged local conservatives. In much of the kingdom, women remain heavily veiled even inside a private home if there is an unrelated man present, and single men are banned from shopping malls.

There are very clear rules about what criticisms can be voiced within the kingdom. These are so widely understood they do not have to be enforced.

Social issues such as bureaucratic incompetence, poverty and corruption can be denounced but only as long as the authority and integrity of the house of Al Saud are not questioned. Widespread anger at graft is thus rarely voiced, even if, as the jigsaw solvers put it, "the ceiling on what can be said has risen a lot".

So an academic who posted an article imagining Saudi Arabia without the royal family on his Facebook page was jailed for three months. So, too, in February and March, were hundreds of Shia demonstrators from the kingdom's eastern oil-rich areas within whose community there is deep resentment at continuing discrimination.

The unpredictability of the far from monolithic authorities also acts as a deterrent. In May, several female drivers were detained, one for 10 days, yet no action was taken against about 40 women who drove two weeks ago. Officials "decided it was better to let their families deal with them", according to General Mansour al-Turki, a spokesman for the interior ministry. But this week, religious police arrested five.

The greatest severity is reserved not for "liberals" – though harassment is continual – but for Shia activists accused of links to Iran, and political Islamists whose organisation, ideology and criticism of the religious legitimacy of Saudi rulers are seen as extremely dangerous.

"The basic watchword is that reforms are to be granted by the king, not won through agitation, organisation and direct action," says one Riyadh-based analyst. "You can make your views known – there is a traditional right of audience and petition which is upheld – but that's it."

Many Saudis do not merely accept this, but welcome it. "It has to be remembered that the royal family are sitting on top of the most conservative society in the region, if not the world, and democracy is a foreign word, whatever is happening elsewhere [in the region]," says a second western Riyadh-based observer. The 87-year-old king remains popular, seen as a grandfatherly patriarch, despite the frequent complaints about his thousands of relatives.

Jamal Khashoggi, a prominent reformist journalist, stresses how the rule of the house of Al Saud is seen as maintaining the cohesion of a relatively new country containing many different communities.

"Egypt has sometimes been smaller or bigger but has not been divided for thousands of years. The Egyptians have their identity," says Khashoggi. "Saudis did not take to the streets demonstrating for change [because] they knew they could never agree. We all want a better country. Some want a more liberal country, some a more conservative country. But we all want a united country."

Others point to the lack of tradition of public protest – political gatherings or parties are illegal – to explain why there has been no "Saudi summer" after the Arab Spring. There is also the clergy's support for the royals in this deeply religious country. In March, senior clerics dutifully issued a fatwa, or religious opinion, stating that it was un-Islamic to demonstrate.

Finally, there is the simple fact that most Saudis are much better off than they were only a few decades ago. The heady rush of the fabulous wealth of the 1970s may be gone, but oil revenue, inflated by recent high prices, still provides vast funds. There are big problems with housing in Saudi Arabia, and youth unemployment is estimated at 30%, but there are also subsidised utilities, a vast range of benefits and huge numbers of easy government jobs with generous pensions. Universities are free, with students paid a monthly stipend. Taxes are minimal. In March the king announced US $130bn worth of new homes and public sector pay rises.

Poverty exists. Turki Faisal al-Rasheed, a businessman and campaigner in Riyadh, calculates that, though 80,000 individuals are worth more than $250m, 3 million are very poor. Starting salaries for teachers are below $6,000, barely a living wage. There are even occasional beggars. But most Saudis, if not the 9 million foreign labourers who do much of the menial work, are at the very least comfortable.

This may eventually change. "At the moment, the macroeconomic picture is just fine, but in the long term something has to give," warns John Sfakianakis, chief economist at the Banque Saudi Fransi in Riyadh. By 2020, the Saudi population will be 35 million, with huge energy demands of its own. Even Saudi oil revenues will not be enough to sustain the current lifestyle of most.

Its leaders are aware of the need for economic reforms, particularly to create jobs for Saudis rather than foreigners, in the private sector. One recent measure was a royal decree to allow women to work in shops serving other women.

"We have to create jobs and to shift the economy into a higher level of productivity, more technology and knowledge-driven and less dependent on oil," Dr Abdul Wahed al-Humaid, the vice-minister of labour, says. One effort involves scholarships worth £20,000 per year for more than 100,000 young Saudis studying overseas, often in the US. A huge new university for women – the biggest in the world – has just opened.

One aim is to stimulate creative, independent thinking, which, Humaid admits, may make young Saudis question authority, particularly if there are economic problems. "With the internet and satellite television, the social change has already taken place," the minister says.

For the moment, however, any real challenge to the house of Al Saud or indeed to the country's strict conservatism appears a distant prospect, whatever is happening in the rest of the region.

"Change will come – it's got to come – but it will be at a pace which suits our society," says Miteb, 23, recently returned from college in California.

The women drivers have been careful to be veiled and accompanied by a family member, as customs demand. Amna stresses how the Bridges bookstore is somewhere to debate and meet but not to challenge social values. Though sexes mix there in a way that would shock some, she and her friends still wear the long black abaya gown.

"People are always trying to categorise liberals and conservatives. It's more complicated. You can be both at the same time but in different ways," she says. "But we definitely want more for our kids than we have."

Jason Burke is a foreign correspondent for the Guardian and Observer

REVOLUTION 2.0

The Facebook generation kickstarts a seismic change

MONA ELTAHAWY · Observer, 30 January

My birth at the end of July 1967 makes me a child of the Naksa, or setback, as the Arab defeat during the June 1967 war with Israel is euphemistically known in Arabic. My parents' generation grew up high on the Arab nationalism that Egyptian president Gamal Abdel Nasser brandished in the 1950s. But we "Children of the Naksa", hemmed in by humiliation, have spent so much of our lives uncomfortably stepping into pride's large, empty shoes.

But here now finally are our children – Generation Facebook – kicking aside the burden of history, determined to show us just how easy it is to tell the dictator it's time to go.

To understand the importance of what's going in Egypt, take the barricades of 1968 (for a good youthful zing), throw them into a mixer with 1989 and blend to produce the potent brew that the popular uprising in Egypt is preparing to offer the entire region. It's the most exciting time of my life.

How did they do it? Why now? What took so long? These are the questions I face on news shows scrambling to understand. I struggle with the magnitude of my feelings of watching as my country revolts and I give into tears when I hear my father's Arabic-inflected accent in the English of Egyptian men screaming at television cameras through tear gas: "I'm doing this for my children. What life is this?"

And Arabs from the Mashreq to the Maghreb are watching, egging on those protesters to topple Hosni Mubarak who has ruled Egypt for 30 years, because they know if he goes, all the other old men will follow, those who have smothered their countries with one hand and robbed them blind with the other. Mubarak is the Berlin Wall. "Down, down with Hosni Mubarak," resonates through the whole region.

In Yemen, tens of thousands have demanded the ousting of Ali Abdullah Saleh who has ruled them for 33 years. Algeria, Libya and Jordan have had their protests. "I'm in Damascus, but my heart is in Cairo," a Syrian dissident wrote to me.

My Twitter feed explodes with messages of support and congratulations from Saudis, Palestinians, Moroccans and Sudanese. The real Arab League;

not those men who have ruled and claimed to speak in our names and who now claim to feel our pain but only because they know the rage that emerged in Tunisia will soon be felt across the region.

Brave little Tunisia, resuscitator of the Arab imagination. Tunisia, homeland of the father of Arab revolution: Mohammed Bouazizi, a 26-year-old who set himself on fire to protest at a desperation at unemployment and repression that covers the region. He set on fire the Arab world's body politic and snapped us all to attention. His self-immolation set into motion Tunisian protests that in just 29 days toppled Ben Ali's 23-year dictatorship. We watched, we said wow and we thought: that's it? Ben Ali ran away that quickly? It's that easy?

Ben Ali called his armed forces for help 27 days into the popular uprising. It took Mubarak just four days into Egypt's revolt to call the army. He had unleashed the brutality of his security forces and their riot police, but they couldn't stem the determination of the thousands who continued to demand his ousting. He put Egypt under information lockdown by shutting down the internet, Burmese-junta style, but still they came.

Ben Ali's fall killed the fear in Egypt. So imagine what Mubarak's fall could do to liberate the region. Too many have rushed in to explain the Arab world to itself. "You like your strongman leader," we're told. "You're passive, and apathetic."

But a group of young online dissidents dissolved those myths. For at least five years now, they've been nimbly moving from the "real" to the "virtual" world where their blogs and Facebook updates and notes and, more recently, tweets offered a self-expression that may have at times been narcissistic but for many Arab youths signalled the triumph of "I". I count, they said again and again.

Most of the people in the Arab world are aged 25 or are younger. They have known no other leaders than those dictators who grew older and richer as the young saw their opportunities – political and economic – dwindle. The internet didn't invent courage; activists in Egypt have exposed Mubarak's police state of torture and jailings for years. And we've seen that even when the dictator shuts the internet down protesters can still organise. Along with making "I" count, social media allowed activists to connect with ordinary people and form the kind of alliances that we're seeing on the streets of Egypt where protesters come from every age and background. Youth kickstarted the revolt, but they've been joined by old and young.

Call me biased, but I know that each Arab watching the Egyptian protesters take on Mubarak's regime does so with the hope that Egypt will mean something again. Thirty years of Mubarak rule have shrivelled the country that once led the Arab world. But those youthful protesters, leapfrogging our dead-in-the-water opposition figures to confront the dictator, are liberating all Egyptians from the burden of history. Or reclaiming the good bits.

Think back to Suez to appreciate the historic amnesia of a regime that cares only for its survival. In cracking down on protesters, Mubarak immediately inspired resistance reminiscent of the Arab collective response to the tripartite aggression of the 1956 Suez crisis. Suez, this time, was resisting the aggression of the dictator; not the former colonial powers but this time Mubarak, the dictator, as occupier.

Meanwhile, the uprisings are curing the Arab world of an opiate, the obsession with Israel. For years, successive Arab dictators have tried to keep discontent at bay by distracting people with the Israeli-Arab conflict. Israel's bombardment of Gaza in 2009 increased global sympathy for Palestinians. Mubarak faced the issue of both guarding the border of Gaza, helping Israel enforce its siege, and continuing to use the conflict as a distraction. Enough with dictators hijacking sympathy for Palestinians and enough with putting our lives on hold for that conflict.

Arabs are watching as tens of thousands of Egyptians turn Tahrir Square into the symbol of their revolt. Every revolution has its square and Tahrir (liberation in Arabic) is earning its name. This is the square Egypt uses to remember the ending of the monarchy in 1952, as well as of British occupation.

The group of young army officers who staged that coup in 1952 claimed it as a revolution, heralding an era of rule by military men who turned Egypt into a police state. Today, the army is out in Tahrir Square again, this time facing down a mass of youthful protesters determined to pull off Egypt's first real post-colonial revolution.

Mona Eltahawy is an Egyptian-American journalist

The uprising isn't born of Twitter or WikiLeaks. But they help

TIMOTHY GARTON ASH • Guardian, 19 January

"The Kleenex revolution"? Somehow I think not. Unless, that is, you follow Libyan president Muammar Gaddafi. In a televised denunciation of the popular uprising that has deposed his friendly neighbouring dictator, he ranted: "Even you, my Tunisian brothers, you may be reading this Kleenex and empty talk on the internet." (Kleenex is how Gaddafi refers to WikiLeaks.) "Any useless person, any liar, any drunkard, anyone under the influence, anyone high on drugs can talk on the internet, and you read what he writes and you believe it. This is talk which is for free. Shall we become the victims of Facebook and Kleenex and YouTube?" To which, since the speaker is another dictator, I devoutly hope that the answer is "Yes". Let Kleenex wipe them away, one after another, like blobs of phlegm.

But will it? What contribution do websites, social networks and mobile phones make to popular protest movements? Is there any justification for labelling the Tunisian events, as some have done, a "Twitter revolution" or a "WikiLeaks revolution"?

A remarkable young Belarussian activist-analyst, Evgeny Morozov, has just challenged the lazy assumptions behind such politico-journalistic tags in a book called The Net Delusion, which went to press before the Tunisian rising. The subtitle of the British edition is "How Not to Liberate the World". Morozov has fun deriding and demolishing the naively optimistic visions which, particularly in the United States, seem to accompany the emergence of every new communications technology. (I remember an article a quarter-century ago entitled "The fax will set you free".)

He shows that claims for the contribution of Twitter and Facebook to Iran's green movement were exaggerated. These new technologies can also be used by dictators to watch, entrap and persecute their opponents. Above all, he insists that the internet does not suspend the usual workings of power politics. It is politics that decides whether the dictator will be toppled, as in Tunisia, or the bloggers beaten and locked up, as in Morozov's native Belarus.

His challenge is salutary but, like most revisionists, Morozov exaggerates in the opposite direction. Tunisia offers a timely corrective to his corrective.

For it seems that here the internet did play a significant role in spreading news of the suicide which sparked the protests, and then in multiplying those protests. An estimated 18% of the Tunisian population is on Facebook, and the dictator neglected to block it in time.

Among the educated young who came out in force, we can be sure that the level of online (and mobile phone) participation was higher. The scholar Noureddine Miladi quotes an estimate that half the Tunisian television audience watches satellite TV, and he notes: "Al-Jazeera heavily relied on referencing Facebook pages and YouTube in reporting the raw events." So professional satellite TV fed off online citizen journalism.

Moreover, these media leap frontiers. A leading British scholar of the Maghreb showed me his Facebook page, which has many of his Maghrebian former students as Facebook friends. Several of the Moroccans had turned their Facebook icons to the Tunisian flag, or a Tunisia-Morocco love-heart, to show their enthusiasm for the first people-power toppling of an Arab dictator in more than 45 years. That's a tiny group, to be sure – but elites matter, in opposition movements as in everything else.

Before Ben Ali's fall, his regime had struck back against the netizens, mounting "phishing" attacks on Gmail and Facebook accounts, harvesting passwords and email lists of presumed opponents, and then arresting prominent bloggers such as Slim Amamou. This reinforces Morozov's point that the internet is a double-edged sword: yet it is also a back-handed tribute to the importance of these new media. As I write, the formerly imprisoned Amamou has become a member of a new, interim coalition government.

Nobody knows what will happen tomorrow, but thus far the Tunisian rising has been a hugely heartening development – especially because it was an authentic, homegrown, largely spontaneous movement, with little active support from western powers. (Sometimes quite the reverse: France was, until the very last minute, offering its security expertise to keep Tunisia's Louis XVI in power. For shame, Madame Liberté, for shame.)

The transformed information and communications technologies of our time played a role in enabling this rising to succeed. They did not cause it, but they helped. Specialists argue that Tunisia, with its small, relatively homogenous, urban, educated population, and (for now) moderate, peaceful, largely exiled Islamists, can become a beacon of change in the Maghreb. If things go well, the internet and satellite TV will spread that news across the Arab world.

So yes, the internet furnishes weapons for the oppressors as well as the oppressed – but not, as Morozov seems to imply, in equal measure. On balance it offers more weapons to the oppressed. I think Hillary Clinton is therefore right to identify global information freedom in general, and internet freedom in particular, as one of the defining opportunities of our time. But there are also dangers here, which Morozov usefully points out.

If the struggle for internet freedom is too closely identified with US foreign policy, and in turn with US companies such as Google, Facebook and Twitter – which in personnel terms are beginning to have something of a "revolving door" relationship with the US government – this can end up damaging the purpose it is meant to serve. Authoritarian regimes everywhere will redouble their efforts to censor and monitor those American platforms that, not accidentally, are among the best and most open we have. Instead, these regimes will promote their own, more restricted native alternatives, such as Baidu in China.

The US government as a whole is also deeply inconsistent in its approach to internet freedom. It berates China and Iran for covert monitoring of opponents while doing the same itself against those it defines as threats to national security. It lauds global information freedom while denouncing WikiLeaks as, in Clinton's extraordinary words, "a threat to the international community".

Again, Tunisia is instructive. Talk of a "WikiLeaks revolution" is as absurd as that of a "Twitter revolution", but WikiLeaks revelations about what the US knew of the Ben Ali regime's rampant corruption did contribute something to the pot of misery boiling over. There was even a special website to disseminate and discuss the Tunisia-related US cables (tunileaks.org). Obviously, Tunisians did not need WikiLeaks to tell them that their presidential family was a goon-protected self-enrichment cartel; but having detailed chapter and verse, with the authority of the US state department, and seeing how much the publicly regime-friendly American superpower privately disliked it, and knowing that other Tunisians must know that too, since the American reports were there online for all to see – all this surely had an impact.

So if Clinton wishes to argue, as I believe she legitimately can, that the American-pioneered infrastructure of global information exchange has contributed to the fragile rebirth of freedom in Tunisia, then she should really put in a word of appreciation for WikiLeaks – or for Kleenex, if you prefer the Gaddafi version. But do not hold your breath.

Timothy Garton Ash is a historian and Guardian columnist

The bloggers' manifesto

YAZAN BADRAN · Guardian, 8 October

If you've been following the so-called Arab Spring you've also probably read an article asking whether Facebook was behind it all. In Washington, in New York, in London and around the world, technologists and sociologists, web developers and foreign policy wonks have deliberated and debated the role of social media in bringing about these momentous events.

What you probably haven't read about though is the history of the painstaking online activism that paved the way for the revolutions that toppled dictators. To hear that story, you needed to be in Tunis this week, where a group of leading bloggers from more than 20 countries across the Middle East and beyond were gathering for the first time since the revolutions began.

There's no doubting the Third Arab Bloggers Meeting was a special event. This was not a conference about the revolutionaries; this was a conference for those very revolutionaries. And more notably, it was the first time we were able to speak publicly and freely in an Arab capital.

Three years ago, in 2008, the first Arab Bloggers Meeting brought together members of the diverse and widespread Arab blogosphere. Many of the bloggers at this year's meeting were in Beirut three years ago for that first event, and remember a very different kind of meeting. Whereas we met this week in jubilation, with our cameras on throughout, that first meeting was private, small and low-key.

Almost a full year after the first protests broke out here in Tunis, they continue to shake the Arab world. We meet now with a completely different set of experiences, and a completely different list of priorities. What has, in Egypt and Tunisia, become reality, and is elsewhere ongoing, was nothing more than aspiration at our first meeting: bloggers talked tactics, laying the groundwork for the revolutions to come.

In 2008, nobody could anticipate these monumental changes that were to sweep across the region two years later. Back then these challenges and our role in overcoming them were very familiar. We had grown up with them; we struggled to organise, to co-ordinate across diverse groups, and to circumvent the dire conditions of censorship and persecution as the first steps to bring about needed changes. The discussions, general and mostly speculative in nature, were about possibilities rather than concrete plans.

But as we sit here and discuss the success stories from around the Arab world, and contemplate how we can contribute this expertise towards the benefit of others still struggling, we have also come to realise that this is only the beginning.

The challenges facing each country in the post-revolution Arab world will be complex, but not dissimilar, whether in Syria – where the revolution is yet to find its final conclusion – or in Tunisia, where elections will take place in just two short weeks, and our roles as bloggers in the coming process of nation-building will have to be adapted to these new realities.

New spheres of expression, long closed and forbidden to us, are now open. Reclaiming, defending and efficiently utilising these spaces to debate and promote our visions of the new Arab world will be our most immediate task. Also vital to our upcoming challenges is establishing a culture of openness and transparency, something that will require us to overcome years of forced secrecy and anonymity in the Arab world.

We are hopeful that when we leave Tunis and go back to our respective bases, we'll bring with us not only the sense of solidarity and comradeship that we've seen in every corner of the Arab world, but also a workable vision that we can all set upon.

Yazan Badran is a Japan-based Syrian blogger. This article was jointly commissioned by Global Voices and Meedan

Experts in messing up hierarchies

PAUL MASON · Guardian, 8 February

"We will fight, we will kiss …" says the poster, over a picture of a single rioter leaping over a line of riot shields. "London, Cairo, Rome, Tunis." It may be a bit over-optimistic about Rome, but it sums up the zeitgeist. What's going on is neither a repeat of 1968 or of the "colour revolutions" that followed the collapse of the Soviet Union. Nor is it enough to observe that "they're all using Twitter" – this misses the point of what they are using it for.

At the heart of the movement is a new sociological type – the graduate with no future. They have access to social media that allow them to express themselves in defiance of corporately owned media and censorship. With Facebook, Twitter, and Yfrog truth travels faster than lies, and propaganda becomes flammable.

More important, they seem immune to hermetic ideologies: Bolshevism, Labourism, Islamism, the myths and legends around constitutional Irish nationalism. Sitting in meetings with the discontented from Athens to Dublin during this crisis, I've noticed how the organised politicos flounder; how they cannot impose their action plans and strategies.

Women are numerous as the backbone of these movements. After 20 years of modernised labour markets and higher education access, the "archetypal" protest leader, organiser, facilitator, spokesperson now is an educated young woman.

But the sociology of the movements is only part of the story. Probably the key factor is "horizontalism", which has become the default method of organising. Technology makes non-hierarchical organising easy: it kills vertical hierarchies spontaneously, whereas the quintessential experience of the 20th century was that movements became hierarchised, killing dissent within, channelling the energies in destructive directions.

In addition, the speed of doing things compensates for their relative lack of organisation: in this the protesters have stumbled upon the principle of asymmetry – a swarm of disorganised people can effect change against a slow-moving hierarchical body.

And then there are "memes". When Richard Dawkins proposed the concept in 1976 – of a cultural genetics in which ideas are spawned, replicate and mutate – he was describing something pervasive in culture. But mass access to information technology, to continue the analogy, may have produced an evolutionary take-off in the speed of replication.

What it means for this generation is that ideas arise, are very quickly market-tested and then either take off, bubble under, insinuate themselves into the mainstream culture or, if they are no good, disappear. And memes are both overt and subtextual: they can be the snatch of a few lyrics from a song; a piece of street art – and they can be as powerful in guiding the actions of people as the old, cadenced and soundbitten public speeches of yesteryear.

On top of that there is the network. It's become axiomatic that the network is more powerful than the hierarchy. But the ad hoc network has become easier to form. So if you "follow" somebody from the UCL occupation on Twitter, as I have done, you can easily run into a radical blogger from Egypt, or a lecturer in peaceful resistance in California with contacts in

Burma. During the early 20th century people would ride hanging on the undersides of train carriages across borders just to make links like these.

Why now? It's a mixture of the unsustainability of regimes based on repression and the sudden uncertainty about the economic future. Modern capitalism demands mass access to higher education. In most of the world this is funded by personal indebtedess – people making a rational judgment to go into debt so they will be better paid later. However, the prospect of 10 years of fiscal retrenchment in some countries means they now believe they will be poorer than their parents. And the effect has been like throwing a light switch; the prosperity story is replaced with the doom story, even if for individuals reality will be more complex.

This evaporation of a promise is compounded in the emerging markets. First, even where you get rapid economic growth, countries like Egypt cannot absorb the demographic bulge of young people fast enough to deliver rising living standards for them. Second, you have states and systems based on the suppression of information. In a suddenly information-rich age, they have struggled to adapt and are mostly dying.

It was Taine who famously described the Jacobin revolution as the product of an impoverished salariat, an oversupply of educated labour: "students in garrets, bohemians in lodgings, physicians without patients and lawyers without clients in lonely Offices ... so many Marats, Robespierres, and St Justs in embryo." Today in their garrets they have laptops and broadband.

The weakness of organised labour means there's a changed relationship between this radicalised middle class, the urban poor and the organised workforce. The world looks more like 19th-century Paris – the predomination of the discontented intelligentsia, intermixed with the urban poor at numerous social interfaces (cabarets then, raves now); meanwhile the solidaristic culture and respectability of organised labour struggles to make an impact.

All this has led to loss of fear among protesters: there is no confrontation they can't retreat from. They can "have a day off" from protesting, occupying. You couldn't "have a day off" from the miners' strike if you lived in a pit village.

And they mix-and-match: they flit between causes: I have met people who do union organising one day, and the next are on a flotilla to Gaza; then they pop up working for a thinktank on sustainable energy; then they're writing a book about something completely different. I was astonished to find people I had interviewed inside the UCL occupation blogging from Tahrir Square.

Ultimately people have a better understanding of power. The activists have read their Chomsky, and their Hardt-Negri, but the ideas therein have replicated and become intuitive. Protesters have become clever to the point of expertise in knowing how to mess up hierarchies. Technology has expanded the power of the individual – their sense of justice, social and personal – and the whole recent history of revolt, from Iran to Egypt to the French banlieues, is driven by this.

Paul Mason is a BBC journalist

TRADE UNIONS
The truly revolutionary social networks
ERIC LEE AND BENJAMIN WEINTHAL · Guardian, 10 February

Perhaps the most overlooked factor in the demise of the authoritarian Ben Ali regime in Tunisia, and the weakening of Hosni Mubarak's grip on state power in Egypt, has been the trade unions in both countries.

While the media has reported on social networks such as Twitter and Facebook as revolutionary methods of mobilisation, it was the old-fashioned working class that enabled the pro-democracy movements to flourish.

As working men and women in Egypt became increasingly vulnerable to exploitation and a deteriorating quality of life, the only legal trade unions – the ones affiliated to the Egyptian Trade Union Federation (ETUF) – proved worthless. The result of all of this was an unprecedented wave of strikes across the public and private sectors that began in 2004 and has continued to the present day. During the first four years of the current strike wave, more than 1,900 strikes took place and an estimated 1.7 million workers were involved.

As one worker in a fertiliser company put it, the effect of going on strike was to convince the employer "that they had a company with human beings working in it. In the past, they dealt with us as if we were not human."

The strikes began in the clothing and textile sector, and moved on to building workers, transport workers, food processing workers, even the workers on the Cairo metro. The biggest and most important took place back in 2006 at Misr Spinning and Weaving, a company that employs some 25,000 workers.

The state-controlled ETUF opposed these strikes and supported the government's privatisation plans. A turning point was reached when municipal tax collectors not only went on strike, but staged a three-day, 10,000-strong sit-in in the streets of Cairo, opposite the prime minister's office.

This could not be ignored, and the government was forced to allow the formation last year of the first independent trade union in more than half a century.

Pro-labour NGOs played a critical role in providing support and guidance to these strikes and protests. As a result, they were targeted by the regime, their offices closed and leaders arrested. The best known of these groups is the Centre for Trade Union and Worker Services (CTUWS), which has been around since 1990.

Groups such as the CTUWS in turn enlisted the support of trade unions in other countries, and that support was invaluable – particularly in persuading the government to ease up on repression.

Those links with the international trade union movement have proven critical in recent days as well. When the Mubarak regime tried to cut off Egypt from the internet, CTUWS activists were able to phone in their daily communiques to the AFL-CIO's Solidarity Centre in Washington. The messages were transcribed, translated from the Arabic, and passed on to the wider trade union world using websites such as LabourStart.

In sharp contrast to the last seven years of Egyptian labour unrest, the Tunisian trade unions played a kingmaker role during the end phase of the uprising.

After decades of lethargy, docility and state domination of the General Tunisian Workers' Union (UGTT), Tunisia's largest employee organisation –with roughly half a million members – helped not only eradicate Ben Ali's regime, but determined the shape of the post-Ben Ali government.

Working-class Tunisians were animated by the same goals as their Egyptian counterparts; namely, the desire to secure dignity and respect, bring about real political democracy, and improve their standard of living.

Mushrooming disapproval of Ben Ali's regime among trade union members, coupled with a vibrant youth movement demanding dignity and greater employment opportunities, seems to explain the shift of top-level UGTT officials who had hitherto been loyal Ben Ali.

Cultivating democracy in Tunisia, and Egypt requires two pre-conditions. First, workers' organisations must remain independent of state control. Second, to blunt the Iranian model, Islamists must be barred from hijacking free trade unions.

This helps to explain the worries of Habib Jerjir, a labour leader from the Regional Workers' Union of Tunis: "That's the danger," he said. "I'm against political Islam. We must block their path."

The UGTT, founded more than 60 years ago, has a history of strike action. Take the examples of the 1977 strike against a state-owned textile plant in Ksar Hellal, and a work stoppage involving phosphate miners in the same year, which secured a victory. The UGTT also called for an unprecedented general strike in 1978.

In a precursor to the December–January protests against Ben Ali's corrupt system, phosphate mine workers in Gafsa waged a six-month battle against a manipulated recruitment process which sparked resistance among young unemployed workers. Rising discontent with the nepotism and cronyism of the state-controlled UGTT prompted workers to occupy the regional office.

This means that participatory economic democracy played a decisive role in Tunisian society before the Jasmine revolution. Ben Ali swiftly suffocated free and democratic trade union activity during his 23-year domination over organised labour. But he could not extinguish democratic aspirations among workers.

There are no exact parallels, but much of this reminds us of what happened in Poland in 1979–80. There, as in Egypt and Tunisia, we saw a mixture of a repressive, single-party state with trade unions that functioned as an arm of the ruling party. But there was also a network of NGOs that quietly worked behind the scenes, in workplaces and communities.

The result was the 1980 strike at the Lenin shipyard in Gdansk, the formation of Solidarnosc, and the end not only of the Communist regime in Poland but of the entire Soviet empire.

Today's pro-democracy revolutions in Egypt and Tunisia are the culmination of that process, and where it will lead we cannot predict – though Poland does provide an appealing model.

The pressing point is that experts misjudged the tumult in Egypt and Tunisia largely because they ignored and overlooked the democratic aspirations of working-class Tunisians and Egyptians. To understand why so many authoritarian Arab regimes remain fragile, one need to only to look through the window on to the court of labour relations.

Eric Lee works in the international trade union movement; Benjamin Weinthal is a Berlin-based journalist

AL-JAZEERA
A revolution in world news

JOHN PLUNKETT AND JOSH HALLIDAY · Guardian, 7 February

Donald Rumsfeld demonised it and George W Bush allegedly said he wanted to bomb it. No one was quite sure whether the then White House incumbent was joking or not, but its offices have been hit by US forces. Twice.

Now something rather strange has begun to happen to the Arabic language news broadcaster al-Jazeera and the English language channel it launched nearly five years ago; American viewers have begun to demand it. It is clear some kind of watershed has been reached when the Kansas City Star publishes a cut-out-and-keep guide to the "easiest way to get al-Jazeera English".

The Qatar-based channel's acclaimed coverage of the Egyptian crisis has been referred to as the broadcaster's "CNN moment", doing for al-Jazeera English what the first Gulf war did for CNN, pushing it to the forefront of the public's consciousness. Put simply, must-see TV. Now the challenge is to translate the plaudits into the major cable or satellite distribution deal the channel has long sought without success in the US.

The New York Times, which praised the channel's "total immersion coverage of news events the whole world is talking about", bemoaned the fact that US cable viewers were able to watch MTV's controversial adaptation of E4's teen drama Skins but not al-Jazeera English. "It seems like a perverse application of free speech," said the paper. "But sex is sexier than foreign affairs and it certainly sells better."

With China investing $7bn in foreign language media, we may also be witnessing the beginning of a shift, albeit slight, in the nature of global TV news and debate. Stephen Claypole, the former senior BBC News and TV news agency executive who is now chairman of the London and Abu Dhabi-based consultancy DMA Media, says: "Al-Jazeera has the game by the throat, both in Arabic and English, and it has certainly lived up to its reputation as the most watched broadcaster in the Arab world in spite of intimidation and violence against its staff in Egypt.

"I have heard that Hillary Clinton watches it constantly and that Barack Obama has been viewing from the situation room. Although al-Jazeera English has been competent since its launch, it has been waiting for a huge story to call its own. Egypt is certainly that," Claypole adds.

Al-Jazeera English is separate from the main al-Jazeera Arabic channel, which began broadcasting in 1996. Staffed largely by western TV journalists, the English-language service leveraged the advantages of its Arabic network and contacts in covering the emerging crisis. For a story of this scale in the Arab world, it absolutely had to be good.

Al Anstey, the former ITN executive who is the managing director of al-Jazeera English, describes it as an "extraordinary week" for the channel and a "truly historical" one for Egypt.

"We are being seen worldwide as a channel of reference on this story," says Anstey. "There has been an exponential increase in the recognition of exactly what it is we do and the quality of our journalism and content. I always say the best way of addressing any misconceptions about al-Jazeera English is to switch on and watch."

Al-Jazeera English is available in around 220m homes in more than 100 countries worldwide. But fewer than 3 million of those homes are in the US including – helpfully for the White House – Washington DC.

The failure to strike a major US distribution deal is partly a result of the political sensitivity that surrounded the perceived negative slant of al-Jazeera Arabic's coverage of the Iraq war. It is also a reflection of the fact that cable operators do not think they can make money from a foreign news network on systems that are already full. BBC World News is distributed to around 6m homes in the US, against more than 10 times that for the entertainment channel BBC America (on which some World News bulletins air).

"For a long time al-Jazeera was seen as the Fox [News] for the bad guys – that's a really unfortunate way of looking at it," says Jon Williams, the BBC's World News editor. "With the change of [US government] administration there's been a slight change of attitude, and if this means that it does now get carriage in the US, then we welcome that. Al-Jazeera has done some great stuff … It wouldn't be fair to single out its Egyptian coverage – it has been doing this for a while."

US viewers have been watching the channel by other means – streamed live on YouTube, on set-top box digital video player Roku and on its own website, which reported a traffic increase of 2,500%, with more than half of the upsurge coming from the US.

Blogger and journalism professor Jeff Jarvis said it was a "sad vestige of the era of 'Freedom Fries'" that the channel was not more widely available on cable, and started a Twitter campaign, #wewantouraje (referencing the line from Dire Straits' "Money for Nothing", but with a twist).

"As much of an internet triumphalist as I am, internet streaming is not going to have the same impact – political and education impact – that putting AJE on the cable dial would have," blogged Jarvis. "It is downright un-American to still refuse to carry it. Vital, world-changing news is occurring in the Middle East and no one – not the xenophobic or celebrity-obsessed or cut-to-the-bone American media – can bring the perspective, insight, and on-the-scene reporting al-Jazeera English can."

Anstey is cautiously optimistic: "I'm confident we will get distribution in the US, it's just a question of when," he says. "It's a very important marketplace for us." Especially in terms of revenue? "It's not about the finances of getting into America, it's about getting the content out there. At this stage of our evolution, the priority for the English channel is about building reputation and reach."

As the broadcaster is bankrolled by the billionaire Emir of Qatar, neither the English nor the Arabic al-Jazeera is under pressure to make a profit any time soon. It has also faced accusations of aligning itself closely to Qatari foreign policy; US embassy cables released by WikiLeaks at the end of last year suggested Qatar was using the Arabic channel as a bargaining chip in foreign policy negotiations with its neighbours.

"Never once has Qatar interfered with our editorial," says Anstey. "It is absolutely not a fair criticism and I can say that with total confidence. We are genuinely independent."

Every global media story produces its winners. Egypt's drawn-out agony is a tailor-made opportunity for al-Jazeera English, which it has seized with careful on-the-ground journalism. If the US cable owners relent to the emerging public pressure, it will mark a coup for a news service that, until recently, was battling to prove it had credibility and salience with many western audiences.

John Plunkett and Josh Halliday are Guardian journalists

THE REVOLUTIONARY MOMENT

This Arab 1848 is a fight against foreign domination

TARIQ ALI· Guardian, 22 February

The refusal of the people to kiss or ignore the rod that has chastised them for so many decades has opened a new chapter in the history of the Arab nation. The absurd, if much vaunted, neocon notion that Arabs or Muslims were hostile to democracy has disappeared like parchment in fire.

Those who promoted such ideas appear to the most unhappy: Israel and its lobbyists in Euro-America; the arms industry, hurriedly trying to sell as much while it can (the British prime minister acting as a merchant of death at the Abu Dhabi arms fair); and the beleaguered rulers of Saudi Arabia, wondering whether the disease will spread to their tyrannical kingdom. Until now they have provided refuge to many a despot, but when the time comes where will the royal family seek refuge? They must be aware that their patrons will dump them without ceremony and claim they always favoured democracy.

If there is a comparison to be made with Europe it is 1848, when the revolutionary upheavals left only Britain and Spain untouched – even though Queen Victoria, thinking of the Chartists, feared otherwise. Writing to her besieged nephew on the Belgian throne, she expressing sympathy but wondered whether "we will all be slain in our beds". Uneasy lies the head that wears a crown or bejewelled headgear, and has billions stored in foreign banks.

Like Europeans in 1848 the Arab people are fighting against foreign domination (82% of Egyptians, a recent opinion poll revealed, have a "negative view of the US"); against the violation of their democratic rights; against an elite blinded by its own illegitimate wealth – and in favour of economic justice. This is different from the first wave of Arab nationalism, which was concerned principally with driving the remnants of the British empire out of the region. The Egyptians under Nasser nationalised the Suez canal and were invaded by Britain, France and Israel – but that was without Washington's permission, and the three were thus compelled to withdraw.

Cairo was triumphant. The pro-British monarchy was toppled by the 1958 revolution in Iraq, radicals took power in Damascus, a senior Saudi prince attempted a palace coup and fled to Cairo when it failed, armed struggles erupted in Yemen and Oman, and there was much talk of an Arab nation with three concurrent capitals. One side effect was an eccentric coup in Libya that brought a young, semi-literate officer, Muammar Gaddafi, to power. His Saudi enemies have always insisted that the coup was masterminded by British intelligence, just like the one that propelled Idi Amin to power in Uganda. Gaddafi's professed nationalism, modernism and radicalism were all for show, like his ghosted science-fiction short stories.

It never extended to his own people. Despite the oil wealth he refused to educate Libyans, or provide them with a health service or subsidised housing, squandering money on absurdist projects abroad – one of which was to divert a British plane carrying socialist and communist Sudanese oppositionists and handing them over to fellow dictator Gaafar Nimeiry in Sudan to be hanged, thus wrecking the possibility of any radical change in that country, with dire consequences, as we witness every day. At home he maintained a rigid tribal structure, thinking he could divide and buy tribes to stay in power. But no longer.

Israel's 1967 lightning war and victory sounded the death knell of Arab nationalism. Internecine conflicts in Syria and Iraq led to the victory of rightwing Ba'athists blessed by Washington. After Nasser's death and his successor Saadat's pyrrhic victory against Israel in 1973, Egypt's military elite decided to cut its losses, accept annual billion-dollar subsidies from the US and do a deal with Tel Aviv. In return its dictator was honoured as a statesman by Euro-America, as was Saddam Hussein for a long time. If only they had left him to be removed by his people instead of by an ugly and destructive war and occupation, over a million dead and 5 million orphaned children.

The Arab revolutions, triggered by the economic crisis, have mobilised mass movements, but not every aspect of life has been called into question. Social, political and religious rights are becoming the subject of fierce controversy in Tunisia, but not elsewhere yet. No new political parties have emerged, an indication that the electoral battles to come will be contests between Arab liberalism and conservatism in the shape of the Muslim Brotherhood, modelling itself on Islamists in power in Turkey and Indonesia, and ensconced in the embrace of the US.

American hegemony in the region has been dented but not destroyed. The post-despot regimes are likely to be more independent, with a democratic system that is fresh and subversive and, hopefully, new constitutions enshrining social and political needs. But the military in Egypt and Tunisia will ensure nothing rash happens. The big worry for Euro-America is Bahrain. If its rulers are removed it will be difficult to prevent a democratic upheaval in Saudi Arabia. Can Washington afford to let that happen? Or will it deploy armed force to keep the Wahhabi kleptocrats in power?

A few decades ago the great Iraqi poet Mudhafar al-Nawab, angered by a gathering of despots described as an Arab Summit, lost his cool:

> *Mubarik, Mubarik,*
> *Wealth and good health*
> *Fax the news to the UN.*
> *Camp after Camp and David,*
> *Father of all your Camps.*
> *Damn your fathers*
> *Rotten Lot;*
> *The stench of your bodies floods your nostrils …*
> *O Make-Believe Summit*
> *Leaders*
> *May your faces be blackened;*
> *Ugly your drooping bellies*
> *Ugly your fat arses*
> *Why the surprise*
> *That your faces resemble both …*
> *Summits … summits … summits*
> *Goats and sheep gather,*
> *Farts with a tune*
> *Let the Summit be*
> *Let the Summit not be*
> *Let the Summit decide;*
> *I spit on each and every one of you*
> *Kings … Sheikhs … Lackeys …*

Whatever else, Arab summits will not be the same again. The poet has been joined by the people.

Tariq Ali is a London-based writer and novelist

ARAB WOMEN

Female protesters are shattering stereotypes

SOUMAYA GHANNOUSHI · Guardian, 11 March

Saida Sadouni does not conform to the typical image of an Arab revolutionary. But this 77-year-old camped out in the bitter Tunisian cold for more than two weeks in front of the prime minister's headquarters, leading the historic Kasbah picket that succeeded in forcing Mohamed Ghannouchi's interim government out of office. "I have resisted French occupation. I have resisted the dictatorships of Bourguiba and Ben Ali. I will not rest until our revolution meets its goals," she told the thousands of fellow protesters who joined her. She is today widely hailed as the mother of Tunisia's revolution, a living record of her country's modern history and its struggle for emancipation.

Sadouni is one of many Arab women from older generations who have joined the revolutions in their countries after decades of political activism. But most women activists today tend to be in their 20s and 30s, highly politicised yet unaffiliated to any organised parties – young women such as Asma Mahfoudh, of Egypt's April 6 movement. This 26-year-old's interests had until recently been no different from those of any woman of her age. While surfing the net in 2008 she stumbled on calls for a general strike to demand an end to government corruption. This initial encounter with protest "marked the beginning of a new chapter" in her life, as she puts it. Ever since, she has been an avid campaigner for change, joining a struggle that culminated in the ousting of President Mubarak.

Even in ultra-conservative Yemen, demonstrations against the rule of President Ali Abdullah Saleh have been led by a young charismatic woman, Tawakul Karman. She has campaigned since 2007 demanding political reform. When she was arrested in January, the authorities were forced to release her following a wave of angry protests in Sana'a. What has inspired these women and thrust them into the heart of protest is the yearning for change and political freedom that is sweeping across the region.

The Arab revolutions are not only shaking the structure of despotism to the core, they are shattering many decades-long myths. Foremost among these is the perception of the Arab woman as powerless and enslaved, forced into a cage of silence and invisibility by her jailor society. That is not the type of woman that has emerged out of Tunisia and Egypt in the last few weeks.

Not only did women participate in the protest movements raging in those countries, they have assumed leadership roles there. The virtual and real battlefields have been incubators of female leadership. Arab women have been proving themselves through continuous action on the ground, rather than in endless polemics behind closed doors.

These revolutions have been characterised by the open politics of the street, through which leaders have been tested, matured and approved. The movements have grown organically from the bottom, unrestricted by party hierarchy, age or outdated gender roles. The open parliaments of Kasbah and Tahrir Square – where people met, communicated and expressed their political views freely – brought everyone closer together, promoting collective identity over divisions of class, ideology, gender, religion and sect.

Another stereotype being dismantled is the association of the Islamic headscarf with passivity, submissiveness and segregation. Surprising as this may be, many Arab women activists choose to wear the hijab. Yet they are no less confident, vocal or charismatic than their unveiled sisters.

This new model of homegrown women leaders represents a challenge to two narratives. The first of these, which is dominant in conservative Muslim circles, sentences women to a life of childbearing and rearing, lived out in the narrow confines of their homes at the mercy of fathers, brothers and husbands. It revolves around notions of sexual purity and family honour, and appeals to tradition and reductionist interpretations of religion for justification.

The other is espoused by Euro-American neoliberals, who view Arab and Muslim women through the narrow prism of the Taliban model: miserable objects of pity in need of their benevolent intervention – intellectual, political, even military – for deliverance from the dark cage of veiling to a promised garden of enlightenment and progress.

Arab women are rebelling against both narratives. They refuse to be treated with contempt, kept in isolation, or be taken by the hand, like a child, and led on the road to emancipation. They are taking charge of their own destinies, determined to liberate themselves as they liberate their societies from dictatorship. The emancipation they are shaping with their own hands is an authentic one defined by their own needs, choices and priorities.

There is, and will be, resistance to this process of emancipation, as recent attacks on female protesters at Tahrir Square indicate. But the dynamic unleashed by the revolution is irreversible. Those who have led the struggle to dismantle the old regimes will no doubt remain at the forefront in rebuilding the new order on its ruins. Tahrir and Kasbah Square are now embedded in the psyche of Arab women, and have given voice to their long-silenced yearning for liberation.

Soumaya Ghannoushi is a researcher at the University of London

We bombed Gaddafi, but now we court Bahrain. Why?

IAN BIRRELL • Guardian, 14 September

The air in Tripoli is heady with optimism. After 42 years of repressive and rapacious rule by Muammar Gaddafi, there is a mood of exhilaration despite the water shortages and power cuts that have plagued the city since the collapse of the dictator's regime.

There is good cause for hope, even as the search for Gaddafi continues. The sensitive note struck by the country's new leader on Monday night in Martyrs' Square underlines the widespread desire for a better future. Mustafa Abdul Jalil spoke in the place where his predecessor delivered many of his most notorious rants, but the tone could not have been more different, nor the sentiments more encouraging.

Problems abound, not least the need to disarm militias with regional loyalties and the difficulties of reviving a resource-rich economy desecrated by one family's kleptocracy without corruption and the creation of a new oligarchy. But for now, Libya has the best chance of emerging the biggest winner from the recent events that have swept north Africa and the Middle East.

Britain, along with France and their Nato allies, can take pride in a timely and restrained intervention that prevented a massacre and helped ensure the success of a popular uprising. This is endorsed by graffiti found in towns across Libya thanking David Cameron and Nicolas Sarkozy for their support; both leaders are probably more popular there than in their native lands at present. And they have rescued the cause of liberal interventionism from the morass of Iraq.

Given the coalition government's stance on Libya, it is disappointing to witness its myopia over Bahrain. First, the prime minister rolls out the red carpet for the crown prince, welcoming him to Downing Street shortly after Saudi tanks rolled in to help quash protests against his family's 200-year rule. Now a country that was recently shooting unarmed protesters in the streets is entertained at an arms fair in London, with an official delegation invited to cast its eye over the latest guns, communications and crowd control devices.

This makes no sense. Since the crackdown began six months ago, the Bahraini government has sought to promote itself as a reformist regime. But any positive steps it has taken have been undermined by its campaign of arbitrary arrests and the dismissal of protesters from their jobs, while there have been allegations of systematic abuse in prisons and a series of show trials before military courts. This is the place, remember, that persecuted doctors who went to the aid of injured protesters.

The situation in Bahrain is muddied by sectarian divisions and the proximity of Iran and Saudi Arabia. But such complications do not excuse Britain from abandoning its support for those seeking to overthrow oppression in the region. After all, we have seen what happens when principles in foreign policy are sacrificed for shady deals with despots, leaving our nation embroiled in torture and appeasing a dictator.

Britain presents an unpredictable face to the world, colluding in Gaddafi's brutality one moment then bombing him the next. Now the mixed messages sent to those seeking fundamental human rights sow further confusion. It can only serve to fuel cynicism that our stance towards the Arab Spring is based more on commerce than ethics.

The coalition government must rescue British foreign policy from the legacy of its predecessor. It showed courage and foresight over Libya – which makes it all the more disappointing to see its encouragement for the monarchy of Bahrain. People fighting for dignity and democracy deserve the same support, whether in Tripoli or Manama.

Ian Birrell is a journalist and former speechwriter for David Cameron

Those who support democracy should welcome the rise of political Islam

WADAH KHANFAR · Guardian, 28 November

An-Nahda, the Islamic party in Tunisia, won 41% of the seats of the Tunisian constitutional assembly last month, causing consternation in the west. But An-Nahda will not be an exception on the Arab scene. Last Friday the Islamic Justice and Development party took the biggest share of the vote in Morocco and will lead the new coalition government for the first time in history. And tomorrow Egypt's elections begin, with the Muslim Brotherhood predicted to become the largest party. There may be more to come. Should free and fair elections be held in Yemen, once the regime of Ali Abdullah Saleh falls, the Yemeni Congregation for Reform, also Islamic, will win by a significant majority. This pattern will repeat itself whenever the democratic process takes its course.

In the west, this phenomenon has led to a debate about the "problem" of the rise of political Islam. In the Arab world, too, there has been mounting tension between Islamists and secularists, who feel anxious about Islamic groups. Many voices warn that the Arab Spring will lead to an Islamic winter, and that the Islamists, though claiming to support democracy, will soon turn against it. In the west, stereotypical images that took root in the aftermath of 9/11 have come to the fore again. In the Arab world, a secular anti-democracy camp has emerged in both Tunisia and Egypt whose pretext for opposing democratisation is that the Islamists are likely to be the victors.

But the uproar that has accompanied the Islamists' gains is unhelpful; a calm and well-informed debate about the rise of political Islam is long overdue.

First, we must define our terms. "Islamist" is used in the Muslim world to describe Muslims who participate in the public sphere, using Islam as a basis. It is understood that this participation is not at odds with democracy. In the west, however, the term routinely describes those who use violence as a means and an end – thus Jihadist Salafism, exemplified by al-Qaida, is called "Islamist" in the west, despite the fact that it rejects democratic political participation (Ayman al-Zawahiri, the leader of al-Qaida, criticised Hamas when it decided to take part in the elections for the Palestinian legislative council, and has repeatedly criticised the Muslim Brotherhood for opposing the use of violence).

This disconnect in the understanding of the term in the west and in the Muslim world was often exploited by despotic Arab regimes to suppress Islamic movements with democratic political programmes. It is time we were clear.

Reform-based Islamic movements, such as the Muslim Brotherhood, work within the political process. They learned a bitter lesson from their armed conflict in Syria against the regime of Hafez al-Assad in 1982, which cost the lives of more than 20,000 people and led to the incarceration or banishment of many thousands more. The Syrian experience convinced mainstream Islamic movements to avoid armed struggle and to observe "strategic patience" instead.

Second, we must understand the history of the region. In western discourse Islamists are seen as newcomers to politics, gullible zealots who are motivated by a radical ideology and lack experience. In fact, they have played a major role in the Arab political scene since the 1920s. Islamic movements have often been in opposition, but since the 1940s they have participated in parliamentary elections, entered alliances with secular, nationalist and socialist groups, and participated in several governments – in Sudan, Jordan, Yemen and Algeria. They have also forged alliances with non-Islamic regimes, like the Nimeiri regime in Sudan in 1977.

A number of other events have had an impact on the collective Muslim mind, and have led to the maturation of political Islam: the much-debated Islamic revolution in Iran in 1979; the military coup in Sudan in 1989; the success of the Algerian Islamic Salvation Front in the 1991 elections and the army's subsequent denial of its right to govern; the conquest of much of Afghan territory by the Taliban in 1996 leading to the establishment of its Islamic emirate; and the success in 2006 of Hamas in the Palestinian Legislative Council elections. The Hamas win was not recognised, nor was the national unity government formed. Instead, a siege was imposed on Gaza to suffocate the movement.

Perhaps one of the most influential experiences has been that of the Justice and Development party (AKP) in Turkey, which won the elections in 2002. It has been a source of inspiration for many Islamic movements. Although the AKP does not describe itself as Islamic, its 10 years of political experience have led to a model that many Islamists regard as successful. The model has three important characteristics: a general Islamic frame of reference; a multi-party democracy; and significant economic growth.

These varied political experiences have had a profound impact on political Islam's flexibility and capacity for political action, and on its philosophy, too.

However, political Islam has also faced enormous pressures from dictatorial Arab regimes, pressures that became more intense after 9/11. Islamic institutions were suppressed. Islamic activists were imprisoned, tortured and killed. Such experiences gave rise to a profound bitterness. Given the history, it is only natural that we should hear overzealous slogans or intolerant threats from some activists. Some of those now at the forefront of election campaigns were only recently released from prison. It would not be fair to expect them to use the voice of professional diplomats.

Despite this, the Islamic political discourse has generally been balanced. The Tunisian Islamic movement has set a good example. Although An-Nahda suffered under Ben Ali's regime, its leaders developed a tolerant discourse and managed to open up to moderate secular and leftist political groups. The movement's leaders have reassured Tunisian citizens that it will not interfere in their personal lives and that it will respect their right to choose. The movement also presented a progressive model of women's participation, with 42 female An-Nahda members in the constitutional assembly.

The Islamic movement's approach to the west has also been balanced, despite the fact that western countries supported despotic Arab regimes. Islamists know the importance of international communication in an economically and politically interconnected world.

Now there is a unique opportunity for the west: to demonstrate that it will no longer support despotic regimes by supporting instead the democratic process in the Arab world, by refusing to intervene in favour of one party against another and by accepting the results of the democratic process, even when it is not the result they would have chosen. Democracy is the only option for bringing stability, security and tolerance to the region, and it is the dearest thing to the hearts of Arabs, who will not forgive any attempts to derail it.

The region has suffered a lot as a result of attempts to exclude Islamists and deny them a role in the public sphere. Undoubtedly, Islamists' participation in governance will give rise to a number of challenges, both within the Islamic ranks and with regard to relations with other local and international forces. Islamists should be careful not to fall into the trap of feeling overconfident: they must accommodate other trends, even if it means making painful concessions. Our societies need political consensus, and the participation of all political groups, regardless of their electoral weight. It is this interplay between Islamists and others that will both guarantee the maturation of the Arab democratic transition and lead to an Arab political consensus and stability that has been missing for decades.

Wadah Khanfar is former director general of the al-Jazeera network

How youth-led revolts shook the world

SHIV MALIK, JACK SHENKER AND ADAM GABBATT
Guardian, 17 December

It could have easily been overlooked. It was not the first time a young, frustrated Arab had taken desperate action to draw attention to the plight of the marginalised millions. But on this occasion the news of a suicide went viral.

A year to the day since Mohamed Bouazizi's self-immolation in a sleepy Tunisian town kicked off a year of revolt, the convulsions have spread further than could ever have been imagined: in the depths of a Russian winter activists are planning their next howl of protest at the Kremlin; in a north American city a nylon tent stands against a bitter wind; in a Syrian nightmare a soldier contemplates defection.

Quietly, a lifetime of old power structures – political, social, ideological – have been dissolved and the certainties of one generation have been replaced by the messy unpredictability of another. Today the furniture of the new sits deliberately beside the supposed certainties of the old. Handmade barricades are bolted to public squares, plastic tents pitched beside stone cathedrals, and the solid steel of a New York bank is harassed by pop-up armies of retweeters.

It began as a Mediterranean revolt spreading on both sides of the sea – from Tunisia through Egypt and Libya and beyond, and from Greece and Spain upwards into Europe. In a million different and fragmented ways, scenes of protest were the narrative backbone to 2011 played out again and again in cities as far afield as Santiago, Stockholm and Seoul.

But to view the activism of 2011 through a nationalist, ethnic or even class lens is to miss its unifying trait – 2011 was the year of a global youth revolt.

The struggles that gave birth to each demonstration, occupation or revolution were separate and yet connected; part of a collective roar from young people who, for the first time in modern history, faced a future in which they would be worse off than their parents.

Kyriakos Chatzistefanou, Greek journalist and director of documentary *Debtocracy*, says it was exactly this awareness that got people into the streets of Athens. "It was mainly middle-class, well-educated people that felt for the first time that they will be what economists now call the lost generation.

"That was a paradigm shift. With small intervals in the second world war and the dictatorship, in general all the generations in Greece had growth and a better future. For the first time after 2008 there is a generation that realises that there is an end to that ... [and] they reacted angrily, violently."

The same prognosis is to be found on the other side of the Atlantic. The lack of opportunities for young Americans has been "a huge part of what's happening", says Laura Long, who has been involved in Occupy Oakland since September.

"We were promised a series of steps on a ladder to climb to get to a point to be successful, and in the last decade especially that ladder has just been pulled up so that we can't even reach the lowest rung basically."

But it is far more than material privation that underlies this year's youth revolt, more than just a question of how to integrate into the globalised economy the talents and expectations of 80 million unemployed young people from the most well-educated generation in human history.

At the heart of this most potent insurrection since 1968 is an expression of the deep uncertainty about how the future will pan out.

"It's the first time in American history that a generation came along and was told: 'No, things are gonna be worse for you than they were for your parents,'" says Jesse LaGreca, a prominent Occupy Wall Street figure who has travelled to occupations across the US.

"I think that has created the necessity for change, and we can no longer wait for political promises – we have to make that change ourselves." And the social problems run deep.

In the US the current crop have been called the boomerang generation due to young people's inability to flee their parents' nest.

The data underscores the problem: more and more young people out of work, more and more of them stuck living with their parents well into their 30s. One in five American men between the age of 25–34 has not yet left home. In Europe the figure is even higher. For Vesna Milosevic, a Slovenian expert on youth employment, statistics like these demonstrate the frustration that young people have with becoming independent adults.

"Young people are postponing the important events or phases in their growing up process. For example, they get a job very much later ... but at first they are stuck in some precarious work or a temporary job.

"The period of 'youth' is extending to the 30s or even towards 35. They have children later ... and [are] moving away from their family and becoming independent later, which is the most important thing.

But, she says, "they don't want to be in this 'mama hotel' ... they have no other choice. This postponement is not voluntary. It's the [economic] situation which forces people to postpone events in their life. It's too expensive to rent an apartment if you don't have a regular job, if you don't know what's going to happen next month," she says.

With the ability to build horizontal links using new technologies, a generation decided this year not to passively embark on a pre-programmed conveyor belt of life under austerity, oppression – or both – but instead opted to come together and attempt an audacious reclamation of autonomy.

Nowhere was this more true than in the Middle East, where Bouazizi's immolation set off an inferno that is still smouldering. On Friday in Cairo, as demonstrators and police again clashed violently, it was as clear as ever that there is plenty of unfinished business in this youth uprising.

"The Arab world was considered a stagnant pond of retardation and tyranny, inhabited by what appeared to be a complacent populace toiling fatalistically under the yoke of their dictators," says Iyad el-Baghdadi, compiler of the canonical Arab Tyrant's Manual.

"Most observers thought this status quo to be stable, if not permanent," adds el-Baghdadi. "What's worst, many Arabs thought so too. Boy, look at us now."

When you speak to those organising the Occupy movement, it is remarkable how important Tunisia and Tahrir were to their own action. No longer was the west to be a democratic beacon to the Middle East. It was very much the other way around.

"Who would have thought that Mohamed Bouazizi would set in motion such a series of events?" says David Osborn from the Occupy Portland movement. He says that many in the west were "deeply moved and inspired" by seeing protests across the Middle East, but that Egypt in particular had captured Americans' imagination.

"To see the movement generally, but in particular the youths, mobilise and really demand the impossible ... to think Mubarak would not have been president more than a few weeks or even a month or two before he actually fell was almost impossible. And yet they asserted that another world without Mubarak was possible, and I think that kind of re-inspired the radical imagination in many of us."

"The lesson of Tahrir Square was that once again, democracy has become a revolutionary force," says Shimri Zameret, who spent four months organising the global day of occupation on 15 October that saw people in more than 900 cities turn the square's tent city into a worldwide phenomenon.

Zameret, who also spent two years in an Israeli jail for refusing to serve in the army, says young people have suddenly reached a tipping point in their acceptance of the status quo.

Suddenly "the natural, everyday has become the historical", he says, adding that there is an awareness that "things can change and change suddenly" when people take to the streets. Civic action, he says, brings a sense of control back into people's uncertain lives.

Zameret also talks of an anger at the way the global leadership has failed to tackle the pressing issues of the day, from corporate greed and banking failure to problems like the environment.

"The demand [by activists] is no longer to go to the IMF or the G8/G20 summit and beg to have this or that issue implemented, it is also not about 'anti-globalisation'. This time it's about 'real global democracy now': we demand the power to fully control the decisions that shape our lives – local, national, European and global."

It is easy to dismiss the interconnectedness of 2011's youth-driven resistance movements; and it is possible even to deny they amount to any kind of identifiable social phenomenon at all.

Certainly, comparisons between the pepper spray of Oakland and the tank shells of Homs can be facetious, and the triumphs of the protester – named this week as Time's "person of the year" – appear scant if limited purely to the arena of formal political change.

But connections there are, not just in mutual recognition and frustration, but in method. The movements that made the headlines in 2011 were largely non-hierarchical, creative and locally autonomous. And consciously so.

Occasionally, a leadership figure peeks through – like Tawakkul Karman in Yemen, Camila Vallejo in Chile or Alexei Navalny in Russia. But on the ground appointed leadership has, it seems, become a shunned concept for fear those at the top of a social movement would soon bow to and barter with an old guard.

As Ganzeer, one of Egypt's most popular street artists, argues, Tahrir has been swamped by all manner of those who speak the language of change but seek ultimately to suppress it by cutting deals with those on the other side of the gate.

"Demonstrations, strikes, and other forms of protest carry on regardless, because today's revolution, unlike revolutions of the past, is leaderless," he claims.

Andres Villena Oliver from the Indignados movement in Spain admits that it is not easy. "It's a very emotional process," he says. "They don't just feel very angry with the economic failures but they want to change the world, in some weeks. It makes it very difficult. The more democratic a movement is, the less efficient it is."

But people will be heard, he says, and on an equal footing as everyone else.

A new political form is being cobbled together by those on the street, and it has come to reflect the horizontal lines of the social media which helps drives so many of today's demonstrations.

But the great revenge is this: the generation that grew up being told they were the heirs to Francis Fukuyama's end of history and victory of a liberal capitalist society, is now working its damnedest to prove how untrue this is, not for the sake of utopian reimagination but to resolve the very serious problems that very system has created.

Where the movement goes next remains to be seen. But as the Jordanian human rights activist Laila Sharaf recently told a group of young people in Beirut, in a statement that could apply universally: "Today the rules of the game have changed, and the ball is in your court."

Or, to put it in the words that are so often held aloft at any street protest today, part in hope, part as threat: "This is just the beginning."

The authors are Guardian journalists based in London, Cairo and New York